ON THE COMPOSITIONAL NATURE
OF THE ASPECTS

.

FOUNDATIONS OF LANGUAGE

SUPPLEMENTARY SERIES

VOLUME 15

ON THE COMPOSITIONAL NATURE
OF THE ASPECTS

by

H. J. VERKUYL

D. REIDEL PUBLISHING COMPANY / DORDRECHT-HOLLAND

Library of Congress Catalog Card Number 77–188006

ISBN 90 277 0227 6

Printed in The Netherlands by D. Reidel, Dordrecht

PREFACE

This book is a thesis submitted to the Faculty of Arts of the University of Utrecht. It was prepared under the supervision of Prof. Dr. H. Schultink. I would like to express my gratitude to him for his criticisms of earlier versions which led to many improvements, in particular with respect to the exposition of the argument.

To my co-referent Dirk van Dalen, reader in the Department of Philosophy ('Centrale Interfaculteit') of the University of Utrecht, I am greatly indebted for his valuable and fruitful suggestions about problems relevant to both linguistics and logic. Several ideas developed in this study owe their present concrete form to our many discussions.

This thesis originates in syntactic research into the Aspects carried out in 1967 under the supervision of Albert Kraak, professor at the University of Nijmegen, who ever since gave much attention to my work in progress. I am very grateful to him for his careful and stimulating criticism as well as for the continuous support he gave me during these years.

The present study closely relates to the work of my colleague Wim Klooster with regard to both its theoretical framework and its subject matter. Our joint work on the measurement of duration in Dutch is an integral part of the argument. I have greatly profited from the numerous discussions we have had.

I am further obliged to my colleague Jan Luif and to Pieter Seuren of Magdalen College Oxford, for their criticisms of earlier drafts and their valuable suggestions, and to all others who have helped me in writing this book.

Finally I want to thank Phil Hyams of the University of Amsterdam, who unweariedly corrected my English, and Peter Nieuwenhuijsen for assisting in compiling the index and the bibliography.

The names mentioned here do not absolve me from the responsibility for errors that remain.

Amsterdam, July 1971   H. J. VERKUYL

CONTENTS

PREFACE   V

ABSTRACT OF THE ARGUMENT   IX

I. ASPECTS AS SEMANTIC PRIMITIVES

1.0. Introduction   1
1.1. Introductory Observations on Aspects   2
1.2. Aspects in *Aspects*   9
     1.2.1. Subcategorization of Lexical Categories in *Aspects*   11
     1.2.2. Some Objections   16
1.3. Aspects in Gruber's Base Component   29
     1.3.1. Polycategorial Lexical Attachment to Semantic Trees   29
     1.3.2. Inherent Subcategorization of Verbs   35

II. ASPECTS AS COMPOUND CATEGORIES

2.0. Introduction   40
2.1. Verbs and Directional Phrases   41
2.2. Strictly Transitive vs. Intransitive Verbs   46
2.3. Pseudo-Intransitive Verbs and Direct-Object Noun Phrases   49
2.4. Pseudo-Intransitive Verbs and Prepositional Phrases   53
     2.4.1. PERFORM-Verbs and Abstract Nouns   54
     2.4.2. TAKE-Verbs and Concrete Nouns   73
     2.4.3. Verbs Occurring with the Accusativus Effectivus   85
2.5. Conclusion   96

III. THE UPPER BOUND OF THE ASPECTS

3.0. Introduction   98
3.1. The Role of the Subject and the Indirect Object in the Composition of the Aspects   100
3.2. The Location of Durational Adverbials and the Upper Bound of the Aspects   109
3.3. A Criterion for Verb Phrase Constituency?   118
     3.3.1. *Doen dat* (do so)-replacement   119
     3.3.2. On the Underlying Category DO   123
     3.3.3. Concerning the Condition of Strict Identity on Co-referentiality   134

3.3.4. The Underlying Structure of Action Sentences   142
3.3.5. Conclusion   155
3.4. Event-Units and Minimal Events   156
3.4.1. On the Logical Structure of Action Sentences   156
3.4.2. The 'All and Only'-Claim by Lakoff and Ross   162
3.4.3. Minimal Scope of Reference   165
3.4.4. Minimal Events and the Upper Bound of the Aspects 174
3.5. Conclusion   176

BIBLIOGRAPHY   179

INDEX   182

ABSTRACT OF THE ARGUMENT

This study aims to make for a better understanding of the term 'Aspects' in linguistic theory. Its most current application is found in studies on Slavonic languages. In the abundant literature on the contrast between the Durative (or Imperfective) Aspect and the Nondurative (or Perfective) Aspect, their occurrence has been taken to be restricted to Slavonic and some other languages, generally speaking to languages whose Verbal systems are morphologically characterized with regard to this opposition.

The central hypothesis of transformational-generative theory that a distinction should be made between the deep structure and the surface structure of a language, entails the possibility for morphological systematicity to be nothing more than a manifestation of a general or even universal regularity expressed, for example, in the syntactic component of grammers of other languages. It will be shown in this study that the opposition between the two Aspects is present in Dutch, and as can be seen from the translated material, also in English, and that it should be described as the expression of regularities of a primarily syntactic-semantic nature.

In Chapter One I shall discuss the plausibility of the view that in non-Slavonic languages generalizations can be made pertaining to phenomena which in Slavonic grammars are generally accounted for in terms of the contrast between the Durative and Nondurative Aspects. As this opposition should be related to the possibility for Durational Adverbials to occur in some sentences and to their exclusion from others, it follows that we cannot consider the Aspects free from selectional relations between these Adverbials and the constituents to which the term 'Aspects' applies.

In Chomsky's *Aspects of the Theory of Syntax* (1965) we meet the claim that Durational Adverbials relate selectionally to Verbs, an opinion which in fact links up with the traditional assumption mentioned above that the Aspects should be assigned to Verbs. Even if we take into consideration recent modifications made by Chomsky in *Remarks on Nominalization* (1968a) many inadequacies inherent to the model proposed in *Aspects* make it rather senseless to pursue other ways of remedying its inherent limitations, notably with respect to the status of Prepositional Phrases, to the organization and the function of the lexicon and to the specification of Verbs and Nouns.

Gruber's abandonment of the principle of monocategorial lexical attachment which states that for every lexical item there is just one categorial node in deep structure to which it can be attached, as well as his basic assumption that no essential difference should be made between syntax and semantics at the level of deep structural representation, should be seen as a basic contribution to what in the work of Lakoff, Ross, McCawley, Postal and others has been developed as an alternative to Chomsky's original and modified conception of transformational-generative theory.

Since Gruber's work is relatively explicit as to the application of the principle of polycategorial lexical attachment, which allows lexical items to be attached to more than one category of the base, and since in his grammar Verbs can inherently be specified in terms of semantic primitives, his framework opens up perspectives for an adequate account of the Aspects in grammar. A brief survey of Gruber's basic assumptions applied to the main theme of this study will follow the refutation of the *Aspects*-model and its extrapolations.

In Chapter 2 the compositional nature of the Aspects will be demonstrated with the help of a number of outwardly diverse sentences, all of which allow for the same generalization regarding the position of Durational Adverbials. The Durative and the Nondurative Aspects in these sentences appear to be composed of a Verbal subcategory on the one hand and a configuration of categories of a nominal nature on the other. Accordingly they can be represented by schemata. Sentences like *Hij speelde een uurlang het celloconcert van Schumann* (lit: He played Schumann's cello concerto for an hour), *Greetje wandelde urenlang een kilometer* (lit: Greetje walked a kilometre for hours), *De muis at een weeklang de kaas* (lit: The mouse ate the cheese for a week), *Hij hoorde urenlang dat De Gaulle was overleden* (lit: He heard for hours that De Gaulle had died), *De chirurg genas een maandlang een hartpatiënt* (lit: Rhe surgeon cured a heart patient for a month), can all be analyzed on the basis of the following Nondurative scheme: $_V[VERB]_V + _{NP}[SPECIFIED\ QUANTITY\ OF\ X]_{NP}$. The asterisk is used to indicate that these sentences are ungrammatical in their single-event reading; they can, however, be interpreted as expressing frequency, though somewhat unnaturally. The category VERB represents one of the categories MOVEMENT, PERFORM, TAKE, ADD TO, TRANSITION, DO, etc., whereas the categories SPECIFIED QUANTITY OF X pertain to the countability, finiteness, or delimitation of X. Thus a cello concerto when performed should be conceived of as a finite piece of musical information, a kilometre when covered as a limited quantity of distance measuring units, a slice of bread when eaten as a specified portion of bread, and so on.

Sentences like *Hij speelde een uurlang cellomuziek* (He played cello music for an hour), *Greetje wandelde urenlang* (Greetje walked for hours), *De muis at een weeklàng van de kaas* (The mouse ate from the cheese for a week), *De muis at een weeklang kaas* (The mouse ate cheese for a week), *De chirurg genas een maandlang hartpatiënten* (For a month the surgeon cured heart patients) and *Hij hoorde urenlang praten over De Gaulle's dood* (He heard people talking about De Gaulle's death for hours) all fit into the Durative scheme $_V[\text{VERB}]_V + _{NP}[\text{UNSPECIFIED QUANTITY OF X}]_{NP}$. Eating from the cheese is to take (separate) an unspecified quantity of cheese from a (specified) quantity of cheese; music can be played for a virtually infinite time, and given the eternal life of Greetje she can walk infinitely. The surgeon restricted himself for a month to curing only members of the set of heart patients. In all these cases the termination of the events is dependent on the length of the stretch of time given in the Durational Adverbials.

In Chapter 3 it will be shown that the Indirect Object, as well as the Subject of the sentence, is also involved in the composition of the Aspects. Thus, in the latter case there is an opposition between sentences like **Er stroomt urenlang een liter water uit de rots* (lit: There is streaming a litre of water out of that rock for hours) and a sentence like *Er stroomt urenlang water uit de rots* (Water is streaming out of that rock for hours), which can be explained in terms of the schemata above. That is to say, the term 'Aspects' applies to configurations of categories of the following form $_{NP}[\text{(UN)SPECIFIED QUANTITY OF X}]_{NP} + _{VP}[_V[\text{VERB}]_V \ (+ _{NP}[\text{(UN)SPECIFIED QUANTITY OF X}]_{NP})]_{VP}$. This very fact invites the question of where the upper bound of the Aspects should be located. Since there are selectional restrictions between the categories fitting into the Nondurative scheme and Durational Adverbials, it can safely be assumed that those constituents which are located "higher" than Durational Adverbials are not involved in the composition of the Aspects. Therefore attention will be given to the status of Durational Adverbials in underlying structure.

In Klooster and Verkuyl (1971) it is argued that sentences containing the Verb *duren* (last) and those containing Durational Adverbials having an Indefinite Determiner are transformationally derived from one underlying source. Both *duren* plus its Specifying Complement and the Durational Adverbial can be considered the Verb Phrase of a sentential structure whose Subject is an embedded S referring to events. In other words, these Durational Adverbials can be taken as predications over events. The rule transforming the underlying Predicate into a Durational Adverbial is called *Adverbialization*.

The Nondurative scheme can be used as a constraint on this transformational rule. This constraint states that if the sentential Subject of a sentence is specified as referring to one single event and if this Subject S dominates categories fitting into the Nondurative scheme, *Adverbialization* cannot take place. This amounts to saying that the VP containing the categories which constitute the input to this rule cannot be transformed into a Prepositional Phrase. Consequently we can block the sentences with the asterisks above in their single-event reading. To account for the tendency to interpret them in a frequency reading we could say that *Adverbialization* may take place if $S_{n>1}$. That is, if the S referring to Nondurative events is pluralized, Durational Adverbials may be derived. This requires that we specify what a single event is, i.e. which unit it is that can be pluralized.

In Lakoff and Ross (1966) attention was given to the question of how to determine the mutual relations between the constituents dominated by the then deep structural category *Predicate Phrase*, among which Durational Adverbials. They proposed a transformational rule, called *Do so-replacement*, which was intended to make explicit a criterion determining which constituents are to be located inside and which outside the Verb Phrase. Their proposal can be taken as an implicit attempt to determine the notion 'event': constituents derived via *Do so-replacement* and necessarily occurring inside the VP seem to make a necessary contribution to the reference to events. Therefore their *do so*-analysis will be closely investigated.

According to Lakoff and Ross Durational Adverbials were, in contrast to Chomsky's position, generated outside the VP. As far as I can see, recent literature offers no serious proposal stating that the node *Predicate Phrase* is a deep structural entity. At best we can consider it a category developed during the transformational derivation. This renders the *Do so*-rule inadequate and consequently we need to restate the generalizations made by Lakoff and Ross.

Starting from a proposal by Staal (1967) the underlying structure of an "action sentence" like *Arie at een haring* (Arie ate a herring) is described as *Arie* + DO + $_S[x$ EAT A HERRING$]_S$, where S represents a propositional function and where DO + EAT form the Verb *eten* (eat). At a further stage of our analysis a more abstract representation of this structure results in a proposal linking up with proposals made by logicians like Reichenbach (1966) and Davidson (1967), the crucial point being that we need to introduce temporal variables into our description. That is, a sentence like *Arie at een haring* (Arie ate a herring) should be analyzed in terms of an existential quantification over events. This point as well as a formalization and extension of the Bach-McCawley proposals about the underlying structure of Noun Phrases in terms of Gruber's framework enables us to relate the sentence under analysis transformationally to such sentences as *Wat Arie deed was een haring eten* (What Arie did was to eat a herring), *Wat Arie at was een haring* (What Arie ate was a herring) and *Degene die een haring at was Arie* (The one who ate a herring was Arie). The structure underlying all four sentences (apart from possible topicalization elements) is roughly of the form $_{NP}$[the x – who is Arie]$_{NP}$ $_{VP}$[DO $_{NP}$[$_{PRO}$[SOME v]$_{PRO}$ $_{REL}$[WH+v BE $_S$[x EAT a y – which is a herring]$_S$]$_{REL}$]$_{NP}$]$_{VP}$, where v is a variable ranging over temporal entities, notably over events. The paraphrase related to this structure is something like 'The one who is Arie occurs as the agens with respect to some event which is his eating something which is a herring'. In this structure DO expresses the relationship of 'agency' between Arie and some event.

By introducing event-variables into our description we obtain the equipment necessary to account for the pluralization of events, for frequency. The term 'frequency' applies to a series of similar events and therefore we ought to know the unit of quantification, the event-unit.

However, as Reichenbach pointed out, the determination of individuals is a matter of convention: we can expand events. This insight is supported by the flexibility of the scope of reference of *dat* (so) in a sentence like *Arie at een haring en Piet deed dat ook* (Arie ate a herring and Piet did so too) and of *wat* (what) in the pseudo-cleft sentence *Wat Arie deed was een haring eten* (What Arie did was to eat a herring). The latter sentence provides a paradigm that can be applied to determine the minimal structure some entity must have to be an event. It is exactly the S referring to minimal events which turns out to be the upper bound of the Aspects.

ASPECTS AS SEMANTIC PRIMITIVES

1.0. INTRODUCTION

In this chapter I shall confront transformational-generative theory with some descriptive problems concerning Durational Adverbials. For these adverbials to be generated properly, it is necessary to develop a selectional system since they cannot occur in all sentences.

By assigning the so-called Durative and Nondurative Aspects to the Verb taking them as semantic primitives, traditional grammarians suggested that the selectional rules involved would have to operate on Verbs and Durational Adverbials. The general attitude among them was to restrict the presence of Aspects to Slavonic and some other languages. By developing Durational Adverbials as sister constituents of Verbs, Chomsky (1965) implicitly adheres to the traditional position that subcategorized Verbs in terms of their compatibility with these adverbials.

In Section 1.1 I shall briefly discuss the main points of view about Aspects in traditional literature, after having shown that in Dutch as well as in some other languages the distinction between a Durative Aspect and a Nondurative Aspect should be accounted for in our grammar. This enables us to raise the question of whether or not Chomsky's grammar developed in *Aspects of the Theory of Syntax* is descriptively adequate with respect to subcategorization and selection. Therefore Section 1.2 treats some possible extrapolations to be made with regard to the restricted domain of cases covered by Chomsky's proposal. I will try to show that his system of subcategorization rules does not work adequately when applied to sentences containing Durational Adverbials. Moreover, it appears to prevent certain generalizations which cannot be ignored in our grammar, such as the relationship between Verbs and Prepositions. In Section 1.3 Gruber's ideas concerning the base component and the function of the lexicon will be sketched. The adoption of the so-called principle of polycategorial lexical attachment as well as the merger of the syntactic and the semantic component seems to provide us with the appropriate descriptive apparatus for dealing with the Durative and Nondurative Aspects in grammar.

1.1. INTRODUCTORY OBSERVATIONS ON ASPECTS

Any grammar of Dutch must deal with the following sentences:

(1a)   Greetje heeft urenlang gewandeld.
        Greetje walked for hours.
(1b)   *Greetje wandelde urenlang een kilometer.
        *Greetje walked a kilometre for hours.
(2a)   De jager verbleef (gedurende) drie weken in die berghut.
        The hunter stayed in that mountain-hut for three weeks.
(2b)   *De jager bereikte (gedurende) drie weken die berghut.
        *The hunter reached that mountain-hut for three weeks.
(3a)   Gloria woonde tot 1965 in Amsterdam.
        Gloria lived in Amsterdam till 1965.
(3b)   *Gloria verhuisde tot 1965 naar Amsterdam.
        *Gloria moved to Amsterdam till 1965.

We need a system of rules generating the a-sentences and blocking the b-sentences. On the face of it, the task of drawing a dividing-line between the a- and b-sentences does not appear to be too difficult. We could make use of a set of selectional rules operating upon Durational Adverbials like *urenlang* (for hours), (*gedurende*) *drie weken* ((for) three weeks), and *tot 1965* (till 1965) on the one hand, and the Verbs of the above sentences on the other, in order to block the derivation of the b-examples.

However, there are some factors which complicate the issue. For by saying that the b-sentences are ungrammatical, we exclude just one reading, in particular the reading corresponding to the a-sentences. For example, sentence (1a) asserts that the period during which Greetje walked had a duration of some hours. Greetje's walk is conceived of as one single event having duration and going on in time continuously. Of course this does not mean that she did not interrupt her walk, but these things do not affect the unity felt between the periods during which she is actually walking; these periods constitute one single durative event. The asterisk in front of (1b) indicates the impossibility of having a reading which corresponds to (1a). That is, sentence (1b) cannot say that a single event, Greetje's walking a kilometre, took place for hours. In other words, it cannot inform us that the period during which Greetje walked a kilometre had a duration of some hours. The same holds, *mutatis mutandis*, for (2b) and (3b).

On the other hand, all b-sentences systematically tend to allow for an interpretation of some sort. For example, (1b) can be used to express that the event 'Greetje's walking a kilometre' took place several times during a certain period having the duration of some hours. Again the same sort of interpretation applies to (2b) and (3b), though it should be stressed that sentences like (1b)–(3b) in their frequency reading are not the most natural sentences for informing us about repetition of given events. Thus, for instance, sentence (2b) is unnatural, though grammatical and perfectly comprehensible; most native speakers prefer to insert Frequency Adverbials like *een paar keer* (several times) or *telkens* (repeatedly): *De jager bereikte drie weken telkens die berghut* (The hunter reached that mountain-hut repeatedly for three weeks). Dutch speakers are also inclined to insert the adverbial *regelmatig* (regularly) in (3b) in order to render this sentence more acceptable. In spite of the decreased acceptability of the b-sentences they should be regarded as grammatical. Or, to describe my interpretation of these sentences precisely, there is no reason for saying that they are ungrammatical in their frequency reading, except for some cases [1].

The above facts are, by no means, new observational data. For instance, Leskien (1919:217) distinguished between the 'imperfective' (German) Verb *jagen* (Dutch: *jagen op*; English: *chase*) and the 'perfective' (German) Verb *erjagen* (Dutch: *vangen*; English: *catch*) by saying that the second of the following two examples:

(4a)   Sie jagten den Hirsch *den ganzen Tag*. (German)
        Ze joegen *de hele dag* op het hert. (Dutch)
        They chased the stag *the whole day long*. (English)
(4b)   *Sie erjagten den Hirsch *den ganzen Tag*.
        *Ze vingen *de hele dag* het hert.
        *They caught the stag *the whole day long*.

is ungrammatical. The italicized constituents are Durational Adverbials just like *urenlang* (for hours) in (1). The asterisk in (4b) expresses Leskien's opinion that one cannot say (4b), in his own words "Man kann (4b) nicht sagen". I think it is justified to translate this latter statement into present-day terms like: sentence (4b) is ungrammatical in the way the presence of the asterisks in (1b)–(3b) is explained above. Sentence (4b) allows for the same sort of interpretation as (1b)–(3b): they express repetition unnaturally. Leskien also discussed sentences like:

(5)   *Das Licht blitzte eine Stunde lang auf. (German)
        *Het licht ging een uur lang aan. (Dutch)
        *The light lit up for an hour. (English)

---

[1] For example, in my dialect the sentence *De jager bereikte een week die berghut* (lit: the hunter reached that mountain-hut a week) is ungrammatical in both its single-event reading and its frequency reading. To obtain the latter we need insert either the Preposition *gedurende* (for) or the morpheme *lang* (lit: long). In sentences like *Jan bleef een week in Engeland* (John stayed in England for a week) the Durational Adverbial can occur without a Preposition or *lang*.

which cannot be said either, unless we want to say that the light lit up repeatedly. Sentence (5) cannot express continuous action, Leskien says, but repeated momentaneous action and, moreover, only the duration of the repetitions[2]. See for similar observations Hermann (1927:207–11).

In discussing the Durative (= Imperfective) and the Nondurative (= Perfective) Aspects, which are considered by many people only to occur in Slavonic languages, we see how easy it is to illustrate the difference between these two with the help of sentences of non-Slavonic languages like Dutch, German and English. Apparently we meet phenomena of a more general nature, though it should be borne in mind that there are many language-specific factors which make it difficult to express generalizations of the kind illustrated in (4) and (5) uniformly. For instance, English requires that the frequency reading of (1b) contain the Plural *kilometres* whereas Dutch can have the Singular form *een kilometer* (a kilometre).

Traditional grammarians like Streitberg (1889), Herbig (1896), Delbrück (1897), Brugmann (1904), Leskien (1919), and many others, most of them belonging to the influential school of the so-called 'Junggrammatiker', were perfectly aware of the fact that their classification of Verbs into Imperfective (or Durative) Verbs and Perfective (or Nondurative) Verbs concerned semantic categories. For instance, Streitberg, who initiated the well-known discussion about the Aspects which lasted some forty years, says: "Three main semantic categories govern the whole Verbal system of the Slavonic as well as the Baltic dialects" (1889:3)[3]. These three categories are (and I follow Streitberg's formulation literally):

(1) The imperfective or durative or continuous aspect which gives the action in its uninterrupted duration or continuity;

(2) the perfective or resultative aspect, which adds the additional notion of termination to the sense of the Verb;

(3) the iterative aspect, which gives the action in its repetition. The second category is divided into (2α) the momentaneous-perfective aspect, which stresses the moment of termination, e.g. in the Old Bulgarian Verb *ubiti* (kill); and (2β) the durative-perfective aspect, which expresses the termination of an action as well as its having a duration, e.g. Slovenian

---

[2] The original text runs as follows: "*Das Licht blitzte eine Stunde lang auf* ist nicht möglich, falls man nicht etwa damit sagen will *es blitzte eine Stunde lang immer wieder von neuem auf*, damit hat man aber nicht eine andauernde Handlung ausgedrückt, sondern eine wiederholte momentane und in dem Zusatz nur die Dauer der Wiederholungen."

[3] The original formulation is: "Drei grosse bedeutungskategorieen beherrschen das gesammte verbalsystem der slavischen und gleicherweise auch der baltischen dialekten." The main participants in this discussion are Streitberg (1889), Herbig (1896), Delbrück (1897), Brugmann (1904), Deutschbein (1917), Leskien (1919), Behaghel (1924), Poutsma (1926), Van Wijk (1928), Hermann (1927), Porzig (1927), Jacobsohn (1926; 1933), Overdiep (1937).

preberem (I read through). The iterative aspect can express repetition of either durative actions or perfective actions (*ibid.*: 4–5).

Ever since Streitberg presented his tripartition a number of other classifications have been proposed. For instance, Poutsma (1926:285–90) says that predications may be divided into: (1) momentaneous predications, i.e. covering one moment; (2) durative predications, i.e. extending over a continuous succession of moments; and (3) iterative predications, i.e. consisting of an indefinitely prolonged succession of like acts[4]. Poutsma's second category is divided into (2α) indefinitely durative predications, i.e. with no particular stage of the predication definitely thought of; (2β) ingressively durative predications, i.e. with the initial stage of the prediction more distinctly thought of than the rest; and (2γ) terminatively durative predications, i.e. with the final stage of the predication more distinctly thought of than the rest. It will be noted that Poutsma's category (2γ) corresponds to Streitberg's categories (2α) and (2β) and that Poutsma's category (2α) is identical to Streitberg's first category.

In this study I shall restrict myself to a classification into Durative, Terminative and Momentaneous Aspects; the latter two can be taken together as Nondurative. Syntactic evidence for the correctness of this classification is given in Verkuyl (1969b; 1970; forthcoming). To promote some familiarity with the terms 'Durative', 'Momentaneous' and 'Terminative', I shall give some examples showing the syntactic motivation for this tripartition.

The Momentaneous Aspect is incompatible with the question *Hoe lang...?* (How long...?) as we can observe in **Hoe lang heeft de generaal zijn trouwe dienstbode vermoord?* (**How long did the general kill his faithful maidservant?*). The same obtains for the Terminative Aspect: **Hoe lang is Greetje naar het strand gewandeld?* (**How long did Greetje walk to the beach?*). By contrast, we find *Hoe lang heeft Greetje gewandeld?* (How long did Greetje walk?) (*Cf.* in this connection Vendler, 1957). Consider also: *Maandag en dinsdag heeft het gemaal gewerkt* (The pumping-engine was working Monday and Tuesday) containing a Durative Aspect, as against *Maandag en dinsdag heb ik een brief geschreven aan mijn tante* (I wrote a letter to my aunt on Monday and Tuesday). The former sentence may pertain to a durative event having the length of forty-eight consecutive hours. That is,

---

[4] The term 'predication' is defined as follows: "A verb is a word by means of which an action, state or quality is predicated of a person or thing, or a number of persons or things. As a general term for the action, state or quality predicated the term *predication* may be used. The word(s) expressing the predication may be called the predicate" (1926:5). Poutsma's use of the term 'predication' can roughly be compared with the current interpretation of the term 'logical predicate'.

the pumping-engine might have been working permanently throughout the two natural days in question. The latter sentence, however, can only pertain to two terminative events, one taking place on Monday, the other one on Tuesday. The same applies to the Momentaneous Aspect in *Maandag en dinsdag heeft de postbode een brief bezorgd* (The postman delivered a letter on Monday and on Tuesday). We know from this sentence that the postman delivered one letter on Monday, the other one on Tuesday, or in other words that there were two momentaneous events 'the postman's delivering a letter', one taking place on Monday, the other one on Tuesday.

The difference between the Terminative and Momentaneous Aspect can be characterized semantically by saying that terminative events have duration and that they necessarily terminate; momentaneous events cover one indivisible moment. The Terminative Aspect in *Ik heb dat artikel in een dag geschreven* (I wrote that article in a day) is compatible with the Temporal Adverbial *in een dag* (in a day) (*Cf.* Kraak, 1967a). This sentence can be paraphrased as 'It took me a day to write that article'. The Momentaneous Aspect in **Peer heeft hem in een dag een stokslag gegeven* (*Peer gave him a stroke of the stick in a day), however, is incompatible with this adverbial. Note also that **Greetje wandelde in een dag* (*Greetje walked in a day) is ungrammatical.

These examples represent a small sample of the material on the basis of which the Aspects can be classified. See for further material Verkuyl (forthcoming). In this study, however, I shall not give much attention to the syntactic evidence for the tripartition into Durative, Terminative and Momentaneous Aspects. Its scope is restricted to the more fundamental problem of how to account for the differences between the Durative Aspect on the one hand, and the Nondurative (Terminative and Momentaneous) Aspects on the other, i.e. for the difference between the a-sentences and the b-sentences of (1)–(5). The opposition between the Durative and Nondurative Aspects in these sentences concerns a basic distinction which underlies more elaborate classifications.

Streitberg's proposal marks the beginning of a period during which very much attention was given to the Aspects of the Verb, and Poutsma's proposal, dating from the time that this discussion was on the ebb, represents the view that investigations into the Aspects should not be restricted to Slavonic languages. I have given their classifications to provide for some information about what can be considered the heuristic stage of the semantic theory available at that time. They fairly represent traditional insights into the nature of the Aspects. It should be said that from the very beginning till its rather abrupt end about 1935 the concept formation regarding the Aspects was characterized by terminological confusion and vague definition, which reveals the inadequacy of the semantic theory implicit in the relevant studies.

So far as I can see the above sketched discussion about Aspects came to an end owing to the lack of an adequate linguistic theory. The point is that morphology played a central role in the whole matter. Most of the scholars participating in the discussion were of the opinion that Aspects could be expressed only in Slavonic languages because their Verbal system *morphologically* distinguished between Durative and Nondurative Verbs. Diachronic research into Indo-European languages had led to the view that, in principle, three morphological expedients could express the presence of Aspects in a Verbal system, namely (a) roots, (b), stems, and (c) composition of Verbs[5]. As far as (a) and (b) are concerned, no Indogermanic language expresses, at present, the Aspects systematically with the help of Verbal roots and stems. Synchronically it is only (c) that is productively present in Slavonic languages. Thus, though *jagen* (chase) in (4a) differs from *erjagen* (catch) in (4b) because the latter Verb contains a prefixed perfective morpheme *er-* the German language was considered as missing a Verbal system having Aspects in that there are no morphological rules uniformly accounting for this difference. That is, there are such pairs as *ziehen* (draw) and *erziehen* (educate) which cannot be forced into an opposition of Aspects, both being Imperfective. The general attitude among the participants in the discussion was that non-Slavonic languages had lost the capacity of expressing Aspects. They did not deny that the semantic categories given by Streitberg, Poutsma, Leskien and others were relevant to the description of all languages, but the majority of scholars required that these categories be expressed by a system of morphological rules.

Anybody who adheres to Chomsky's central hypothesis that each sentence of a given language must be given a deep structure and a surface structure will agree upon the view that regularities of morphology are at best considered reflections of certain underlying regularities[6]. The absence, in a language L_i of a system of rules expressing, for example, the perfective sense of a verbal prefix and the presence of such a system in a language L_j,

---

[5] *Cf.* Porzig (1927:153), Jacobsohn (1926:380–1; 1933:292–4), Behaghel (1924:96), Van Wijk (1928).

[6] The term 'deep structure' can be used in its strict technical sense when pertaining to the structure generated by the syntactic component (the base) of the grammar developed in Chomsky (1965) and modified recently. In rejecting deep structure as an independently motivated, intermediate syntactic level of representation between semantic representation and surface structure, generative semanticists like McCawley, Lakoff, Gruber and others do not abandon Chomsky's hypothesis that linguistic description should not be restricted to surface structure. In its non-technical sense the term 'deep structure' is often replaced by the term 'underlying structure'. I shall use the term 'deep structure' in its non-technical sense, unless mentioned specifically.

cannot be regarded as a proof that the underlying structure of L_i does not correspond to the underlying structure of L_j. In other words, Dutch and English can have developed other, non-morphological, means of expressing the same kind of information as given by e.g. the perfective morpheme *otu* in *otúnesti* (carry away) and *u* in *ubiti* (kill) in Oldbulgarian.

In my opinion, the lack of an adequate linguistic theory prevented most of the participants from giving a correct account of the Aspects. Notable exceptions to the claim that Aspects were a matter of morphology and semantics were Herbig (1896), Poutsma (1926), Jacobsohn (1933) and Over-diep (1937). They were able to look upon morphological phenomena as a matter of secondary importance for generalizations about the perfective and imperfective categories and they introduced arguments of a predomi-nantly syntactic nature [7]. I shall have the opportunity of referring to some of these scholars again below when discussing some of their examples or problems relevant to their views.

Returning now to our examples (1)–(5) we are facing the task of describing these sentences against the background of the problems raised by the above mentioned discussion. Many observations and generalizations, though made from what can be considered nowadays a wrong angle, are of very great relevance to the analysis of sentences like (1)–(5) generated by the grammar of a non-Slavonic language. That is, in this respect there are some descriptive problems associated with our examples which were also implicit in the literature on the Aspects and which strongly suggest that any attempt to describe sentences containing Temporal Adverbials cannot ignore Aspects. First of all, we have to block the single-event reading of sentences like (1b)–(3b) and of the Dutch sentences (4) and (5). Secondly, we have to account for frequency in terms of the co-occurrence of Durational Adverbials with certain constituents of the Predicate. Thirdly, the b-sentences pro-vide an argument for differentiating between such Adverbials as *urenlang* (for hours), *tot 1965* (till 1965), etc. on the one hand, and *gisteren* (yesterday), *in die tijd* (at that time), etc. on the other. For sentences like

(1c)   Greetje heeft gisteren gewandeld.
        Greetje walked yesterday.

[7] To my knowledge, Kraak (1967a) was the first who made an attempt to describe the opposi-tion between the Nondurative and Durative Aspects within transformational-generative frame-work. In fact, he made explicit the Chomskian position sketched in Section 1.2 by maintaining that a syntactic distinction should be made between Nondurative and Durative Verbs. Kraak explicitly reverts to Overdiep (1937) in considering 'Durative' and 'Nondurative' syntactic notions. In Van Es (to appear) Aspects are characterized as syntactic functions from the "stilistic" point of view, i.e. within the theoretical framework of Overdiep and Van Es. Van Es' survey of the discussion about the Aspects does not essentially differ from the sketch given here. See also Vendler (1957) and Gruber (1967a). A recent paper on the Aspects in Russian within the transformational-generative framework is Miller (1970).

(1d)   Greetje heeft gisteren een kilometer gewandeld.
        Greetje walked a kilometre yesterday.
(3c)   Gloria woonde in die tijd in Amsterdam.
        Gloria lived in Amsterdam at that time.
(3d)   Gloria verhuisde in die tijd naar Amsterdam.
        Gloria moved to Amsterdam at that time.

do not call for a distinction of the sort shown in the a- and b-sentences of (1)–(3). Neither (1d) nor (3d) have an interpretation comparable with that of their corresponding b-sentences. The above c- and d-sentences are all interpreted in exactly the same way as far as reference to single or multiple occurrence of events is concerned.

At present we find ourselves in the situation of having a corpus of observational data, a number of generalizations based upon an inadequate linguistic theory and the impression that some of the above mentioned scholars had an excellent idea of what was at issue in spite of the terminological confusion and their poor analytical tools. Transformational-generative theory has presented itself as a theory that adequately deals with many linguistic problems which were left unsolved in traditional grammar. Yet, as far as I know, virtually no attention has been paid to problems raised in connection with sentences like (1)–(5) by transformationalists. Since no linguistic theory, in my opinion, may ignore these problems we may confront transformational-generative theory with them so as to see whether this theory is adequate. It can easily be seen that Chomsky's grammar in *Aspects* illustrated descriptive solutions to problems which had nothing to do with the Aspects of the Verb. However, we must demand that Chomsky's underlying linguistic theory provide tools for extrapolating from the domain of cases by the rules given in Chomsky (1965).

Therefore, the relevant question at present is: can Chomsky's grammar deal adequately with such sentences as (1)–(5)? And if the answer is in the negative, can transformational-generative theory provide for a grammar which describe them adequately? The negative answer to the first question will be given in the subsequent section. The present study is an attempt to provide for a positive answer to the second.

1.2. ASPECTS IN 'ASPECTS'

My reasons for taking the position held by Chomsky in *Aspects of the Theory of Syntax* as the point of departure are the following. Firstly, this position happens to represent the traditional view that Aspects are a matter of the Verb, as was made explicit in Kraak (1967a). Secondly, it forms the point of application for a better understanding of Gruber's framework developed shortly after Chomsky (1965). Thirdly, the modifications proposed in Chomsky's *Remarks on Nominalization* do not affect the main line of argument pursued in this and the subsequent section, namely that both Verbs and Nouns should be subcategorized inherently as well as context-dependently. Fourthly, apart from Lakoff and Ross (1966), Chomsky's *Aspects* contains the only explicit proposal about the location of Durational Adverbials in deep structure. Fifthly, the modifications proposed in Chomsky's *Remarks* concern only part of the grammar sketched in Chomsky (1965). Particularly, the status of Prepositional Phrases, among which Durational Adverbials, have remained the same and consequently selectional problems inherent to the conception underlying *Aspects* have not yet disappeared and can best be demonstrated with the help of the clearest of the two proposals.

In Chomsky's base component we find two types of rewriting rule, namely *branching rules* and *subcategorization rules*, which are restricted to lexical categories and which introduce syntactic features. Both types of rule may be context-free or context-sensitive. Among the context-sensitive rules we find *strict subcategorization rules*, "which subcategorize a lexical category in terms of the frame of category symbols in which it appears" and *selectional rules*, "which subcategorize a lexical category in terms of syntactic features that appear in specified positions in the sentence" (Chomsky, 1965:112–3).

In order to show the exact nature of the difficulties we face when adopting Chomsky's proposal I shall briefly sketch how a sentence like

(2c)   De jager verbleef gedurende een week in die berghut.
        The hunter stayed in that mountain-hut for a week.

would be derived with the help of the above mentioned base rules. I shall only stress the points relevant to the exposition of the descriptive problems raised in Section 1.1, assuming some familiarity with the organization of the base component anno-1965 (Chomsky, 1965:84–111).

It should be pointed out here that Chomsky also sketched the outline for an alternative organization of the base. In this conception subcategorization rules are not part of the base but they are assigned to the lexicon (Chomsky, 1965:120–3; see also Botha, 1968:26–32). However, the point at issue in this section, the selectional relationship between the Durational Adverbials and Verbs, remains the same in either of the two alternatives, the main point being that in Chomsky's conception Verbs can only be subcategorized in terms of context-sensitive subcategorization rules.

1.2.1. *Subcategorization of Lexical Categories in 'Aspects'*

To account for the information that *jager* (hunter) is a Common Noun (as distinct from the Proper Noun *Teun*), a Count Noun (as distinct from the Non-Count Noun *water*), an Animate Noun (as distinct from the Non-Animate Noun *geweer* (rifle), a Human Noun (as distinct from the Non-Human Noun *hert* (stag), etc. Chomsky extended his system of rewriting rules developed in *Syntactic Structures* (1957) so as to contain a set of non-branching context-free subcategorization rules attaching this information in the form of syntactic features to the node *Noun*. The first rule of this set provides for the connection between these features and the categorial node *Noun* because it has *Noun* on the left of the arrow, e.g. Noun→[+N, +Common]. The syntactic features dominated by one node *Noun* form a complex symbol, this being "a collection of specified syntactic features" (Chomsky, 1965:84). Thus, for instance, structure (I) being derived before lexical attachment takes place, contains a complex symbol

(6)   [+N, +Common, +Count, +Animate, +Human,...]

where the dots represent further information characterizing the Noun in question:

(I)

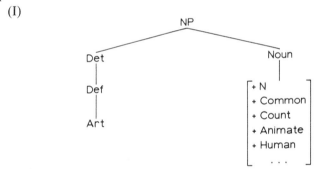

After structure (I) is generated, lexical attachment may take place. Each lexical entry is defined as a pair (D, C), "where D is a phonological distinctive feature matrix 'spelling' a certain lexical formative and C is a collection of specified syntactic features (a complex symbol)" (Chomsky, 1965:84). Lexical attachment takes place if C is not distinct from the complex symbol generated by the base component. Thus, in our case the lexical entry for *jager*, having the following form:

(7)   (*jager*, [+N, +Common, +Count, +Animate, +Human,...])

contains a lexical formative *jager* (hunter) which can be inserted in the position of the complex symbol of (I), because the information between the square brackets in (7) is not distinct from the information given in (6).

The syntactic information of complex symbols subcategorizes the Noun inherently, i.e. independently of any contextual information. Though the status of features like [+Count] and [−Animate], etc. is defined in Chomsky (1965) as being of a syntactic nature, it is very much under attack at present. I shall not give attention here to the question of how these features should be conceived of so far as their status in syntax or semantics is concerned. That is, though there are many arguments for the view that the features in question are of a semantic nature, I shall not question here the validity of Chomsky's decision to consider them as belonging to the domain of syntax in this section[8].

It stands to reason that, within Chomsky's framework, Nouns like *week* should be specified inherently as [+Temporal] and [+Duration] in addition to features discussed above. [+Temporal] is necessary to distinguish *week* from *jager* (hunter), [+Duration] to make a distinction between *week* and *uur* in *botsing* (collision) which would have to be specified as [−Duration] or [+Moment][9].

As far as the Verb *verblijven* (remain) in sentence (2c) is concerned, Chomsky decided not to specify Verbs inherently rather by contextual information. Subcategorization of Verbs takes place in terms of the frames in which Verbs can occur[10]. The complex symbol of V contains syntactic information about its sister constituents in terms of categorial nodes (e.g.

---

[8] In McCawley (1968a; 1968c; 1968d) Chomsky's selectional system is subjected to heavy fire. McCawley is of the opinion that "selectional restrictions are actually semantic rather than syntactic in nature, that the full range of properties which figure in semantic representations can figure in selectional restrictions and that only semantic properties figure in selectional restrictions, and that it is the semantic representation of an entire syntactic constituent such as a noun phrase rather than (as implied by the proposals of *Aspects*) merely properties of the lexical item which constitutes its 'head' that determines whether a selectional restriction is met or violated" (1968c:265). McCawley's point that selection is a matter of non-lexical categories, notably of those which can have referents, prepared the ground for the position held by Fillmore and sketched in McCawley (1968c:267; 1968a:128ff.) that selectional restrictions are, in fact, a matter of reference, i.e. of our knowledge of the world. The present study can be taken as an attempt to produce some independent evidence for the view that selection takes place between non-lexical categories, in particular NP's and S's (See also footnote 21 of this chapter).

[9] Note that Chomsky does not give a criterion for determining whether we need a minus- or a plus-specification. I shall assume that [+Moment] is equivalent to [−Duration].

[10] Chomsky writes: "Observe that the feature specification [+Transitive] can be regarded as merely a notation indicating occurrence in the environment —NP. A more expressive notation would simply be the symbol "—NP" itself. Generalizing, let us allow certain features to be designated in the form [X— Y], where X and Y are strings (perhaps null) of symbols. We shall henceforth call these *contextual features*. Let us regard Transitive Verbs as positively specified for the contextual feature [—NP], pre-Adjectival Verbs such as *grow*, *feel* as positively specified for the contextual feature [—Adjective], and so on. We then have a general rule of subcategorization to the effect that *a Verb is positively specified with respect to the contextual feature associated in which it occurs*" (1965:93) [Chomsky's italics].

about whether V occurs with a Direct-Object NP, a Directional Prep Phrase, etc.) as well as information about the inherent features of either these sister constituents or constituents outside the VP (e.g. about whether the Indirect Object NP must be [+Human] or whether the Subject NP must be [+Animate], etc.).

Now, in order to derive sentences like (2c) the base component was designed so as to generate first all syntactic information about categorial nodes and inherent syntactic features. The context-dependent syntactic specification of the Verb can only be filled in after the context has been generated. The pre-terminal base structure of sentence (2c), i.e. the structure immediately before lexical attachment takes place, would have the form of structure (II) if the syntactic information about the Verb has not yet replaced the symbol *CS*.

(II)

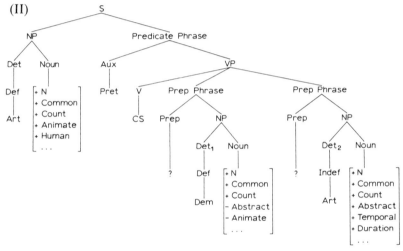

The complex symbols of the Nouns which are involved in the selection of the Verb, in this case all Nouns of structure (II), are incorporated into the complex symbol of V. The selectional rules operating upon the Verb assign each feature of the Nouns involved in the selection to the Verb and determine "an appropriate selectional subclassification of it" (Chomsky, 1965:97). In the same way as (6) relates to the syntactic information of the lexical entry (7), the newly formed complex symbol of the Verb relates to the syntactic information contained by the lexical entry for Verbs. Thus, in the case of sentence (2c) the CS of V will have a form not distinct from the complex symbol of the following lexical entry:

(8)   (*verblijven*, [+V, +—Prep Phrase$_{Place}$ (+Prep Phrase$_{Duration}$),
       ..., +[+Animate, ...] Aux—... Det$_1$ [+Place, ...]
       Det$_2$ [+Temporal, +Duration, ...] ...])

If so, then *verblijven* (remain) can be inserted in the position of the complex symbol[11]. Lexical entry (8) expresses that *verblijven* must occur with Prep Phrase$_{Place}$ and that it can appear optionally with Prep Phrase$_{Duration}$. This is marked with the help of round brackets.

As far as the question-marks in (II) are concerned, Chomsky restricts himself to an illustrative fragment which contains subcategorization rules covering only the relationship between Verbs on the one hand, and the head Nouns of Noun Phrases having the function of Subject or Direct Object. He does not indicate how the relationship between the Prepositional Phrases belonging to the VP and the Verb of this VP should be expressed in grammar, neither does Kraak (1967a). Consequently, we have to call on extrapolations based upon the discussion leading to this fragment in *Aspects*.

As far as I can see, from the moment we extend the domain of cases illustrated by Chomsky's fragmentary base component so as to cover Prepositional Phrases as well, we can no longer adhere to his idea of dealing with selection with the help of rules operating upon features of Verbs and Nouns only. That is, it seems wrong to specify a selectional relationship between the Verb *verblijven* and the Noun *week* in the Durational Prep Phrase of sentence (2c). The relevant syntactic features involved in this selection are [+Temporal] and [+Duration], for we do not have **Hij verbleef daar gedurende zijn humeur* (*He remained there for/during his mood) nor **Hij verbleef daar gedurende half twaalf uur precies* (*He remained there for half past eleven precisely). However, a feature like [+Duration] cannot be involved in the selectional relationship between the Verb of (3) and the Noun of the Durational Adverbial *tot 1965* (till 1965). For Durational Adverbials with *tot* (till), *sinds* (since), *vanaf* (from), etc. can contain Temporal Nouns which are inherently specified as having a syntactic feature [+Moment][12]. For instance, the Durational Adverbial *sinds die botsing* (since that collision) contains a Temporal Noun *botsing* (collision) pertaining to a Momentaneous event and having a feature [+Moment]. This feature is incompatible with Verbs like *verblijven* which require a selectional

---

[11] Subscripts like *Place* and *Duration* do not occur in Chomsky's complex symbols. They are needed here to determine which Prep Phrases we are dealing with. They abbreviate selectional information (i.e. information given by selectional rules) whose storage would unduly complicate our exposition. As a matter of fact, Chomsky does not give clear instructions for how to store selectional features in the lexical entries for Verbs in their relationship to corresponding strict subcategorizational features, neither in *Aspects* nor in later work. The examples given in *Aspects* are, in fact, too simple since they concern only selectional information about the Subject and the Direct Object. Difficulties arise as soon as we try to describe more complicated sentences like those under analysis here.

[12] The NP *tot 1965* does not contain a Noun in surface structure. We can certainly assume the presence of an underlying Noun *jaar* (year). However, the underlying structure of this Adverbial presumably has the following form: till the moment at which the year 1965 began.

relationship to Nouns specified as [+Duration]. Nevertheless *sinds die botsing* can occur quite freely with this Verb. Consider in this connection:

(2d)   De jager verbleef sinds die botsing in het ziekenhuis.
         The hunter had remained in hospital since that collision.

(2e)   *De jager verbleef gedurende die botsing in het ziekenhuis.
         *The hunter remained in hospital for (the duration of) that collision.

(2f)   De jager verbleef na die botsing in het ziekenhuis.
         The hunter remained in hospital after that collision.

(2g)   *De jager overleed sinds die botsing in het ziekenhuis.
         lit: the hunter has died in hospital since that collision.

(2h)   De jager overleed na die botsing in het ziekenhuis.
         The hunter died in hospital after that collision.

Sentence (2d) containing a Durational Adverbial *sinds die botsing* is grammatical, whereas (2g) which has the same Adverbial, is ungrammatical. Note that *overlijden* (die) in (2g) pertains to a Momentaneous event, just like *botsing*. Consequently, if it were the head noun of a Prep Phrase which is involved in selection, then we would not be able to explain why (2g) is ungrammatical and why (2d) is grammatical. Apparently, the relevant selectional feature [+Duration] which should be compatible with the Verb *verblijven* and incompatible with *overlijden* cannot be assigned to the Noun *botsing*. This is also shown by (2e). This sentence is ungrammatical owing to the incompatibility of *gedurende* with *die botsing*. The preposition *gedurende* requires that the Noun of the NP be specified as having a feature [+Duration][13]. The latter fact shows that there are also selectional rules operating upon the constituents dominated by the node *Prep Phrase*. Now, the point is that the selectional rules governing the relationship between the Verbs of (2d)–(2h) and their sister constituent *Prep Phrase*$_{Duration}$ can only operate upon a selectional feature [+Duration]. And we have seen that this feature cannot be present in the Noun. Consequently it should be assigned to the Preposition or to the entire Prep Phrase. Note that *verblijven* (remain) as well as *overlijden* (die) can occur with *na die botsing* in (2f) and (2h), which is also indicative of the fact that selectional rules include information about the Preposition.

At this point some solutions to the problem of how to extend Chomsky's grammar on the basis of principles formulated or suggested by himself,

---

[13] *Cf.* Verkuyl (1969b; 1970) where it was argued that *gedurende* (for the duration of) should be taken as an universal quantifier ranging over the smallest temporal entities when occurring in Durational Adverbials having a Definite Determiner. Its correct paraphrase is 'for all moments of (a given interval)'. See also Section 3.2 (and footnote 6 to Chapter III).

present themselves. One is to regard Prep Phrases as constituents being derived from underlying sentential structures[14]. In that case *Prep* could, for example, be considered a transform of a Verb and this would explain the ungrammaticality of (2e): the syntactic information of this underlying Verb would then be incompatible with the syntactic feature specification of the Noun *botsing*. Another solution would be to allow for selection between non-lexical categories[15]. I shall return to both solutions, which are not mutually exclusive, below in the discussion about the inadequacy of Chomsky's subcategorization rules.

To indicate my uncertainty about which solution would be preferred by Chomsky as a natural consequence of the considerations leading to his illustrative fragment, I have used question-marks in structure (II) attached to Prep.

1.2.2. *Some Objections*

As far as the descriptive problems raised in Section 1.1 are concerned, Chomsky's fragmentary grammar presented in *Aspects*, appears to be inadequate or incomplete in three respects:

(A) There are some strong arguments supporting the view that adverbials like *Duration* have a position in the base component differently than is suggested by Chomsky (1965:102).

(B) Chomsky's decision to distinguish between context-free subcategorization rules assigning inherent syntactic subcategorization features to Nouns and context-sensitive subcategorization rules assigning contextual features to Verbs should be rejected since it prevents an adequate account of the Aspects.

(C) Chomsky's grammar cannot account for the repetition expressed by the b-sentences of (1)–(4) and by (5).

As far as (A) is concerned, Lakoff and Ross (1966) showed convincingly to my mind that a base rule like:

(9)   VP→V(NP) (Prep Phrase$_1$) (Prep Phrase$_2$) (Manner)

occurring in Chomsky (1965:102), where one of the Prep Phrases can be a

---

[14] Lakoff (1965; 1967; 1968) developed the idea that Adverbials are derived from a higher simplex sentence than the one occurring as the main clause in surface structure. Thus e.g. a sentence like *He beats his wife in the yard* is analyzed as IT – *he beats his wife* – IN *the yard*, where IN is analyzed as an underlying Verb (1965:F-17). In Lakoff (1968) the Instrumental Adverbial *with a knife* was said to relate transformationally to the Verbal constituent *use a knife to*.

[15] See footnote 8. In Chomsky (1968a:207) certain selectional features are allowed to be associated with non-lexical categories. This step brings Chomsky nearer to the theoretical framework of Gruber as we shall see in Section 1.3. Chomsky does not, however, make explicit how his modification should be conceived of.

Durational Adverbial, fails to account for some generalizations which cannot be ignored in our grammar without falling foul of descriptive inadequacy. They argued that the Pro-VP *do so* in the second of the conjoined sentences:

(10)   John *worked on the problem* for eight hours but I *did so* for only two hours.

occurs in surface structure with the help of a transformation, called *Do so-replacement*, which substitutes *do so* for the VP *worked on the problem* in S_2 on account of its being referentially identical to the italicized constituent in S_1, this being the VP. If *for eight hours* were inside the VP of S_1 replacement of the VP by *do so* in S_2 on the basis of referential identity would give:

(10a)   ... but I [worked on the problem for eight hours] for only two hours.

The point made by Lakoff and Ross is very strong and though their *Do so-replacement* is not without difficulties, one thing seems reasonably clear: rule (9) cannot adequately account for the relationship between Durational Adverbials on the one hand and the Verb and other constituents on the other. Since I shall have the opportunity, in Chapter 3, to discuss *Do so-replacement* in detail and to support the validity of the point made by Lakoff and Ross (1966) as far as the higher location of Durational Adverbials is concerned, I would like to confine myself here to saying that Chomsky's system of strict subcategorizational and selectional rules appears to be in need of revision on the basis of empirical evidence. The rules developed by Chomsky to specify the relationship between Verbs and Durational Adverbials should at least be adapted to the facts and the generalizations presented by Lakoff and Ross and supported by the subsequent sections of the present study on independent grounds. In other words, the proposal by Lakoff and Ross can be taken to suggest that there are Durative as well as Nondurative Verb Phrases, because if Durational Adverbials are located outside the VP it is the VP as a whole which selectionally relates to these Adverbials. It appears as if there is a selectional relationship between a constituent $_{VP}[Verb+X]_{VP}$ and Durational Adverbials, where X is a variable which may be null and which ranges over constituents dominated by the node VP. In Chapter III some evidence is given for the view that the generalizations made by Lakoff and Ross apply to derived structure rather than to deep structure.

At any rate, if it can be shown that Durational Adverbials are restricted in their occurrence by certain configurations of categories rather than by the Verb, then it will be clear that Chomsky's proposal to specify Verbs like *verblijven* (remain) in terms of contextual information can only encounter severe difficulties. For if it is true that Durational Adverbials have a selectional relationship to configurations of categories rather than to one lexical category, then the relevant selectional information will concern these configurations as a whole.

Summarizing, we can say that the proposal by Lakoff and Ross incorporates the claim that selectional information should sometimes be assigned to non-lexical categories. Consequently it is highly improbable that Verbs should be subcategorized as is done in (7).

Our second objection (B) concerns strict subcategorization and selection viewed from another angle. Let us, for the moment, look away from the fact that Lakoff and Ross (1966) may be right with respect to the hierarchical status of Durational Adverbials, and let us continue to generate them with the help of rules like (9), i.e. within the VP. Then an inadequate account of descriptive problems raised by sentences like (2c) and (1)–(5) would provide independent arguments for rejecting Chomsky's proposal. Point (B) concerns the inadequacy of rules assigning contextual features to Verbs. It will be argued that there are no valid grounds for the position to specify Verbs exclusively in terms of contextual features as was held by Chomsky and by Kraak (1967a). First of all, consider the following sentences:

(1a)   Greetje heeft urenlang gewandeld.
        Greetje walked for hours.
(1e)   Greetje heeft een kilometer gewandeld.
        Greetje walked a kilometre.
(1f)   Greetje is naar het strand gewandeld.
        Greetje walked to the beach.
(1g)   Greetje is tot de derde boom na het kruispunt gewandeld.
        Greetje walked as far as the third tree after the intersection.

The lexical entry for *wandelen* (walk) in (1a) would have the following form:

(11)   (*wandelen*, [+V, +—(Prep Phrase$_{\text{Duration}}$)#, +...,
                +[+Human, ...] Aux—... Det+[+Temporal,
                +Duration, ...]...])

The complex symbol of (11) contains the information that *wandelen* can be inserted in the environment of a Durational Adverbial. The contextual feature [+—Prep Phrase$_{\text{Duration}}$] indicates that we can have a string of the form $V \frown Prep\ Phrase_{\text{Duration}}$, where V is *wandelen*. Entry (11) also specifies that the Noun occurring in the Durational Adverbial is a Temporal Noun expressing duration. Sentences like (1e)–(1g) would require the following subcategorization features, respectively:

(11a)   (*wandelen*, [+V, +—(Measure Phrase)#, ...])
(11b)   (*wandelen*, [+V, +—(Prep Phrase$_{Direction}$)#, ...])
(11c)   (*wandelen*, [+V, +—(Prep Phrase$_{Goal}$)#, ...])

Chomsky's grammar locates Measure Phrases like *een kilometer* in (1e), Directional Phrases like *naar het strand* in (1f) and Prep Phrases of Goal like *tot de derde boom na het kruispunt* in (1g) within the Verb Phrase, which seems to be correct. Lakoff and Ross (1966:6) also conclude that these constituents belong to the VP.

In order to avoid the necessity of having a lexicon containing at least four entries *wandelen*, Chomsky stored all information about subcategorization of Verbs in one and the same lexical entry. Thus, we would obtain:

(11d)   (*wandelen*, [+V, +—(Prep Phrase$_{Duration}$)#, +—(Prep
          Phrase$_{Direction}$)#, +—(Measure Phrase)#,
          +—(Prep Phrase$_{Goal}$)#, ...])

where just as in the case of (11a)–(11c) selectional information is not represented in the form given in (11) or (8). See also footnote 11.

Entry (11d) could, in principle, deal with (1a) and (1e)–(1g) because the lexical attachment rule matches the appropriate lexical feature, e.g. [+ −Measure Phrase], with a corresponding feature i.c. [+ −Measure Phrase] contained by the Complex Symbol of the Verb in the base tree generated. Note in passing that (11d) informs us four times that *wandelen* is an Intransitive Verb. Notice also that entries for Verbs essentially differ from entries for Nouns in that only some of the features collected in their Complex Symbol can be attached, whereas all inherent features of Nouns find a corresponding feature in the base tree. In my opinion, one should aim at lexical entries whose complex symbols all match in the same way with the complex symbols of the base according to one principle of lexical attachment[16].

---

[16] In Chomsky (1968a) derived nominals and corresponding Verbs are given one lexical entry containing selectional and strict subcategorization features and unspecified as to the categorial features [+ Noun] or [+ Verb]. For example, there would be a lexical entry for *verblijv*-(remain; stay) containing selectional information. Morphological rules change this neutral lexical entity into either a Noun *verblijf* (stay) or into a Verb *verblijven* (remain). However, Verbs having no corresponding derived nominals are not discussed so it stands to reason to assume that Chomsky did not change his position. If he would, then the *order* of selection (i.e. Verbs can be attached only if the nominal categories have already been attached) would become a problem for him. (*Cf.* 1965:115).

Consider now the following sentences:

(1h)   *Greetje heeft de hele dag een kilometer gewandeld.
        *Greetje walked a kilometre for the whole day.
(1i)   *Greetje is urenlang naar het strand gewandeld.
        *Greetje walked to the beach for hours.
(1j)   *Greetje heeft gedurende een uur tot de derde boom na het kruis-
        punt gewandeld.
        *Greetje walked as far as the third tree after the intersection
        for an hour.

At this stage it is necessary to realize that (11d) contains only positively specified contextual features, whereas Nouns can be specified negatively, e.g. [−Count]. As far as lexical entries for Verbs are concerned, it was only to exclude mutually inconsistent features from being paired simultaneously with features of the base tree that Chomsky (1965:110–1; 164–70) decided to specify them "negatively for features corresponding to contexts in which they may not occur" (p. 110). Chomsky illustrates the necessity of introducing negative features supplementary to positive features with the help of the Verb *hit*, which can only occur with a Manner Adverbial if the Direct Object-NP is also generated. Thus we do not find in English *He hit carefully*. In order to prevent lexical attachment of *hit* to a base structure in which *Manner* has been generated, the lexical entry for *hit* will have to contain a negative feature [−−Manner] in addition to the positive feature [+—NP Manner] which accounts for the lexical attachment in the case of *He hit him carefully* (1965:166*ff.*).[17]

Thus we can extend (11d) so as to obtain also information pertinent to (1h)–(1j). We should then obtain:

(11e)   (*wandelen*, [+V, +—(Prep Phrase$_{Duration}$)#, +—(Prep
         Phrase$_{Direction}$)#, +—(Measure Phrase)#,
         +—(Prep Phrase$_{Goal}$)#, −—Prep Phrase$_{Direction}$Prep
         Phrase$_{Duration}$, −—Measure Phrase⌒Prep Phrase$_{Duration}$,
         −—Prep Phrase$_{Goal}$Prep Phrase$_{Duration}$, ...])

Note however, that we do not have either:

(1a′)   *Greetje heeft het strand urenlang gewandeld.
         *Greetje walked the beach for hours.

Following Chomsky we would have to add the negative feature [−—NP⌒Prep

---

[17] It should be mentioned here that Chomsky restricted himself to just one of four possible routes sketched on page 111 of *Aspects*. However, the objections raised also apply to the three other possibilities.

Phrase$_{Duration}$] to (11e). Now, the point to be made is the following: Chomsky's lexicon is, at present, the only place where a generalization with respect to the ungrammaticality of (1h)–(1j) could be made. However, it is not possible at all to express the fact that (1h)–(1j) are ungrammatical for the same reason; our lexical entry (11e) will also contain negative features hampering a proper generalization: the negative feature of (1a') differs from the negative features of (1h)–(1j) because *wandelen* (walk) cannot occur with a Direct Object NP. But since they all have the same form [——X̄ Prep Phrase$_{Duration}$] we cannot account for the fact that the ungrammaticality of (1a') is different from the ungrammaticality of (1h)–(1j). Consequently, we miss an important generalization in our grammar with respect to (1h)–(1j). In *Remarks on Nominalization* Chomsky did not change his position with regard to negative specifications.

I shall now discuss a second group of examples to show some of the consequences of adopting Chomsky's proposal concerning subcategorization of Verbs. Consider the following sentences:

(12a)   Ze dronken.
        They were drinking.
(13a)   Ze dronken een liter whisky.
        They were drinking a litre of whisky.
(14a)   Ze dronken whisky.
        They were drinking whisky.

The following lexical entry:

(15)   (*drinken*, [+V, + — —(Noun Phrase)#, ...+[+Animate, ...]
        ux — —Det+[+Mass, +Fluid...]...])

would account for (12a) and (14a). We might add a feature like [+Quantity] to (15) in connection with the presence of *een liter* in (13a). Consider also the following sentences:

(12b)   Ze dronken urenlang.
        They were drinking for hours.
(13b)   *Ze dronken urenlang een liter whisky.
        *They were drinking a litre of whisky for hours.
(14b)   Ze dronken urenlang whisky.
        They were drinking whisky for hours.

In order to account for the Durational Adverbial in the b-sentences, we have to extend our lexical entry (15). The additional information concerns the positive specification that *drinken* as well as *whisky drinken* can occur with Durational Adverbials, and the negative specification that *een liter whisky drinken* cannot occur with them. In Chomsky's terms, the Verb *drinken* should be subcategorized negatively with respect to the contextual frame '—$_{NP}$[Det⌢Quantity Noun⌢of⌢Mass Noun]$_{NP}$Prep Phrase$_{Duration}$'. Note, however, that the Quantity Noun in question must be singular, since sentences like:

(13c)   Ze dronken urenlang liters whisky.
         They were drinking litres of whisky for hours.

are grammatical. Having the same sort of reading as (14b), sentence (13c) refers to a continuous event 'their drinking litres of whisky'. Another complicating factor which must be expressed by means of negative strict subcategorization features is the ungrammaticality of:

(13d)   *Ze dronken urenlang een glas whisky.
         *They were drinking a glass of whisky for hours.

How do we specify the Noun *glas*? By assigning to it a feature [+Quantity]? Then we would have different Nouns *glas*, because the sentence:

(13e)   *Ze braken urenlang een glas waar whisky in zat.
         *They broke a glass containing whisky for hours.

being ungrammatical in the same way as (13d), cannot contain *glas* as a Noun specified as [+Quantity]. Rather should we use the specifications [+Concrete] and [+Object] in this case. Nevertheless, (13d) and (13e) correspond as to the nature of the selectional restriction. Apart from the obvious difficulty of capturing the relevant generalization by means of Chomsky's context-sensitive subcategorization rules, we can confront his context-free subcategorization rules assigning inherent features to Nouns with the task of accounting for the fact that the feature involved in the selectional restrictions in (13b), (13d) and (13e) is located at a higher level of constituency than the Noun. In other words, the feature in question should not be assigned to the Nouns *liter* (litre), *glas* (glass) or *whisky* but rather to the Noun Phrases *een liter whisky*, *een glas whisky* or *een glas waar whisky in zat* (a glass containing whisky). Comparing (13b) with (13d) we observe that the relevant features are 'Singular' and 'Plural'. Thus we are in conformity with McCawley's contention that the opposition between Singular and Plural is a matter of the NP rather than of Nouns (1968a). Comparing (14b) with (13d) we can observe that the relevant selectional features are 'Mass' (or 'Non-Count') and 'Count', which should also be assigned to the whole Noun Phrase as will be shown in Chapter 2. In my opinion both the context-sensitive subcategorization rules and the context-free subcategorization rules are inadequate with respect to features assigned to non-lexical categories. It is suggested by sentence (13e) that we should analyze *een glas waar whisky in zat* as 'Physical Object containing a quantity of fluid'. Thus, we could explain the ungrammaticality of (13e) in terms of that in (13b) and (13d). However, it is virtually impossible, at any rate extremely clumsy to store this sort of information in the lexical entry of *drinken* (drink) or *breken* (break).

In addition to this, it should be pointed out that the selectional restrictions of (13b), (13d) and (13e) primarily concern the constituents *een liter whisky, een glas whisky* and *een glas waar whisky in zat* on the one hand and *urenlang* on the other. *Urenlang* can occur with *drinken* in (12b) as well as with *whisky drinken* in (14b) and *drinken* can occur freely with *een liter whisky* as we see from (13a). Only if the singular NP *een liter* (a litre) is inserted in its position in (12b), is it necessary to state a restriction. Apparently, there is some syntactic information present in *een liter* (a litre) which is incompatible with *urenlang*. In my opinion, it is unnatural to burden the syntactic information about the subcategorial status of the Verb *drinken* with a selectional restriction between *een liter* and *urenlang*: *een liter* and not *drinken* appears to contain the element which is incompatible with *urenlang*. By storing this sort of information in the entry of *drinken* as well as in the entry of *breken* (break) in (13e), one fails to make a generalization. Moreover, any explanation of the correspondences between (13b), (13d) and (13e) and between (14b) and (13c) is blocked.

In conclusion of our-introductory-analysis of the sentences under discussion we shall slightly modify the picture given in the preceding paragraph. Sentences like:

(13f)   Ze zagen urenlang een liter whisky.
         They saw a litre of whisky for hours.

are grammatical. We meet here the situation that a Verb like *drinken* in (13b) as it were activates a syntactic feature present in *een liter* thus forming a combination which cannot occur with *urenlang* whereas a Verb like *zien* in (13f) does not activate this feature. To my mind, this can only mean that selection may be dependent on information contained by more than one lexical category, in (13f) by *zien* (see), and by *een liter (whisky)*. The difference between (13f) and (13b) could be explained by the fact that *drinken* and *zien* differ in their relationship to the contextual frame $[\alpha \text{—}_{NP}[\text{Det Quantity Noun of Mass Noun}]_{\overline{NP}} \text{Prep Phrase}_{Duration}]$. The former Verb would, in Chomsky's proposal, have a negative specification in its entry, the latter a positive. It will be clear that these specifications do not reveal the essence of the difference between the two Verbs in question. We want to know *why* they cannot both occur in the same contextual frame rather than confine ourselves to observing *that* they cannot both occur in it. In Chapter 2 I shall return to sentences like (13) and (14).

The third illustration of the inadequacy of Chomsky's subcategorization rules coming under point (B) links up with the two possible extensions of Chomsky's grammar discussed at the end of Section 1.2.1. Let us first consider the possibility of deriving Prep Phrases from underlying sentences to see whether Chomsky's system of selectional rules can be simplified, and then discuss the possibility of stating selectional restrictions in terms of non-lexical categories. Both in recent literature and in the following section arguments can be found for the correctness of the view to consider Prep Phrases transforms of underlying sentences and to deal with selection at the level of major categories. I shall now argue that in both cases Chomsky's selectional system does not work adequately.

Suppose that Prepositional Phrases can indeed be considered transforms from underlying structures of a sentential nature. Then it stands to reason that the Preposition itself will presumably be derived from an underlying Verb. We know from sentences like (2e) *De jager verbleef gedurende die botsing in het ziekenhuis* (*The hunter remained in hospital for that collision) that *gedurende* requires a NP containing a Noun expressing duration. That is, the Preposition appears to govern selection just as the Verb *duren* (last) with respect to its complement: both the Preposition and the Verb require a Noun specified as [+ Duration]. At any rate, there are may independent indications that Prepositions are more-place predicates[18].

On the face of it, the fact that Prep Phrases can be derived transformationally from underlying sentences seems to simplify Chomsky's selectional system. For if Prepositions are Verbs, we can state the internal selectional relationships of Prep Phrases in terms of Chomsky's subcategorization rules operating upon Verbs and Nouns. Thus, for example, instead of stating a selectional restriction between *gedurende* (for) and *botsing* (collision) in (2e), we state it between the underlying Verb *duren* (last) and *botsing* (collision): *gedurende een botsing* (*for a collision) is ungrammatical for exactly the same reason that *... duurde een botsing* (*... lasted a collision) is ungrammatical (Cf. Klooster and Verkuyl, 1971).

---

[18] See e.g. Lakoff (1965). In footnote 14 the Preposition *in* occurring as a higher Verb IN is a two-place predicate. In logical analyses Prepositions are either incorporated into the Predicate or considered more-place Predicates themselves, e.g. in Davidson (1967). See also Section 3.4.1. Traditional grammarians like Den Hertog were perfectly aware of the correspondences between Verbs and Prepositions (1903: 208–13).

However, it is possible to show that Chomsky's subcategorization rules no longer work satisfactorily if Prep Phrases are derived from underlying sentences. As it stands now Chomsky's proposal necessarily leads to either a paradox or to the situation that selectional information is inaccessible. I shall demonstrate this point with the help of sentence (2c). If *gedurende een week* (for a week) indeed is a transform, then structure (III) seems a reasonably adequate representation (see Section 3.2).

(III)

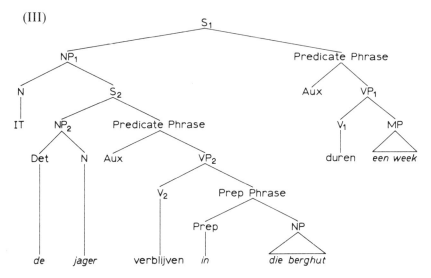

A transformational rule would have to change the structure of the form *IT ... duurde een week* (IT ... lasted a week) so as to obtain a Prepositional Phrase attached to VP_2 as a Durational Adverbial.

If the basic assumption leading to a structure like (III) is correct, i.e. if it is, in principle, right to express the transformational relationship between the Prep Phrase *gedurende een week* (for (the duration of) a week) and VP_1 ... *duurde een week* (lasted a week) with the help of (III), then we have to specify selectional restrictions between the Verb *duren* and the Sentential Subject S_2. We do not find:

(15)   *De jager overleed gedurende een week.
         *The hunter died for a week.

which would wrongly fit into the categorial string

(15a) $[_{NP_1} IT [_{S_2} [_{VP_2} NP_2 [_{VP_2} V_2 X]]_{S_2}]_{NP_1} [_{VP_1} V_1 MP]_{VP_1}$

where MP is a Measure Phrase and X is a variable.

As Chomsky's subcategorization rules are supposed to operate before the application of transformational rules there is no *a priori*-reason for their operating cyclically. Thus, let us suppose that they do not first apply to S_2 and subsequently to S_1. In that case V_1 and V_2 are mutually dependent. *Duren* can only occur as V_1 if Verbs appearing as V_2 are Verbs like *verblijven* (stay), *wonen* (live), *slapen* (sleep) and not Verbs like *schrikken* (take fright), *struikelen* (stumble), *overlijden* (die) etc. Or, conversely, *verblijven*, etc. can only appear as V_2 if V_1 is a Verb like *duren*. To my mind, it is impossible to specify Verbs like *verblijven* and *duren* syntactically with the help of context-dependent strict subcategorization features without running into a paradox. One cannot fill out the lexical entry for *verblijven* with syntactic information about its possibility of occurring with *duren*, which itself depends on syntactic information of *verblijven*. Nevertheless, structure (III) demands this as a natural consequence of Chomsky's system of subcategorization of Verbs.

We can avoid this paradox by stating that the subcategorization rules should first operate upon S_2[19]. *Verblijven* can be inserted because it has neither restrictions with NP_2 nor with Prep Phrase. If lexical attachment has taken place in S_2, the subcategorization rules apply to S_1. The selectional information of V_1 concerning the subject-S_2 is, however, information about V_2. We can show this with the help of sentences like

(2i)   Het verblijf van de jager in die berghut duurde een week.
        The hunter's stay in that mountain-hut lasted a week.
(15b)   *Het overlijden van de jager in die berghut duurde een week.
        lit: The hunter's dying in that mountain-hut lasted a week.

which differ from each other because in (2i) the derived nominal *verblijf* can occur with *duren* whereas the nominalized form of the Verb *overlijden* in (15b) cannot appear in the Subject-position of *duren*[20].

Now, the crucial point is that in Chomsky (1965) as well as in Chomsky (1968a) the relevant selectional information is inaccessible. As far as strict subcategorization is concerned, there is no opportunity to subcategorize *verblijven* as a Durative Verb and *overlijden* as a Nondurative Verb since the lexical entries for these Verbs can only contain strict subcategorial information about constituents dominated by VP_2, according to Chomsky's general condition on strict subcategorization rules (1965:99). However, this subcategorization should follow from rules like (9). The selectional rules would have to specify items like *verblijven* in terms of the

---

[19] I am indebted to Jan Luif for his criticism of the present point in its earlier version.
[20] Unlike its English counterpart *to die* the Dutch Verb *overlijden* can pertain only to momentaneous events. The English Verb *to die* in its terminative sense corresponds to the Dutch Verb *sterven*.

syntactic frames in which they can occur. But the syntactic frame concerning the VP$_1$ of structure (III) contains information about *duren* which itself is entirely dependent on selectional information contained by S$_2$, particularly by V$_2$. Hence, Chomsky's proposal concerning selection and strict sub-categorization can be shown to be inadequate as soon as we consider Prep Phrases transforms.

The above difficulties could be avoided by stating that *duren* in (III) should not be lexicalized before the relevant transformational rules shaping the Preposition *gedurende* apply. This would mean two things: either selection would take place after VP$_1$ is incorporated into VP$_2$ as Prep Phrase$_{\text{Duration}}$, which is rather unlikely in view of the fact that Chomsky's selectional rules operate pre-transformationally (if it were, we would face again the question-marks of structure (II)); or selectional rules are operative upon base structures before lexical attachment takes place, which would bring on a radical departure from Chomsky's model *anno*-1965 and from its modified version.

The second possible extension of Chomsky's proposal is to allow for se-lection between non-lexical categories so as to remedy the inadequacies that arise if we were to restrict selectional rules so that they only operated upon Nouns and Verbs. In fact, this is what Chomsky proposed to do in *Remarks on Nominalization*. It can be shown, however, that if Verbs are exclusively subcategorized context-dependently and if Prep Phrases are treated like in *Aspects*, then we face the same problem as described above.

We could avoid the difficulties given in structure (II) and illustrated by sentences like (2d)–(2h), by assuming that the relevant features de-termining selection should be assigned to such categories as NP, S, VP, Prep Phrase, etc., in general to non-lexical categories. If so, let us ten-tatively assume that there is a selectional relationship between the VP *verblijven in die berghut* (remain in that mountain-hut) in (IVa) and the Prep Phrase *gedurende een week* (for a week) in (IVb), where [X] and [Y] represent the relevant selectional information coming from the categories dominated by VP and Prep Phrase, respectively.[21] Then it will become ex-tremely complicated to store context-dependent information of the Verb *verblijven* in [X] so as to be part of the input to selectional rules governing the relationship between [X] and [Y]. In other words, selectional features

---

[21] In fact, this would represent the position held by Lakoff and Ross (1966). In Chapter III it will be argued that selectional relations can only hold between NP's or S's. Sentence (2c) expresses a binary relation between an event 'The hunter's staying in that mountain-hut' and a temporal entity 'a week', where *gedurende* is a two-place predicate. Selectional restrictions concern the relationship between the Predicate and its arguments.

like [X] and [Y] will be composed of syntactic features of the categories
dominated by the nodes VP and Prep Phrase.

To my mind, it is unlikely that e.g. [X] would contain some information
about features inherent to the Noun *berghut* (mountain-hut) together with
contextual features of the lexical entry of *verblijven*. The rules collecting
this incongruous information are likely to be extremely clumsy. Moreover,

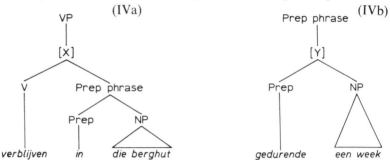

the relevant information about the compatibility of [X] and [Y] cannot
be stored in [X] if this information is context-dependent. For it is exactly
the information contained by [Y] which is necessary for [X] to be compatible
with [Y]. Thus we face again the problem of inaccessibility of information
arising from the decision to specify Verbs only in terms of contextual
features. Only if we subcategorize Verbs also inherently, can we collect
selectional information in [X] which is either compatible or incompatible
with [Y].

We have now seen that our objection (B), i.e. our criticism of Chomsky's
subcategorization rules, rests upon several points of support, the most
important being that we miss generalizations, that we burden the lexical
entries for Verbs with information that does not primarily concern the
Verb itself, and that we cannot extend Chomsky's grammar without running
into unnecessary complications. In general, point (B) concerns the artificial
and unmotivated distinction between the inherent specification of Nouns
and context-sensitive specification of Verbs. This distinction leads to
descriptive inadequacy as I have tried to show.

As far as (C) is concerned, i.e. the frequency expressed by (1b)–(4b),
Chomsky's grammar cannot account for the frequency expressed by the sentences under discussion in Section 1.1. Of course, we cannot demand this.
Besides, we first need to have a better selectional system before we can
hope to attain descriptive adequacy. It is very difficult to describe the
underlying structure of these sentences, as will gradually become clear in
the course of this study. At any rate, it is necessary to investigate the exact

nature of the Nondurative Aspect which is present in the b-sentences of
(1)–(4), because this Aspect will certainly be involved in the description
of these sentences in their frequency-reading.

In conclusion, the objections raised to Chomsky's positions discussed
here turn on two points. Firstly, the hierarchical status of Durational
Adverbials is very likely to be different from what is stated by rules like (9),
which introduce the necessity of extending the application of subcategorization rules so as to let them operate upon higher constituents. This being so,
it is no longer possible to say that only Verbs and Nouns are specified as
having features relevant to selection. Secondly, the lexical entries for
Nouns and Verbs should not be as incongruous as in Chomsky's proposal.

1.3. Aspects in gruber's base component

In this section I shall give a brief sketch of Gruber's ideas on the base
component and its relationship to the lexicon, as his work is scarcely known
on account of its not being published. I would refer to Gruber (1967a),
De Rijk (1968), Klooster (1971), and Klooster and Verkuyl (1971) for
further information.

In 1.3.1 the principle of polycategorial lexical attachment well known in
generative semantics and first formulated by Gruber (1967a) will be explained. For this to be possible it will be necessary to relate this principle
to some of the other basic assumptions underlying Gruber's work. In 1.3.2
I shall discuss the inherent subcategorization of Verbs, which is a natural
consequence of the manner in which Gruber designed his lexical entries. In
preparation for the analysis to come in Chapter 2 I shall tentatively and
provisionally assume that Verbs can be subcategorized into Durative,
Terminative and Momentaneous Verbs, thus adopting the traditional position. It will be demonstrated that selection takes place in terms of the compatibility of nodes present in base structure rather than in terms of negative
features.

It must be remarked that some exegetic proficiency will be required in
order to develop a consistent view upon Gruber's framework, as in many
places his *Functions of the Lexicon in Formal Descriptive Grammars* is
rather loosely formulated.

1.3.1. *Polycategorial Lexical Attachment to Semantic Trees*

The basic assumption underlying Gruber's work and determining the degree
of deviation from Chomsky's position, can be formulated as follows:

(i) the relationship between the base component and the lexicon rests
upon the principle of polycategorial lexical attachment;

(ii) for this principle to be possible, it is necessary to present syntactic information uniformly. In other words, no distinction should be made between categorial nodes and syntactic features, since the latter entities can be taken as categories generated by branching rules;

(iii) since syntactic features can be eliminated from our base component in favour of categorial nodes, selection and strict subcategorization will no longer depend on negative specifications;

(iv) since selectional and co-occurrence relationships between constituents appear to be semantic rather than syntactic in the sense defined by Chomsky (1965), the base trees can be considered members of a semantic language. In other words, Gruber wants to regard the base as "generating the very semantic language by which meaning is formalized in language, so that semantics and syntax are merged at this level" (Gruber, 1967c:19).

Gruber's option for a base component generating semantic categories receives support from the fact that there appear to be no reasons for expressing selectional restrictions in the syntactic component. Ross and Lakoff and after them McCawley (1968a; 1968c) argue that selectional restrictions are of a semantic nature: "there are no cases on record of a verb which will exclude a lexical item as the head of its subject but allow the subject to be a noun phrase which splits the same semantic information between the head and the modifier; for example, there are no verbs on record which exclude *a bachelor* as subject but allow *an unmarried man*" (McCawley, 1968a:133–4).

Since co-occurrence relationships between constituents exist when the same selectional restrictions are involved, they are also semantic, according to Gruber (1967c:18). In his opinion, co-occurrence relationships were

the syntactic motivation for setting up a common syntactic base, since only the syntactic base could incorporate within it as much structure as was needed. On the other hand, co-occurrence relationships came to appear quite obviously semantic, yet not interpretively semantic. What seems to be lurking here is that semantics itself came to appear syntactic: It seemed that the language in which meaning is to be formalized must itself have a syntactic structure. There is a conflict only so long as semantics is thought of as interpretive. If semantics is generative, then the common syntactic base tree underlying sentences mutually involved in a co-occurrence relationship could be regarded as a member of the semantic language. The base itself can be regarded as generating the very semantic elements that characterize meaning in language. But with such a base, we must have polycategorial lexical attachment, because there is a many-one relationship mapping the elements of linguistic meaning (i.e. the highly structured base tree itself) into a less structured tree terminating in morphemes. The component which accomplishes this task is the lexical attachment component; the lexicon at this stage we can call the translational lexicon, translating the underlying semantic language into a language in terms of the traditional elements of syntax, the morphemes. (*ibid.*:19)

The "very semantic elements that characterize meaning" can be considered irreducible semantic primitives organized on syntactic principles.

Polycategorial lexical attachment is the opposite of monocategorial lexical attachment. The lexical item *jager* (hunter) in entry (7) is mono-categorially attached to structure (I): just one lexical category, the Noun, is involved. The principle of polycategorial lexical attachment asserts that "lexical items can be attached below more than one lowest lying category in the derived tree" (*ibid.*: 7). For example, the lexical item *enter* can be attached to the tree represented as (Va), where GO and INTO represent

(Va)   (Vb)

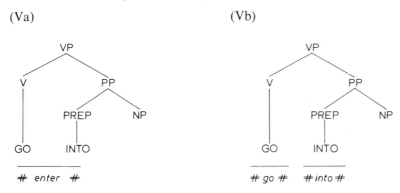

sets of categories which characterize the Verb *go* and the Preposition *into*, respectively. The lexical item *enter* is attached to the categories GO and INTO, i.e. to the Verb and the Preposition. In (Vb) we see that the lexical item *go* is monocategorially attached to V and the lexical item *into* to PREP. The principle of polycategorial lexical attachement enables us to express the close correspondence in meaning between such sentences like *He entered the church* and *He went into the church*. In Chomsky (1965) it is not possible to look upon *enter* and *go into* as alternative representations of the same underlying categorial tree because Chomsky's monocategorial attachment rules cannot attach the item *enter* to a structure identical to the structure which *go into* can be attached to. I shall return to this point in Section 2.1.

The principle of polycategorial lexical attachment demands that the base component be homogeneous as far as the entities occurring in it are concerned. It is not possible to attach items to more than one node if we have non-branching rules introducing syntactic features next to brancing rules introducing categories. Gruber argued that there are no valid reasons for introducing features below lexical categories like Noun and Verb. We can continue to use branching rules. Thus, for example, the syntactic feature [+ Common] can be taken as a (sub)category COMMON dominated by the node NOUN. The rewriting rules introducing subcategories like COMMON, ANIMATE, FEMALE, etc. can branch and consequently they can introduce structure. That is, the information regarding sub-categorization and playing a role in selection can be ordered without calling on the intricate system of redundancy rules advocated by Chomsky (1965:164–70). For instance, on the basis of the following rules:[22]

(16)   NOUN→(PROPER) (MASS) (CONCRETE)
        CONCRETE→(ANIMATE)
        ANIMATE→(HUMAN)

Gruber generates base structures of the sort presented in (VIa) and (VIb), thus accounting for the semantic relationship between *cow* and *livestock* in terms of the semantic categories they have in common.[23] Of course, it is possible to rearrange the non-branching rules introducing inherent features so as to obtain structure (i.e. to reflect the rules that generated them), but this structure "is not significant in that it is not used for any stage in the generation of a sentence subsequent to lexical attachment" (Gruber, 1967c:22).

(VIa)   N   (VIb)   N
               | ╱   ╲
         CONCRETE   MASS   CONCRETE
               | |
          ANIMATE   ANIMATE
         _____   _____
          # cow #   # livestock #

In this connection it should be noted that Chomsky (1968a) also accepted the view that the base component should be homogeneous with respect to the entities occurring in it, his argument being that we should allow for selectional restrictions between non-lexical categories in certain cases. He states that 'the distinction between features and categories is a rather artificial one' and that "there is no reason to retain the notion of category at all, even for the base. We might just as well eliminate the distinction of

---

[22] The rules given in (16) violate an important condition on Phrase Structure Grammars stated in Chomsky (1965) and earlier work and in Postal (1964). In rewriting rules of the form '$A→Z/X—Y$' it is required that Z be a nonnull string of symbols. Gruber does not discuss this violation, nor does he explicitly characterize the rules of his base component. Some passages in Gruber (1967c) notably on pages 37 and 60 strongly suggest, however, that his base rules should be taken as *node admissibility conditions* in the sense described by McCawley (1968c:247). On page 60 Gruber (1967c) states: "if we have a base rule with the categories A and B, e.g., A→(B) then the semantic significance of this is that A is a necessary condition for B (i.e. 'if B then A')."

[23] Gruber (1967c:23) says: "We allow morphemes to be attached to strings containing more than one category, and hence can account for the cross-classification of words by being able to refer to a word by any of the categories dominated by it". It will be clear that rules like (16) are provisionally formulated since a fully equipped base component is beyond our reach for the time being. The same holds good, however, for Chomsky's system of syntactic features which is also illustrative and suggestive rather than complete.

feature and category, and regard all symbols of the grammar as sets of features" (1968a:208). Chomsky evades giving any argument for generating sets of features rather than categories nor does he give any information about the internal structure of these sets of features.

The optionality of the rules in (16) takes the place of the $[\alpha F]$-specification in Chomsky's rules. The absence of a category in the base indicates the nonspecification of some particular quality. "This is opposed to a binary system, one of whose values (formally, the presence of a negatively marked feature) is interpreted as a specification for the contrastive condition to some quality" (*ibid.*:23). The claim inherent to this position is that a word should never be specified by its lack of a quality (e.g. non-concrete, non-mass). Recall to mind that Chomsky's system needs negative specifications in order to exclude mutually exclusive positive specifications. Thus, in the case of (11) we had $[+ \text{—Prep Phrase}_{\text{Direction}}]$ and $[+ \text{—Prep Phrase}_{\text{Duration}}]$, but since Directional Prep Phrases and Durational Prep Phrases cannot occur together with certain Verbs we had to call on the negative specification $[- \text{—Prep Phrase}_{\text{Direction}} \text{Prep Phrase}_{\text{Duration}}]$. By eliminating negative features Gruber does not have to burden his lexicon with supplementary negative specifications about the base tree configurations to which the lexical item in question cannot be attached. His lexical entries contain only information about the constituents with which lexical items can occur. The absence of certain specifications in the lexical entry means that the lexical item in question cannot be attached to certain configurations of the base. The principle of polycategorial attachment takes over the function of Chomsky's convention which had to supplement the positive subcategorization features with negative ones. The greater flexibility we obtain by attaching morphemes to more than one category generated by the base enables us to use the lexicon as a filter without making use of negative specifications.

Lexical entries in Gruber's system have the form of tree diagrams associated with phonologically specified strings. The phonological part of an entry is called a 'lexical item'. The tree diagrams themselves are referred to as 'the lexical environment', i.e. "the semantic and syntactic associate of the lexical entry is called the 'lexical environment' of the lexical item" (*ibid.*:5). The lexical environment is divided into a simultaneous environment, i.e. "the part to which the lexical item is directly attached" (*ibid.*: 66) and the peripheral environment, i.e. the rest of the tree in the lexical entry. For example, the lexical entry for *enter* will be represented as in (VII).

The simultaneous environment of *enter* is the boxed-in configuration of (VII). Its peripheral environment is the NP. The peripheral environment in Gruber's lexical entries consists of the semantic-syntactic information needed for the selection of the lexical item in question.

Lexical attachment to a subpart of the base tree can take place if "this subpart includes the categorial tree associated with that lexical item in some entry" (*ibid.*:63). In other words, the set of categories constituting the lexical environment of an entry may be identical to the set of categories forming a generated subtree or may be a proper subset of it. Never can a subpart of the base tree be a proper subset of the lexical environment

(VII)

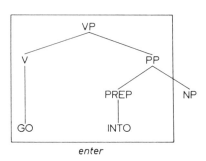

enter

of an entry. For example, if the base component generates the categories CONCRETE and ANIMATE, lexical items associated with lexical environments containing the nodes CONCRETE, ANIMATE and HUMAN cannot be attached because the node HUMAN is not present in the base (*ibid.*:66).

During the process of lexical attachment some restructuring conventions applying to the base structure are necessary. "There seems to be a condition that the result of the attachment of a single lexical item must be a phonological form having a node that dominates this phonological form only. This is necessary in order that transformations that apply subsequently can apply correctly, and also in order that the final word may belong to the appropriate category" (Gruber, 1967c:130). For example, if the lexical item *enter* in (VII) were attached to the base tree of (Va) without any modification of (Va), we would not have a category which exclusively dominates V and PREP, and not also NP. "In order for transformations to be able to apply, there must be such a node defining the word" (*Ibid.*). Gruber argues that in this case this must be a Verb, "because tense is attracted to it, it passivizes, etc." (*Ibid.*).

Restructuring of (Va) takes place as follows. The node PREP is detached from the node PP as is represented in (Vc).

Next, PREP is Chomsky-adjoined to a new node V thus becoming a sister of the original node V. The encircled node PP is left as a non-branching node which can be pruned. The resulting tree is (Vd).[24] After this the order

---

[24] For the notion 'Tree Pruning' see Ross (1966), who formulated this convention concerning derived structure as follows: "An embedded node S is deleted unless it immediately dominates

of V and PREP will be inverted during affixation; since it does not play any role in the present study the order of reversion of categories will be left out

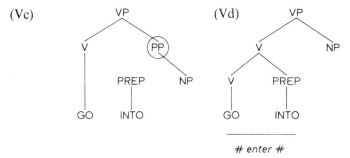

(Vc)   (Vd)

enter

of consideration her. For a detailed discussion of restructuring rules see Klooster (1971a; 1971b).

1.3.2. *Inherent Subcategorization of Verbs*

Gruber (1967a; 1967c) subcategorizes Verbs inherently: in diagram (VII), which is taken from Gruber (1967c:130), GO represents inherent subcategorial information. Of course, the symbol 'GO' does not reveal anything that could be used in our grammar to make generalizations and it should be replaced by inherent nodes subcategorizing Verbs. Thus, for example, we could say that *enter* as well as *go* are Movement Verbs (as distinct from *look*) just as we say that *hunter* and *rifle* are Count Nouns (as distinct from *water*). It will be clear that a simultaneous environment ("the semantic field of a word" – Gruber, 1967c:85) cannot be empty. It will also be understood that some of the context-dependent subcategorial information of Chomsky's lexical entries of Verbs is taken as inherent information in entries like (VII). The advantage of this transfer seems to be a more well-balanced distribution of the information needed for subcategorization.

By subcategorizing Verbs with the help of inherent categories as well as their peripheral environment our grammar gains more generalizing power, since it can account for the relationship between Verbs in terms of the subcategories they have in common, just as we could account for the correspondence between (VIa) and (VIb), but also in terms of the selectional information they share. In Chomsky (1965) subcategorization of Verbs could only be expressed in terms of the syntactic frames in which they can and cannot occur.

VP and some other constituent" (IV-18). Gruber extended the application of this convention by changing it into a convention covering all nodes in derived structure that do not branch any longer after certain transformations have taken place.

Chomsky-adjunction is an elementary transformation creating a new node *A'* when another node *B* is adjoined as the sister node to *A*, where *A'* immediately dominates *A* and *B*.

It stands to reason that the choice of the inherent subcategories assigned to Verbs depends on the generalizations made possible by them. But this is also the case with the inherent specification of Nouns: we justify the presence of a category like COUNT in our base component by reason of the fact that it is of use to express in our grammar that some Nouns can occur with an Indefinite Article whereas some other Nouns cannot. Likewise, there appear to be reasons to assume that it is helpful to have a category MOVE-MENT in our base component, as we shall elucidate below. We can extend our lexical entry (VII) as shown in (VIIa), where GO now represents all information characteristic for the Verb *go* and differentiating it from all other Movement Verbs.

(VIIa)

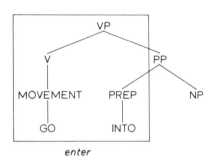

enter

Returning now to the descriptive problems raised in the preceding sections and preparing the analysis to come in Chapter Two, we can say that within Gruber's framework a solution to them could be found by subcategorizing Verbs in terms of nodes like DURATIVE, TERMINATIVE and MOMEN-TANEOUS. Thus we could, tentatively and provisionally, represent Verbs like *wandelen* (walk) in (1a), *verhuizen* (move) in (3b) and *bereiken* (reach) in (2a) as shown in (VIII), where X is a variable representing the peripheral environment dominated by VP. The nodes WALK, MOVE and REACH represent sets of inherent categories characterizing the Verbs *wandelen* (walk), *verhuizen* (move) and *bereiken* (reach) and containing the categories DURATIVE, TERMINATIVE and MOMENTANEOUS, respectively.

(VIIIa)   (VIIIb)   (VIIIc)

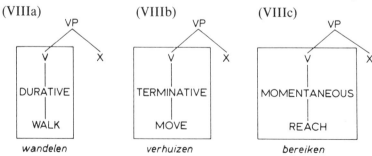

wandelen   *verhuizen*   *bereiken*

Assuming the correctness of the view that Verbs are also subcategorized inherently I shall now briefly describe how selection takes place in Gruber's grammar with the help of the base structure underlying (2c). Let us tentatively adopt structure (IX) as correctly representing the base structure underlying (2c), where X, Y and Z are variables representing parts of the tree which are irrelevant to the selectional relationships illustrated.[25] Note that (IX) expresses that PREP PHRASE$_{Duration}$ is a sister constituent of the VP, but this is not relevant to the point at issue.

(IX)

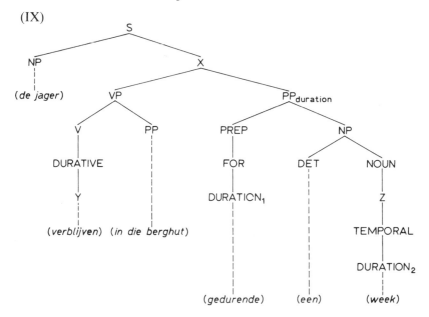

Selection of the lexical items in question depends on the compatibility of the nodes DURATIVE, DURATION$_1$ and DURATION$_2$. The lexical entries of *gedurende* and *week* will have the form given in (Xa) and (Xb), where X, W and Z are variables. W may be null.

The lexical item *week* can be attached to the base tree in (IX). Its simultaneous environment is identical to the rightmost branch of (IX) and its peripheral environment is a (proper) subset of the set of categories generated by the base: the selection of *week* depends on the presence of a Determiner rather than on the presence of an Article. In other words, *week* can also be attached if the Determiner is developed into a Demonstrative Pronoun. Note also that it is not necessary to have information about PREP in the

---

[25] Henceforward I shall use dotted lines connecting underlying structures with lexical items, when these structures are represented at a stage at which lexical attachment has not yet taken place. The lexical items are added in the diagrams for the sake of convenience.

peripheral environment of entry (Xb): Noun Phrases like *een week* (a week) need not only occur in Prepositional Phrases.

In diagram (Xa) it is expressed that *gedurende* can occur with Nouns like *week*. If the base component would generate Noun Phrases dominating nodes like TEMPORAL and MOMENT so that a Noun like *botsing* (collision) rather than *week* could be attached to the rightmost branch of (IX), the peripheral environment of (Xa) would prevent the lexical at-

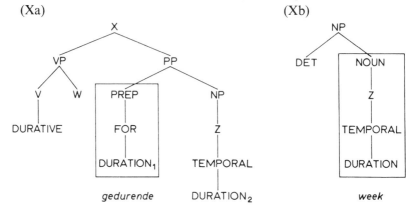

tachment of *gedurende* to this categorial tree. Hence ill-formed strings like **gedurende die botsing* (for that collision) in sentences like (2e) on page 15 are blocked.

As far as the category DURATIVE is concerned, it should be noted that the Chomskyan position discussed in the preceding section can easily be accounted for. If Prep Phrase$_{\text{Duration}}$ were a sister constituent of the Verb rather than of the Verb Phrase, then we could simply replace X by VP in both (IX) and (Xa). The general idea is that it is the presence of the inherent node DURATIVE which makes it possible to attach Durational Adverbials to the base structure. The presence of the nodes TERMINATIVE or MOMENTANEOUS in the base tree would automatically exclude the Preposition *gedurende* from being attached to this tree to the effect of blocking the single-event reading of the b-sentences of (1)–(3). The presence of nodes like TERMINATIVE and MOMENTANEOUS, abbreviated as NONDURATIVE, also gives us the opportunity to express frequency.

Structure (IX) as well as the diagrams (Xa) and (Xb) are highly tentative and provisional in that they provide only for the basis upon which the analysis to come in the subsequent chapters will rest. In fact, they represent the position that Aspects are a matter of the Verb in terms of Gruber's framework, the main point being that Verbs are to be specified inherently as well as context-dependently. Descriptively, (VIII)–(X) will be shown to be inadequate, since there are reasons to assume that there are no Durative or Nondurative Verbs. The labels DURATIVE, TERMINATIVE and MOMENTANEOUS pertain to major categories, as I will try to show. Moreover, the lexical entry for *gedurende* in (Xa) will be changed beyond recognition (See diagram (XXVIf) on page 115).

It will be understood that in the course of this study many things concerning Gruber's framework will receive a fuller explanation than has been given here. The descriptive results presented in Chapters Two and Three will have to support the correctness of the basic assumptions discussed in this section. To my mind, Gruber's base component in which the distinction between syntax and semantics is dissolved, tends to do more justice to a description of the Aspects than Chomsky's system of syntactic features, the reason being that Aspects appear to be semantically relevant – an opinion which was already held in traditional grammar.

CHAPTER II

ASPECTS AS COMPOUND CATEGORIES

2.0. INTRODUCTION

The basic idea developed in this chapter is that the categories DURATIVE
and NONDURATIVE should not be considered semantic primitives assigned to Verbs but that they should rather be assigned to a higher node than
V. In other words, I shall try to show that the terms 'Durative Aspect' and
'Nondurative Aspect' apply to configurations of underlying categories
among which necessarily a subcategory of V. The mechanism underlying the
composition of the Aspects can most clearly be demonstrated by assuming
– provisionally – that they should be assigned to the VP. This assumption
states that it is only constituents belonging to the VP which attribute to the
composition of the Aspects. This position was held in Verkuyl (1969b; 1970)
where a distinction was made between Durative and Nondurative Verb
Phrases. In Chapter 3 we shall see that in some particular cases the Subject
of the sentence can also contribute to the composition of the Aspects. In
the majority of cases, however, the opposition between the Durative and
Nondurative Aspects manifests itself most clearly as an opposition between
constituents dominated by the VP.

On the face of it, the composition of the categories DURATIVE and
NONDURATIVE seems to involve ingredients of a rather diverse nature:
on the one side we find subcategories of what appears as a Verb in surface
structure, on the other side Prepositional Phrases, Noun Phrases and
Measure Phrases. There appears to be one underlying principle, however,
on the basis of which we can homogeneously describe the composition of the
Durative and Nondurative Aspects in sentences containing Verbs plus
Directional Phrases (in Section 2.1), Verbs plus Noun Phrases, Verbs
plus Prepositional Phrases and Verbs plus Quantifying Complements
(in Sections 2.3 and 2.4).

It should be borne in mind throughout the rest of this study that given
the fact that the Aspects should be assigned to non-lexical categories, we
can seriously question whether there are such entities as Aspects. To say
that they are compound categories implies that they ought to be given the
same status as categories like S, NP, VP, etc. We can evade this by saying
that the term 'Aspects' applies to configurations of categories fitting into
certain schemata. If categories come under these schemata we can say that

the node dominating these categories is the node to which the Aspects should be assigned. Thus, in our linguistic theory the term 'Aspects' can be considered a derived notion.

2.1. VERBS AND DIRECTIONAL PHRASES

Consider the following sentences:

(1a)   Greetje heeft urenlang gewandeld.
         Greetje walked for hours.
(1k)   *Greetje heeft urenlang van de Munt naar de Dam gewandeld.
         *Greetje walked from the Mint to the Dam for hours.

The grammaticality of (1a) could be explained by the presence of a category DURATIVE dominated by the node V to which the lexical item *wandelen* (walk) can be attached. The lexical entry for *wandelen*, reflecting this position, is given in (VIIIa). The ungrammaticality of (1k) in the single-event reading could be attributed, as we have seen, to the presence of a category which is incompatible with the node DURATION inherent to Durational Adverbials. The same category could be held responsible for the frequency reading. I shall refer to this categorial node as NONDURATIVE.

Let us assume that it is correct to class *wandelen* (walk) in (1a) as a Durative Verb. Then we could expect that the category DURATIVE also be present in the simultaneous environment of the Verb *wandelen* in (1k) because this Verb closely corresponds to the Verb *wandelen* in (1a) as far as meaning is concerned. However, the incompatibility of *van de Munt naar de Dam* (from the Mint to the Dam) with *wandelen* in (1k) can be explained by the incompatibility of the nodes DURATION (occurring in the Durational Adverbial) and NONDURATIVE. So, since for the moment, we have agreed upon the status of the latter category as being inherent to Verbs, we are forced to assign it to *wandelen* in (1k). Consequently, we have two Verbs *wandelen*, one Durative, the other Nondurative (i.e. Terminative).

This analysis is to be rejected since it is not clear at all why there should be more than one Verb *wandelen*. There are no non-arbitrary reasons nor independent grounds for duplicating lexical entries for Verbs in respect of our wish to block (1k) and to generate (1a). Moreover, the difference between these sentences appears to be caused by the presence of the constituent *van de Munt naar de Dam* in (1k) rather than by a Nondurative Verb *wandelen*.

We could therefore consider the possibility of assigning the category NONDURATIVE to the Prep Phrase *van de Munt naar de Dam*. We would then be able to regard the category NONDURATIVE as neutralizing the category DURATIVE inherent to the Verb *wandelen*. By adopting this position we eliminate the difficulty of distinguishing between a Durative and a Nondurative Verb *wandelen* since we restrict ourselves to one (Durative) Verb *wandelen* only. On the basis of these considerations, we could represent the Verb Phrase of (1k) as in (XI), where X and Y are variables representing the categories constituting the complex Prep Phrase. The node NONDURATIVE must be "somewhere" in the internal structure of this Prep Phrase. Structure (XI) should be accompanied by a condition:

(17)   If a Durative Verb occurs with a constituent containing the node NONDURATIVE, then the node DURATIVE is neutralized by the latter.

It should be pointed out here that this position was, in fact, already held

(XI)

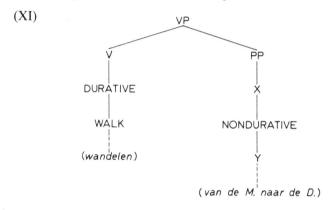

by Poutsma (1926), who stated "that the normal aspect of a verb is often modified or even utterly changed by the context" (1926:291). In a section under the heading "The Context imparting a Terminative Aspect to Indefinitely Durative Verbs" he illustrated his statement with the help of examples like *I made a mistake in searching you out*, where *out* modifies the meaning of the Durative Verb *search* (*ibid.*:300). The basic idea underlying Poutsma's analysis is that every Verb has a "normal" or "basic" Aspect and that this Aspect can be modified by the context, i.e. by the presence of constituents with which the Verb occurs. A similar position was held by Jacobsohn (1933) as we shall see in Section 2.4.3.

An analysis leading to representations like (XI) and conditions like (17) can be countered by the following objections:

(i) we lose a relevant generalization by extending the domain of such categories as DURATIVE and NONDURATIVE so as to cover non-verbal constituents by creating the peculiar situation that the Aspect of the Verb turns out to be exclusively the Aspect of the complement of the Verb;

(ii) we need a special rule or condition to neutralize the category DURATIVE of the Verb;

(iii) the complement of the Verb *wandelen* in sentence (1k) does not contain the category NONDURATIVE as an inherent node: *van de Munt naar de Dam* can occur in sentences without causing ungrammaticality of the sort illustrated in (1k). There are sentences like:

(18)   *Van de Munt naar de Dam* stond een lange rij politieagenten met helmen en knuppels.
         From the Mint to the Dam stood a long line of policemen with helmets and cudgels.

(19)   Het is vijfhonderd meter lopen *van de Dam naar de Munt.*
         It's a 500 metres walk *from the Mint to the Dam.*

Both sentences contain the constituent under discussion, but in both cases the presence of a category NONDURATIVE in the italicized constituents is irrelevant to our description of the structure of these sentences. The italicized constituents pertain to a certain topological entity rather than to a temporal entity. From a certain point of view this is also the case with *van de Munt naar de Dam* in (1k). Nevertheless, this sentence is to be analyzed differently than (18) and (19).

In order to establish the nature of this difference we should compare (18) with (1k). The constituent *stond* pertains to a durative event just as *wandelen*. A sentence like *Hij stond daar urenlang* (He stood there for hours) indicates that *staan* (stand) can be subcategorized as being Durative. We can also insert a Durational Adverbial like *urenlang* in (18) without causing frequency and without blocking the single-event reading as in (1k). We could assume then that since *wandelen* is a Movement Verb, the category NONDURATIVE is actualized with respect to the constituent *van de Munt naar de Dam*. Or, in other words, the Prep Phrase in (1k) is temporalized, i.e. it receives a temporal specification when co-occurring with the Verb *wandelen* (see Section 2.4.3). In (18) the italicized constituent has only a locative sense. The same holds for (19), where the Verb *zijn* (be) is not a Movement Verb. Consequently, we could argue that the Nondurative Aspect of sentence (1k) is composed of a meaning element MOVEMENT and a meaning element DISTANCE BETWEEN TWO POINTS.

(iv) Our last objection to (XI) and (17) is that we would miss an important generalization with respect to the relationship between constituents like *van de Dam naar de Munt wandelen* in (1k) and *vallen* (fall), *struikelen* (stumble), etc. For consider the following sentences:

(20)   Urenlang *viel* de guillotine met een klap die mij telkens deed huiveren.

For hours the guillotine *fell* with a thud that made me shudder every time.

(21)   Greetje heeft urenlang *van de Munt naar de Dam* gewandeld en merkwaardig genoeg stond ze telkens bij het Spui even stil. Greetje walked for hours *from the Mint to the Dam* and strangely enough she stopped every time just for a moment at the Spui.

Both sentences can only be interpreted in their frequency reading: the presence of *telkens* (every time) is permitted only because the events in question took place several times.

In my opinion, it would be wrong to assign the category NONDURATIVE to *van de Munt naar de Dam* in (21) and to *viel* in (20). For this would imply that we have two kinds of categories NONDURATIVE, one inherent to Verbs like *vallen* (fall), the other one occurring in sister constituents of Verbs and transferred ("imparted") to Verbs like *wandelen* when occurring in sentences like (21). The former category would be inherent to the Verb *vallen* (it would appear in the simultaneous environment of its lexical entry), whereas the latter one would be an accidental category coming from the sister constituent of the Verb *wandelen*. The correspondence between (20) and (21), i.e. their sharing a frequency reading due to the presence of a Nondurative Aspect, would have to be explained as a correspondence between an inherent Verbal category NONDURATIVE in (20) and an accidental category NONDURATIVE coming from the complement of *wandelen*. This sounds highly improbable.

(XIIa)   (XIIb)

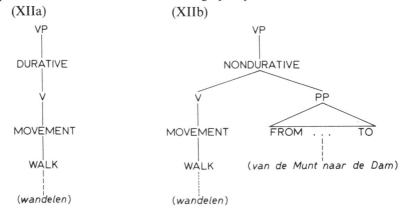

In view of the above objections there are some reasons to represent the Verb Phrases of (1a) and (1k) as in (XII), where the complex Prep Phrase contains the Prepositional nodes FROM and TO. By adopting this position, we are able to eliminate objections (i)–(iv). First of all, we need not distinguish between a Durative Verb *wandelen* and a Nondurative Verb *wan-*

delen, nor do we have to distinguish between an accidentally Nondurative Verb *wandelen* and a "real" Nondurative Prep Phrase *van de Munt naar de Dam*. The categorial node NONDURATIVE dominates V as well as the Directional Prep Phrase. Secondly we do not need to call on conditions like (17) which transfer information from one constituent to its sister constituent. Instead we can say that the node NONDURATIVE in (XIIb) is composed of categories which are dominated by it. Thirdly, we do more justice to the empirical data since we can explain the difference between sentences like (18) and (19) on the one hand and (1k) on the other in terms of the presence of a node MOVEMENT in (1k). The nodes FROM ... TO are generated in (18) and (19) as well as in (1k). Both *wandelen* (walk) and *staan* (stand) can take Durational Adverbials. Consequently, it cannot be Verbal nodes like NONDURATIVE or DURATIVE which can be held responsible for the fact that (1k) must be blocked whereas (18) can be generated. Fourthly, one can cut down to one category NONDURATIVE in (20) and (21) since this category dominates V as well as the Directional Prep Phrase. The correspondence between (20) and (21) is reflected by the correspondence between (XIIb) and (XIIc).

(XIIc)

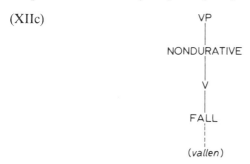

In this connection I would like to call to mind the principle of polycategorial lexical attachment applied to the account of the correspondences between such Verbs as *enter* and *go into*, represented in (Va) and (Vb). This principle turns out to conform with the position developed in the present section, namely that nodes like NONDURATIVE and DURATIVE subcategorize Verb Phrases rather than Verbs. Consider the following sentences:

(22)   *He entered the church until twelve o'clock.
(23)   *He went into the church until twelve o'clock.
(24)   He looked into the church until twelve o'clock.
(25)   He went on with his walk until twelve o'clock.

Both (22) and (23) are ungrammatical for exactly the same reason that

(1b)–(4b) are ungrammatical. It is apparent that *into* must have something to do with the ungrammaticality of (23) because *on* in (25) can occur with *go* without causing any trouble. On the other hand, we cannot say that *into the church* should be specified as containing a node NONDURATIVE since *into the church* can occur with *look* in the grammatical sentence (24). Gruber (1967a) made clear that *look* cannot be considered a Movement Verb. By contrast, *go* can be subcategorized as a Movement Verb. Consequently, we could argue that MOVEMENT + INTO forms a Nondurative Aspect, whereas NONMOVEMENT + INTO forms a Durative Aspect. The former combination of nodes is incompatible with Durational Adverbials, whereas the latter one can occur freely with them. Now, if we want to explain the ungrammaticality of (22) and (23) uniformly, we cannot say that (22) contains a Nondurative Verb *enter* and that (23) contains a Nondurative combination *went into the church*, because in that case we would have two different types of Aspects, one assigned to Verbs, the other one to Verb Phrases. If we generate structures like (Va′) and (Vb′), to which *enter* as well as *go into* can be attached with the help of different lexical attachment rules, then we can uniformly account for the ungrammaticality of (22) and (23).

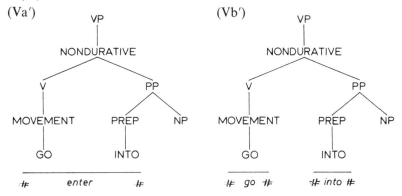

I would conclude this section by saying that Verb Phrases containing Directional Prep Phrases appear to fall under the opposition between the Durative and Nondurative Aspects. I shall return to these VP's in Section 2.4.3 after having discussed the general principles underlying the composition of the Aspects. These can best be demonstrated with the help of the relationship between the Verb and its Direct Object.

2.2. STRICTLY TRANSITIVE VS. INTRANSITIVE VERBS

In this section I shall discuss some of the consequences of the principle of polycategorial lexical attachment for the interpretation of the terms 'Transitive Verb' and 'Intransitive Verb'. It will be seen that these terms apply to derived structure. Consequently, the expression 'the Aspects are assigned to the Verb' is rather ambiguous. It appears necessary to disambiguate the term 'Verb'. Consider the following sentences:

(26)   *Luns heeft maandenlang die verklaring over Nieuw-Guinea afgelegd.
        *For months Luns made that declaration about New Guinea.
(27)   *Wekenlang stuurde Gustaaf zijn ex-geliefde een brief waarin hij haar smeekte hem weer te accepteren.
        *For weeks Gustaaf sent his ex-love a letter in which he begged her to accept him.

We must take these sentences in their frequency reading. Sentence (26) asserts that Luns repeatedly made that declaration about New Guinea. Sentence (27) informs us about Gustaaf's sending several letters to his ex-love. Both sentences are characterized by the presence of a Nondurative Aspect.

The following methodological problem comes up for discussion here. On the basis of which criterion could we assign a Nondurative Aspect to such Verbs as *afleggen* (make) and *sturen* (send) in (26) and (27)? In traditional grammar it was implicitly taken for granted that there was a criterion. So far as I can see, the underlying argument ran as follows. Since we can assign a Nondurative Aspect to intransitive Verbs like *vallen* (fall), *ontploffen* (explode), *struikelen* (stumble), etc., we are allowed to infer from the presence of this Aspect in these Verbs that strictly transitive Verbs like *afleggen* (make) and *sturen* (send) also have an Aspect. Since intransitive Verbs are unanalyzable, i.e. cannot be regarded as having a complex structure, all semantic properties e.g. their having an Aspect, are taken to be unanalyzable. Since intransitive Verbs are the same sort of entity as transitive Verbs, the inference can be made that transitive Verbs also have an Aspect.

The above line of argument, which is implicit in traditional literature on Aspects, does not take into account the fact that strictly transitive Verbs never occur alone and that consequently the inference that certain properties of intransitive Verbs are the same as certain properties of transitive Verbs is rather arbitrary. Strictly transitive Verbs form a syntactic-semantic unit with their Direct Object. Semantic properties of this unit can be scattered over the whole VP. Therefore, it can be questioned whether the inference sketched above is a valid one.

What does it mean to say that transitive Verbs have the same semantic properties as intransitive Verbs? Or, what does it mean to say that intransitive and transitive Verbs are the same sort of entity? The underlying assumption of any statement asserting that they are similar entities is that we compare certain lexical categories on the basis of their sharing a node V. The principle of monocategorial lexical attachment implies that the difference between transitive and intransitive Verbs is a matter of deep structure because the categorial tree consists of nodes having a one-to-one relationship with lexical items. That is, there is a node V to which a given lexical item is attached and this node V is specified as [+ Transitive] if the categorial tree generates a Direct Object. The category V is specified as [− Transitive] if there is no such category.

The principle of polycategorial lexical attachment, however, allows for the lexical attachment of items to sets of categories among which V. For example, the lexical entry for *enter* contains information about the node PREP as well as the node V, as shown in diagram (VIIa) on page 36. Thus it appears that the node VP (or part of it) can serve as the node in respect of which lexical categories can be characterized. As a matter of consequence, we cannot simply create an opposition between *enter* as a transitive Verb and *go* as an intransitive Verb in deep structure. It is only after lexical attachment has taken place that we can use the terms 'transitive Verb' and 'intransitive Verb', particularly after the lexical restructuring rules changing structures like (Va) on page 31 into structures like (Vc) and (Vd) on page 35 have been operative. Intransitive Verbs could, in principle, be attached to a VP having a Direct Object which does not lexicalize separately. Thus we can account for the synonymity of some intransitive Verbs with transitive Verbs plus their Direct Objects in terms of alternative lexicalizations of an identical categorial tree as is suggested by the following examples: *boeren* (belch) − *een boer laten* (lit.: bring up a belch); *gillen* (scream) − *een gil geven* (give a scream); *wandelen* (walk) − *een wandeling maken* (take a walk); *appear* − *make one's appearance; springen* (jump) − *een sprong maken* (take a jump), etc.

Returning now to the Aspects, we can see the inference mentioned above is not justified at all, since the Aspects are semantically relevant, i.e. at a level of underlying structure at which neither *vallen* (fall), *ontploffen* (explode), *struikelen* (stumble) nor *afleggen* (make), *sturen* (send) can be identified as intransitive or transitive Verbs, respectively. Consequently, there are no *a-priori*-reasons to assume that the Aspects are a matter of the deep structural category V alone on the ground that it is intransitive Verbs which Aspects are assigned to.

In view of the above considerations it is necessary to disambiguate the term 'Verb'. At present it may refer to the node V at that stage of the derivation at which lexical attachment has not yet taken place, and it may refer to a derived structural node which itself dominates the node V as well as other non-verbal nodes such as NP or PREP, at that stage of the derivation at which lexical restructuring rules demonstrated in (Vc) and (Vd) have operated. Henceforward I shall use the symbol 'V' or capitalized categories such as MOVEMENT, TAKE, DO, etc. to refer to Verbal nodes at their pre-lexical stage; the term 'Verb' will be used for referring to what appears as a Verb in surface structure, i.e. to what falls under the distinction between 'transitive' and 'intransitive'.

Neither Verb Phrases containing strictly transitive Verbs nor Verb Phrases containing intransitive Verbs facilitate the inquiry into the nature of the Aspects because they present themselves as syntactic-semantic units which can hardly be broken down into underlying categories so that we can determine, in a non-arbitrary way, which of these categories are involved. By contrast, Verb Phrases containing pseudo-intransitive Verbs (i.e. Verbs which may or may not occur with a Direct Object) provide for a clue to the exact role of the Verb and its underlying V because we are able to isolate its Direct Object. Consequently, the view that the Durative and Nondurative Aspects are composed of more elementary categories scattered over constituents dominated by the node VP (or higher nodes) is brought in question in the case of Verb Phrases containing pseudo-intransitive Verbs. In the next two sections I shall discuss sentences containing pseudo-intransitive Verbs which can occur with Direct-Object NP's as well as with Prepositional Phrases.

2.3. PSEUDO-INTRANSITIVE VERBS AND DIRECT-OBJECT NOUN PHRASES

Consider the following sentences:

(28a) Koos en Robby *aten* urenlang.
Koos and Robby *ate* for hours.
(29a) Katinka *breide* wekenlang.
Katinka *knitted* for weeks.

The italicized constituents could be specified as Durative Verbs. Neither (28a) nor (29a) necessarily express frequency; they have a single-event reading like (1a)–(4a).

On the other hand, sentences like:

(28b) *Koos en Robby aten urenlang een boterham.
*Koos and Robby ate a sandwich for hours.
(29b) *Katinka breide wekenlang een Noorse trui.
*Katinka knitted a Norwegian sweater for weeks.

are ungrammatical in their single-event reading. If taken in their frequency reading they say that Koos and Robby repeatedly ate a sandwich, and that Katinka knitted several sweaters or that she repeatedly knitted one and the same sweater which she unpicked every time she completed it.

To say that Aspects should be assigned to Verbs would force us to distinguish between Nondurative Verbs *eten* (eat) and *breien* (knit) on the one hand, and Durative Verbs *eten* and *breien* on the other, the former occurring in the b-sentences, the latter in the a-sentences. Consider also:

(28c)   Koos en Robby aten urenlang boterhammen.
         Koos and Robby ate sandwiches for hours.
(29c)   Katinka breide wekenlang Noorse truien.
         Katinka knitted Norwegian sweaters for weeks.

These sentences are interpreted in the same way as the above a-sentences. They do not express repetition of the same sort as the b-sentences. For instance, (29c) does not say that Katinka repeatedly knitted batches of Norwegian sweaters, which would be the case in:

(29d)   *Katinka breide wekenlang tien Noorse truien.
         *Katinka knitted ten Norwegian sweaters for weeks.

Sentence (29d) is ungrammatical in the single-event reading: it cannot say that the total number of Norwegian sweaters knitted by Katinka was ten. It says that Katinka knitted several batches of Norwegian sweaters, each batch consisting of ten sweaters.

The point to be made here is that apparently the nature of the Direct Object has much bearing on the presence or absence of the Nondurative Aspect. The difference between the c-sentences and the b-sentences is not a difference between Durative Verbs (*eten, breien*) in the former two and Nondurative Verbs (*eten, breien*) in the latter, which would follow from the position that Aspects should be assigned to Verbs. The difference in question is rather a difference between the Plural NP (*boterhammen, Noorse truien*) and the Singular NP (*een boterham, een Noorse trui*).

On the other hand, sentences like (29d) suggest that it is not only the opposition between categories like SINGULAR and PLURAL that is crucial to the opposition between Nondurative and Durative in the sentences under discussion. For we see that the single-event reading of (29d) is blocked owing to the presence of a Nondurative Aspect. It appears that it is rather the c-sentences containing an Indefinite *unspecified* Plural which is of key importance. In this connection it is relevant to the present analysis to note that sentence

(28d)   Koos en Robby aten urenlang iets.
         Koos and Robby ate something for hours.

should be analyzed on a par with the a-sentences and the c-sentences: no
repetition is expressed and the sentence can be interpreted in a single-
event reading. Koos and Robby were continuously involved in eating something. The pronoun *iets* (something) is specified as being INDEFINITE. In
addition it can be analyzed as having an unspecified reference to entities: it
may have a singular or a plural reference, or, in other words, it is "neutral
as to number in meaning" (Chomsky, 1964:39). One of the semantic charac-
teristics of *iets* seems to be the specification 'UNSPECIFIED QUANTITY
OF X'.[1] This is exactly what is the case in the c-sentences. The categories
INDEFINITE and PLURAL constitute the specification 'UNSPECIFIED
QUANTITY'.

We cannot maintain that it is only the nature of the Direct Object that
decides upon the question of which Aspect is present in the sentences
under discussion. For, sentences like:

(28e)   Koos en Robby zagen urenlang een boterham.
         Koos and Robby saw a sandwich for hours.
(28f)   Koos en Robby zagen urenlang boterhammen.
         Koos and Robby saw sandwiches for hours.

have underlying structures corresponding to those of the c- and a-sentences
rather than those of the b-sentences. Verbs like *breien* (knit) and *eten*
(eat) can, tentatively and provisionally, be specified as containing a node
AGENTIVE in their simultaneous environment, whereas *zien* (see) can be
characterized as a Nonagentive Verb (Gruber, 1967a:944). Apparently, the
categories $_V$[AGENTIVE]$_V$ + $_{NP}$[INDEFINITE + PLURAL]$_{NP}$ make up
the Durative Aspect inherent to the VP of the c-sentences just like the
categories $_V$[NONAGENTIVE]$_V$ + $_{NP}$[INDEFINITE + PLURAL]$_{NP}$ in
(28f). By contrast, $_V$[AGENTIVE]$_V$ + $_{NP}$[INDEFINITE + SINGULAR]$_{NP}$
constitute the Nondurative Aspect inherent to the VP's of the b-sentences,
whereas $_V$[NONAGENTIVE]$_V$ + $_{NP}$[INDEFINITE + SINGULAR]$_{NP}$ form
the Durative Aspect in sentences like (28e). We can represent the Verb
Phrases of the b- and c-sentences as in (XIIIa) and (XIIIb), respectively.[2]

The analysis leading to such structures as (XIIIa) and (XIIIb) rests on the
basic assumption that both DURATIVE and NONDURATIVE should

---

[1] A more detailed analysis of *iets* (something) will be given in Section 2.4.1, pages 68–70 where it
is shown that *iets* cannot always be characterized in terms of the specification 'UNSPECIFIED
QUANTITY OF X'.
[2] For a detailed analysis of such Verbs like *breien* (knit) and *eten* (eat) see Section 2.4.3. and
2.4.2, respectively.

(XIIIa)

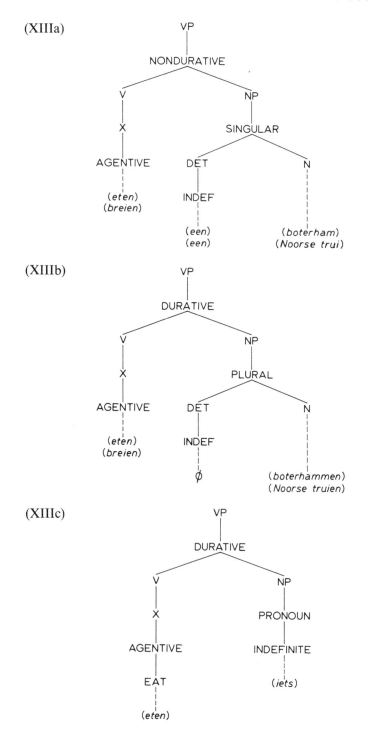

(XIIIb)

(XIIIc)

be homogeneously assigned to the same sort of constituent, in particular to the VP. In view of this we could represent the VP of (28d) by (XIIIc).

I have said that the node AGENTIVE is provisionally introduced to account for a certain meaning element in the Verbs under discussion. It will be shown that there are reasons to describe the composition of Aspects in terms of more elementary semantic categories. For this to become possible it will be necessary to discuss the relationship between pseudo-intransitive Verbs and the Prepositional Phrases with which they can occur.

2.4. PSEUDO-INTRANSITIVE VERBS AND PREPOSITIONAL PHRASES

In this section I shall discuss the following sentences:

(30a)   De Machula *speelde* urenlang *uit het celloconcert van Schumann.*
           De Machula *played from Schumann's cello concerto* for hours.
(31a)   Karel *dronk* urenlang *van de whisky.*
           lit: Karel *drank from the whisky* for hours.
           Karel took draughts from the whisky for hours.
(28g)   Koos en Robby *aten* urenlang *van een boterham.*
           lit: Koos and Robby *ate from a sandwich* for hours.
           Koos and Robby were taking bites from a sandwich for hours.
(29e)   Katinka *breide* wekenlang *aan een Noorse trui.*
           lit: Katinka *knitted at a Norwegian sweater* for weeks.
           Katinka *was knitting a Norwegian sweater* for weeks.

One of the main descriptive problems on which we have to focus our attention is the question of how to account for the relationship between these four sentences and their counterparts in which the Preposition does not occur, for example, the relationship between (28g) and (28b) *Koos en Robby aten urenlang een boterham* (*Koos and Robby ate a sandwich for hours). The italicized constituents in the above sentences are compatible with Durational Adverbials and consequently we can interpret them as pertaining to one single event. As soon as we drop the Prepositions *uit* (from), *van* (from) and *aan* (at, to), the remaining part of the italicized constituents can no longer occur with Durational Adverbials.

In Section 2.4.1 I shall analyze the Verb *spelen* as containing an underlying semantic category PERFORM. This enables us to consider *celloconcert* an Abstract Quantity Noun. In 2.4.2 I shall discuss the Verbs *drinken* and *eten*. It will be argued that they share a node TAKE. This explains the presence of the Preposition *van* (from). In Section 2.4.3 I shall connect (29e) with the discussion about the so-called *Accusativus effectivus* (Jacobsohn,

1933:297), which occurs in sentences like *Katinka breide een Noorse trui* (Katinka knitted a Norwegian sweater) where the referent of the Direct Object comes into existence as a result of the activity mentioned by the Verb.

It will be shown that there are reasons to assume that the surface structural configuration $_{VP}$[Verb + Prep Phrase]$_{VP}$ is derived from an underlying structure in which V occurs with a (Direct Object) NP which is a Dummy Pronoun. I shall argue that the description of the sentences under analysis will be simplified by adopting the view that the Aspects should be assigned to the VP rather than to V.

2.4.1. *PERFORM-Verbs and Abstract Nouns*

Consider the following sentences:

(30a)   De Machula speelde urenlang uit het celloconcert van Schumann.
De Machula played from Schumann's cello concerto for hours.

(30b)   *De Machula speelde urenlang het celloconcert van Schumann.
*De Machula played Schumann's cello concerto for hours.

(30c)   De Machula speelde urenlang in het Concertgebouw.
De Machula played in the Concertgebouw for hours.

Sentence (30b) is ungrammatical in its single-event reading and can only be interpreted as expressing frequency. Both (30a) and (30c) have a single-event reading and consequently we may assume that they both contain a Durative Aspect.

Three questions will be at issue in respect to (30a)–(30c):

(A) Should we assign the Nondurative Aspect in (30b) as a semantic primitive to the Verb *spelen*, and are the Verbs *spelen* in (30a) and (30c) accordingly Durative Verbs?

(B) What is the structural status of the Preposition *uit* (from)? Should (30a) be analyzed as having a VP consisting of the Verb *spelen* (play) and the Prep Phrase *uit het celloconcert van Schumann* (from Schumann's cello concerto) or can we say that the constituent *spelen uit* (play from) occurs with the NP *het celloconcert van Schumann*?

(C) How do we account for the opposition between (30a) and (30c) on the one hand, and (30b) on the other in terms of the distinction between the categories DURATIVE and NONDURATIVE?

As far as (A) is concerned we can say that the relationship between (30b) and (30c) corresponds to the relationship between (1a) and (1k) on page 41. Like *van de Munt naar de Dam* in (1k), *het celloconcert van Schumann* in

(30b) can be said to contribute to the Nondurative Aspect. We find sentences
like:

(30d)   Frits haatte jarenlang het celloconcert van Schumann.
         Frits hated Schumann's cello concerto for years.

which we must interpret as asserting that Frits' hate was continuously
present for some years. Note that *het celloconcert van Schumann* in (30d)
cannot be specified as for its containing a node TEMPORAL, because
Frits' hate does not concern the performance or performances of the
concerto in question but an abstract object having a linear structure that
does not pertain to time; that is, in sentence (30d) it is not representable
as a part of the Time axis.

If we were to assign a Nondurative Aspect to the Verb *spelen* in (30b)
and a Durative Aspect to the Verb *haten* in (30d), we would not be able to
account satisfactorily for the fact that the Direct-Object NP in the former
sentence requires another specification than its equivalent in the latter.
In (30b) *het celloconcert van Schumann* is temporally relevant in occurring
with *spelen*: it can be represented as an interval having duration. By regarding *haten* (hate) and *spelen* (play) as being in opposition to each other
in terms of the two Aspects under discussion we would miss the opportunity
of characterizing the nature of the difference between the two Direct-Object
NP's with which they occur. And it appears that it is this difference which
explains the ungrammaticality of (30b) in its single-event reading. In order
to make this clear let us consider the following sentences:

(30e)   Tijdens het concert begon Peter te schreeuwen.
         During the concert Peter started to yell.
(30f)   Tijdens het (cello)concert begon Peter te roepen.
         During the (cello) concerto Peter started to call out.
(30g)   *Zij speelden het concert.
         *They played the concert.
(30h)   Zij speelden het (cello)concert.
         They played the (cello) concerto.

The Noun *concert* is ambiguous in Dutch. It means either 'performance of
music' (in English: *concert*) or 'piece of music being performed' (in English:
concerto). Sentence (30e) asserts in its most natural interpretation that
Peter started to yell at some moment of an event referred to as *het concert*
(the concert). By contrast, (30f) asserts that Peter disturbed the performance of a concerto. Thus we can say in Dutch *Tijdens het concert werd het
(derde piano-)concert van Bartok uitgevoerd* (During the concert Bartok's
(third piano) concerto was performed). The asterisk in (30g) indicates that

spelen is not compatible with *het concert* in its 'performance of music'-reading. This sentence is grammatical only when *het concert* refers to a piece of music performed during a concert like in (30h). *Het (cello)concert* in (30h) corresponds to *het concert* in (30f) rather than to *het concert* in (30e).

There are some problems connected with (30f) and (30h). From (30f) we know that the concerto was being played when Peter started to yell. Nevertheless, the Verb *spelen* (play) does not occur in surface structure, whereas it does in (30h). So either we have to take *concert* (concerto) in (30f) as having the meaning 'performance of an abstract non-temporal object having linear structure', or we have to derive the Temporal Adverbial in (30f) from a structure corresponding to the following string:

> (30i)   Tijdens *het spelen van* het (cello)concert ...
>   During *the playing of* the (cello) concerto ...

The former solution would force us to distinguish between *concert* (concerto) in (30h), meaning 'abstract non-temporal object having linear structure' and *concert* (concerto) in (30f), meaning 'performance of an abstract non-temporal object having linear structure'. Such a distinction is neither necessary nor adequate. Sentence (30f) can be derived by deleting the italicized constituent in (30i) or by preventing lexicalization. In Verkuyl (1969b) it was argued that we are in need of such rules to account for Adverbials like *na dat huizenblok* (after that block) and *tijdens Johnson* (lit: during Johnson). Note in this connection that in (30f) Peter may be a musician participating in the performance of the concerto in question: he might be the logical subject of the element PERFORM underlying *het (cello)concert* in (30f). In (30e) Peter cannot be the logical subject of *het concert* (the concert). An analysis based upon the idea that (30f) is derived from the structure underlying (30i) would account for this fact.

Furthermore, if we analyze (30f) as being derived from a string having the form *tijdens* + PERFORM + *het celloconcert* (during + PERFORM + the cello concerto) where *celloconcert* is specified as 'abstract non-temporal object having linear structure', we can properly account for the difference between (30d) and

> (30j)   De Machula speelde het celloconcert van Schumann.
>   De Machula played Schumann's cello concerto.

in terms of a difference between the Verbs *spelen* (play) and *haten* (hate). The latter sentence is identical to (30b) except for the absence of the Durational Adverbial. I shall investigate into the structure of the VP of (30j) on the basis of the above considerations concerning (30e)–(30h).

We have seen that we cannot simply specify *het celloconcert van Schumann* in (30j) as containing such nodes as TEMPORAL or EVENT, because it is only with the Verb *spelen* that the NP is temporalized. Likewise we do not attribute these nodes to *het (cello)concert* in (30i) and (30h).

Somehow or other we have to express that the meaning of (30j) relates closely to the meaning of the expression:

(30j′)   De Machula caused the abstract linearly structured object 'Schumann's cello concerto' to be mapped into the Time-axis.

whereas in the case of *haten* (hate) this linear entity remains a-temporal.

If the present analysis is right, we can take one further step. Consider the following sentences:

(30k)   *Hij hoorde urenlang dat concert.
         *He heard that concerto for hours.
(30l)   Hij hoorde urenlang muziek.
         He heard music for hours.
(30m)   De Machula speelde urenlang muziek.
         De Machula played music for hours.

Sentence (30k) is ungrammatical in its single-event reading.[3] It can only assert that he repeatedly heard a concerto. By contrast, (30l) does not express repetition; the same obtains for (30m). Note that *muziek* in (30l) and (30m) is a Noncount Mass Noun, whereas *concert* in (30k) is a Count Noun. Let us characterize the meaning of *muziek* as 'virtually infinite set of auditively experienced vibrations', thus putting aside esthetic and other qualifications which make up the meaning of this word but are not relevant to our discussion. The above characterization is partly reflected by such nodes as INDEFINITE and MASS inherent to the NP *muziek*. These nodes could explain why Durational Adverbials can appear in sentences like (30l) and (30m).

Given the fact that both *spelen* (play) and *horen* (hear) bestow temporal relevance to their Direct-Object NP's, we could say that the NP *muziek* in (30l) and (30m) refers to a linearly ordered virtually infinite set of

---

[3] It should be realized that a concerto, though having a beginning and an end, may last virtually indefinitely when performed, due to the presence of recursive rules (just as in the case of sentences). Suppose that there is a concerto having a length of several hours (or weeks, or months) and that (30k) pertains to that concerto. Then *horen* (hear) can only be interpreted as meaning 'listen to', i.e. not in its normal sense. There are differences between *horen* (hear) and *luisteren naar* (listen to); the former can be described as Stative, the latter as Nonstative. The meaning of *luisteren naar* (listen to) can be described as 'move between the initial point and the terminal point of some auditively perceived quantity of information'. As such it can be considered related to constituents like *wandelen naar* (walk towards), *breien aan* (be knitting, be at work on).

auditively experienced vibrations which can be mapped into the Time axis.
If this is correct, we could equally well say that *het concert* in (30k)
refers to a bounded subset of the set of vibrations referred to as *muziek*.
That is, *een concert* is a piece of music, a certain quantity of music, just
like *tien boterhammen* (ten sandwiches) is a subset of the universal set of
sandwiches. Sentences like (30l) and (30m) allow for the following re-
presentationally significant paraphrases:

(30l′)   He perceived an unspecified quantity of music.
(30m′)   De Machula performed an unspecified quantity of music.

whereas *Hij hoorde dat concert* (He heard that concerto) and *Hij speelde dat
concert* (He played that concerto) can be paraphrased as: *He perceived a
specified quantity of music* and *He performed a specified quantity of music*,
respectively. In all these cases we can represent the referents of *muziek*
and *dat concert* in terms of the Time axis. In both (30l′) and (30m′), however, we have to do with intervals whose initial and terminal points are
not given. In the other two paraphrases the referents of *dat concert* are
bounded intervals. It should be pointed out here that we already met a
similar situation in connection with sentence (1k) and structure (XIIb) on
page 44 where the initial and terminal point of the interval in question
were given by the nodes FROM and TO.

Looking away from an account of the constituents *van Schumann*
(Schumann's) and *cello* in (30j) we can represent the remaining VP *het
concert spelen* (play the concerto) as shown in diagram (XIV).

In explanation of this diagram the following can be said. The Noun
Phrase *het concert* (the concerto) is analyzed as having an underlying struc-

(XIV)

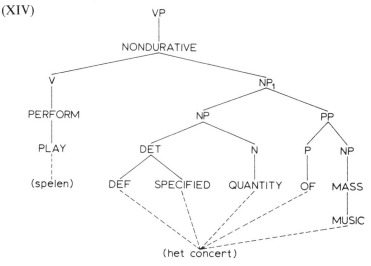

ture of the form DEF SPECIFIED QUANTITY OF MUSIC. The Determiner consists of two nodes DEF and SPECIFIED. If we were to substitute INDEFINITE for DEF, we would obtain the Noun Phrase *een
concert* (a concerto).

Note in this connection that the Noun *muziekstuk* (piece of music) in
which the category QUANTITY manifests itself in surface structure as *-stuk*
(piece), closely corresponds in meaning to *concert* (concerto). The latter
Noun is more fully specified than the former as to certain information concerning performance, which I shall not discuss here (for example, a concerto
is normally performed by an orchestra and one or more soloists). Note in
passing that we also find such Nouns as *dichtstuk* (piece of poetry) as
against *gedicht* (poem), and *toneelstuk* (stage-play) as against *drama* or
blijspel (comedy), where *dichtstuk* and *toneelstuk* have a more general
meaning than *gedicht, drama* or *blijspel*.

The node SPECIFIED calls for some further explanation. Nodes like
FINITE or BOUNDED would come close to the meaning of SPECIFIED;
however, UNSPECIFIED cannot be identified with INFINITE. The category SPECIFIED could be characterized as 'giving the bounds of the
temporal interval in question'; the category UNSPECIFIED as 'not giving
the bounds of the temporal interval in question'. Since the expression
'giving the bounds of an interval' involves referential information, SPECI-
FIED is provisionally located in the Determiner. The point is that *het concert*
(the concerto) and *een concert* (a concerto), when occurring in sentences like
(30j) refer to bounded or finite intervals on the Time axis. Only because
these intervals are bounded can we isolate them as temporal entities
distinguishable from sortlike entities; and only because they are bounded
can we count them.

At this point it will have become clear that what we have been doing here
is to analyze such categories as COUNT into more elementary categories
scattered over the whole Noun Phrase, whereas Chomsky (1965) assigned
the syntactic feature [+Count] to the Noun. It is of importance to bear in
mind that the node COUNT (i.e. the categories into which COUNT can be
analyzed) plays a crucial role in the description of the Aspects. Its presence
accounts for the fact that sentences containing a Nondurative Aspect can
express frequency if they also contain Durational Adverbials. Nodes which
exclude COUNT, e.g. MASS, do not cause repetition, as we see from (30m).

I shall elaborate the point at issue in the preceding paragraphs somewhat
further. Compare the following sentences:

(30b)   *De Machula speelde urenlang *het celloconcert van Schumann*.
         *De Machula played *Schumann's cello concerto* for hours.

(30n)   De Machula speelde urenlang *celloconcerten van 19e eeuwse componisten.*
De Machula played *cello concertos by composers of the 19th century* for hours.

The opposition between (30b) and (30n) cannot be explained in terms of the presence of the category SINGULAR in (30b) as against PLURAL in (30n), because it remains the same if we substitute such Noun Phrases as *die twee celloconcerten* (those two cello concertos), *drie romantische celloconcerten* (three romantic cello concertos), *enkele van Boccherini's cellosonates* (some of Boccherini's cello sonatas), etc. for *het celloconcert van Schumann* in (30b). Just as in the case of (29d) the resulting sentences would express repetition of sets. For example, in the case of *die twee celloconcerten* (those two cello concertos), (30b) would state that De Machula repeatedly played those two cello concertos.

The opposition between (30b) and (30n) can also not be explained in terms of the distinction between DEFINITE and INDEFINITE, because *drie romantische celloconcerten* (three romantic cello concertos) which occurs in the group of Noun Phrases substituting for *het celloconcert van Schumann* in (30b) is INDEFINITE, just as the italicized constituent in (30n). Moreover, the NP *zijn eigen cello concerten* (his own cello concertos) can substitute for the italicized constituent of (30n) without changing the Durative Aspect. The resulting sentence can include the information that De Machula played his own compositions without repeating any of them. He just played an unspecified quantity of his own cello concertos. Note that the Definite Determiner *zijn* (his) does not interfere with the information 'UNSPECIFIED'.

It is strongly suggested by sentences like (30m), (30n), (28d), etc. that the opposition between the Durative and the Nondurative Aspects can at least partly be explained in terms of such categories as MASS (i.e. NONCOUNT), PLURAL (which is also NONCOUNT) and COUNT. Specifications like COUNT and NONCOUNT are usually assigned to Nouns. Thus, Nouns like *vrouw* (woman), *concert* (concerto), *gedicht* (poem), *kaas* (cheese) in one of its senses, etc. are called Count Nouns because they can occur with an indefinite Article, and hence with Numerical elements: *een gedicht* (a poem), *tien gedichten* (ten poems). Nouns like *water*, *muziek* (music), *informatie* (information), *kaas* (cheese) in its other sense are Non-Count: **een muziek* (a music), **drie waters* (three waters), etc. Plural Nouns like *notulen* (minutes), *hersenen* (brains) are also considered Non-Count (See e.g. Chomsky, 1965; Kraak and Klooster, 1968).

The description of the opposition between sentences like (30b) and (30n), and in general the description of sentences expressing frequency, make it necessary to relate the opposition COUNT-NONCOUNT to a distinction between Noun Phrases rather than between Nouns. Thus, for example, the ungrammaticality of *Sinds zijn drie jeugden was hij een veelbelovende jongen (*Since his three youths he was a most promising boy) containing the Non-Count Noun jeugd (youth), is of exactly the same nature as the ungrammaticality of *Sinds hij drie keer jong was, was hij een veelbelovende jongen (*Since he was young thrice, he was a most promising boy). Drie keer (thrice, three times) cannot occur with hij was jong (he was young) for the same reason that drie (three) cannot occur with zijn jeugd (his youth). If it is true that hij was jong and zijn jeugd relate transformationally (as is the case in Toen hij jong was (When he was young) and tijdens zijn jeugd (during his youth)), then it is highly improbable that the property 'Countability' should be assigned to the Noun jeugd (youth), whereas it is also assigned to an S in hij was jong (he was young).[4]

By levering up the distinction between COUNT and NONCOUNT to the level of the NP we can better explain the opposition between (30b) and (30n) with respect to the diversity of Noun Phrases which can replace their italicized constituents. The presence of such Numerical elements as een, twee (two), sommige (some), enkele van (some of), etc. indicates that the NP refers to entities which can be quantified. If these elements are absent as in the case of (30m), (30n), etc. we simply cannot count. Countability is a matter of reference and hence it should be accounted for at the level at which constituents can refer to things. I shall return to this point in Chapter III.

In this connection I would like to give some attention to sentences like

(30p)   *Hij hoorde urenlang dat Jan ziek was.
        *He heard for hours that Jan was ill.

which are ungrammatical in the same way as (30k) *Hij hoorde urenlang dat concert (*He heard that concerto for hours), the more so as the sentence Hij hoorde dat concert (He heard that concerto) sounds elliptical to me in the same way as (30f) Tijdens het concert ... (During the concerto ...). We might provide some more general support for the present analysis by a proper account of (30p) so that we can capture (30k) and (30f) under the same generalization.

Sentence (30p) can be interpreted as asserting that he heard several times someone giving the information 'John is ill'. We cannot simply analyze (30p) in terms of an underlying structural string of the form NP+

---

[4] Cf. in this connection Bowers (1969) who argued for similar reasons that Nouns like virtue, death and hence jeugd (youth) should not be specified as [+Abstract].

$_{VP}$[HEAR + S]$_{VP}$, where the embedded S is the Direct-Object of the VP, because this string would not express the fact that he heard sentences being uttered containing the information that John is ill.

Ross (1968) argued convincingly, to my mind, that every sentence can be regarded as a Direct-Object S of a Verb Phrase in which a so-called Performative Verb (*say, declare, ask, demand, forbid, require*, etc.) occurs. Thus a sentence like *Jan is ziek* (Jan is ill) is analyzed as NP$_1$ + $_{VP}$[PERFORMATIVE + NP$_2$ + $_S$[JAN IS ILL]$_S$]$_{VP}$, where NP$_1$ represents the speaker, NP$_2$ the hearer, and S the sentence *Jan is ziek*. The Performative used here is a Declarative Performative corresponding to Verbs like *say* or *declare*. Consequently, we can represent the differences between sentence-types (declaratives, questions, imperatives) in terms of different Performatives. Ross' analysis also accounts for the speaker (the highest NP of a tree), the hearer (the second NP of a tree) and what is said in a sentence. See also McCawley (1968a:155–8) for a perspicuous exposition of Ross' analysis.

Sentence (30p) provides an independent argument for the correctness of Ross' position. Consider structure (XV), underlying *Hij hoorde dat Jan ziek was* (He heard that John was ill), which corresponds to a sentence

(XV)

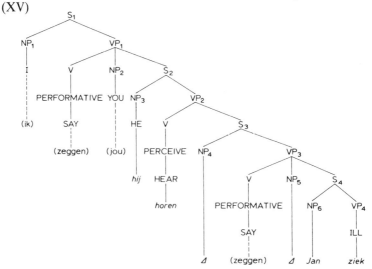

where the Performatives occur in surface structure:

(30p′)   Ik (NP$_1$) zeg jou (NP$_2$) dat hij (NP$_3$) hoorde dat iemand (NP$_4$) zei tegen iemand (NP$_5$) dat Jan (NP$_6$) ziek was.

I say to you that he heard that someone said to someone that Jan was ill.

The crucial point here is that *urenlang* (for hours) cannot occur with *zeggen* without causing repetition. Thus, the sentence **Ik zeg urenlang tegen jou dat hij ziek is* (*I say to you for hours that he is ill) can only be interpreted as asserting that I repeatedly give the information that he is ill. Apparently, we can analyze the construction *zeggen* + S (say + S), or more generally, PERFORMATIVE + S as constituting a Nondurative Aspect. I think it will not be too far-fetched to relate the underlying string PERFORMATIVE + S to structures like (XIV) and to assume that in both cases the Nondurative Aspect is formed on the basis of one and the same principle.

Of course, Performatives can occur in embedded sentences as well. In structure (XV) the node NP_4 represents the speaker (speakers) of sentence S_4. Now, the restriction between the Durational Adverbial and the Nondurative Aspect in sentence (30p) concerns the VP_3 of (XV). To my mind, the nodes PERFORMATIVE and S_4 constitute the Nondurative Aspect which is incompatible with the Durational Adverbial in (30p) in the single-event reading; for a sentence as an expedient for exchanging information can be considered a piece of linearly ordered information, i.e. an abstract object having linear structure. As such this object corresponds to a concerto. The information contained by the sentence *Jan is ziek* (Jan is ill) is a certain quantity of auditive information. To hear a sentence is to perceive the temporal realization of an abstract object having linear structure, just as hearing a concerto is to perceive auditively the temporalization, i.e. the performance, of a piece of music. To say a sentence is to temporalize (to "perform") a piece of information. We relate its linear structure to the Time axis. In the same way as the concerto in (30j) can be considered a certain quantity of music being performed, a sentence can be regarded as a certain quantity of information being performed. *Informatie* (information) is a Mass Noun just like *muziek* (music). In fact, music can be considered a special type of auditively perceived information. On the basis of these considerations we can analyze (30p) in terms of an underlying string roughly having the following form:

(30p″)   HE + AUDITIVELY PERCEIVED +$_s$[$\varDelta$ + PERFORMATIVE + $\varDelta$ + PIECE OF INFORMATION]$_s$.

It is strongly suggested by the above analysis that S-nodes occurring after Performatives should be specified somehow for pertaining to tokens rather than to types. That is, it should be expressed that S_2 and S_4 in structure (XV) differ from S_1 and S_3 in that they pertain to propositions which are uttered, i.e. realized in time. This marks the difference between such sentences as *Hij dacht urenlang dat De Gaulle was overleden* (He thought

for hours that De Gaulle had died) and *Hij zei urenlang dat De Gaulle
overleden was (*He said for hours that De Gaulle had died). The S following *denken* (think) need not be specified as for its pertaining to a token.
So far as I can see, the node SPECIFIED should contain information about
token-reference; the node UNSPECIFIED expresses information about
type-reference. I shall not go into the question of how the nodes SPECIFIED
and UNSPECIFIED should be stored in S-structures.

The Verbs *horen* (hear), *zeggen* (say) and *spelen* (play) apparently all
share the property of performing some mental or physical activity. To account for this correspondence we can say that Performatives like *zeggen*
(say) as well as Verbs like *spelen* (play) and *horen* (hear), which are not
Performatives in the sense meant by Ross, all belong to a category of Verbs
which contain an underlying node PERFORM. In this they resemble very
much the Verb *wandelen* (walk) which "temporalizes" Directional Phrases
like *van de Munt naar de Dam* (from the Mint to the Dam), as we see from
Section 2.1, particularly from page 43. If we break down the node
MOVEMENT into more fundamental nodes, one of which is the node
PERFORM, we would obtain a generalization which covers cases like
van de Munt naar de Dam wandelen (walk from the Mint to the Dam), *een
concert spelen* (play a concerto), *een zin zeggen* (say a sentence), *een concert
horen* (hear a concerto). All these cases can be analyzed in terms of an underlying structure of the form 'PERFORM + SPECIFIED QUANTITY
OF X'.

Summarizing point (A), i.e. the question of whether or not we should assign the Aspects to Verbs like *spelen* in (30a)–(30c), we can say that this
would force us to assume that there are several Verbs *spelen* (play). Furthermore, it would prevent the above made generalizations, which are based on
the assumption that Aspects can be regarded as entities of a compositional
nature. If the above analysis is correct, the following statements emerge
from it:

(32)   The Nondurative Aspect in the sentences under discussion is
        composed of:
        $_{VP}[_V[PERFORM]_V + _{NP}[SPECIFIED \ QUANTITY \ OF \ X]_{NP}]_{VP}$

(33)   The Durative Aspect in these sentences is composed of the
        following categories:
        $_{VP}[_V[PERFORM]_V + _{NP}[UNSPECIFIED \ QUANTITY$
        $OF \ X]_{NP}]_{VP}$

Both (32) and (33) enable us to approach the problem formulated under
point (B), i.e. the problem of how to describe the underlying structure of

sentences like (30a) *De Machula speelde uit het celloconcert van Schumann* (De Machula played from Schumann's cello concerto), with respect to the structural status of the Preposition *uit*.

As far as the position of *uit* (from) with respect to *spelen* (play) and *het celloconcert van Schumann* (Schumann's cello concerto) is concerned, there seem to be two possible arguments. Either we analyze (30a) in terms of a strong degree of cohesion between *spelen* and *uit* which is expressed by regarding them as being dominated by the same node, or we adopt the view that *uit* belongs to a Prep Phrase whose NP is *het celloconcert van Schumann*. I shall argue in favour of the latter view.

The first position is represented in structure (XVI).

(XVI)

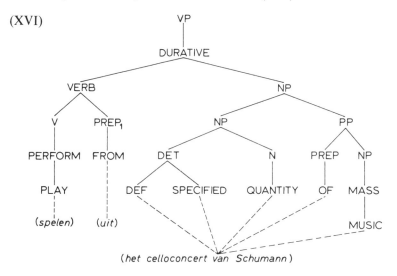

This structure suggests that we need a lexical entry for *spelen uit* (play from), to be taken as one Verb. The Durative Aspect is assigned to the VP a little previously, at any rate ahead of the argument. Let us therefore again broach the question of whether the category DURATIVE should indeed be assigned to the VP or not. This is of importance in view of our desire to reject the configuration $_{\text{VERB}}[\text{V}+\text{PREP}_1]_{\text{VERB}}$ as the underlying structure of *spelen uit* (play from).

As far as I can see the Durative Aspect in (30a) could be only assigned to the VP or to VERB, not to the node V or to PREP$_1$. If the Durative Aspect were assigned to the node V, we would not be able to explain the difference between (30a) and (30b), unless we would distinguish between two Verbs *spelen*. As a matter of fact, the presence of the Preposition *uit* has something to do with the fact that the Durational Adverbial can occur freely in (30a) and not in (30b).

We cannot assign the Durative Aspect to PREP₁ either: *uit* (from) is not a Temporal Preposition, whereas Aspects are to be considered entities having to do with time. Moreover, we would need a rule neutralizing the effect of combinations like those given in (32). In other words, *spelen* contains a node PERFORM, and *het celloconcert van Schumann* can be analyzed as having an underlying structure of the form SPECIFIED QUANTITY OF MUSIC. Both specifications appear to constitute an element which is incompatible with Durational Adverbials. If the Durative Aspect were inherent to PREP₁ in (XVI), we would have to neutralize the effect of the combination PERFORM + SPECIFIED QUANTITY OF MUSIC; we would need a special type of rule for which no other empirical justification can be found. Consequently, I reject the idea of assigning the Durative Aspect in (30a) to PREP₁.

Now, if the above argument can be agreed upon, we could consider the possibility of assigning the Durative Aspect to VERB. Note, however, that if we do this, we immediately adopt the position developed in the present Chapter, namely that Aspects are of a compositional nature and that they are not semantic primitives. As soon as we are ready to assign the Durative Aspect to VERB in (XVI) and thus accept the principle of analyzing Aspects into more elementary categories (in this case V and PREP₁), we reach the position where an alternative solution can be offered, namely of assigning the Durative Aspect to the VP on the basis of the same principle. This solution is represented by (XVI). The question of whether the Durative Aspect should be assigned to the VP or to VERB in (XVI) will be postponed until we have represented the second possibility with respect to the status of *uit*, namely the possibility of its being a sister constituent of the NP *het celloconcert van Schumann*. Thus we could, for instance, say that the underlying structure of the VP in (30a) is of the form shown in structure (XVII).

I have assigned the Durative Aspect to VP and not to V for several reasons, all having been under discussion above. Summarizing the preceding considerations we seem to face three possibilities: (a) the Durative Aspect can be assigned to the node VERB in (XVI); (b) it could be assigned to the node VP in (XVI); and (c) it occurs as sketched in (XVII).

I shall now present an analysis of sentence (30a) which shows that (c) should be preferred to (a) and (b), but which also indicates that structure (XVII) can at most be regarded as derived from an underlying structure in which the Prep Phrase *uit het celloconcert van Schumann* is part of a Noun Phrase which is the Direct Object of the Verb Phrase *spelen uit het celloconcert van Schumann* (play from Schumann's cello concerto). This analysis appears to do more justice to the empirical data presented in this section

(XVII)

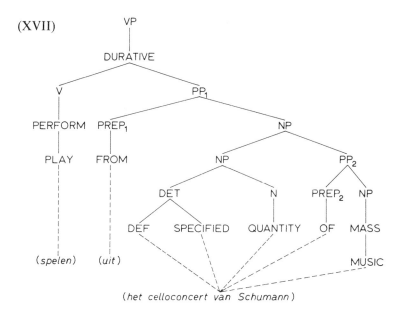

in that it enables us to account for the relationships between (30a), (30b) and (30c) homogeneously: we can restrict ourselves to one single Verb *spelen* in all three sentences; we will be able to explain the opposition between (30a) and (30c) on the one hand, and (30b) on the other; we can generalize our findings under point (A) as well as the results of our analysis of sentences like (28) and (29) in section 2.4.3; and finally, as far as (b) and (c) are concerned, it will become clear that structure (XVI) could, in principle, be derived from structure (XVII) by a restructuring rule operative in the lexical component. Consequently, the analysis to come will automatically exclude (a) as an inadequate solution to the descriptive problems under discussion; (b) and (c) are not, in fact, alternative solutions but represent different stages of the derivation of (30a).

It seems not unreasonable to analyze (30a) in terms of a synonymity relationship with a sentence like:

(30q) De Machula speelde urenlang stukken/delen uit het celloconcert van Schumann.
De Machula played pieces/parts from Schumann's cello concerto for hours.

In a certain way (30q) could be considered a correct paraphrase of (30a). Accordingly, we could explain why (30a) and (30q) are similar, both containing a Durational Adverbial without having a frequency reading of the sort given in (30b). The Plural NP *stukken* behaves like *boterhammen* (sandwiches) in (28c) *Koos en Robby aten urenlang boterhammen* (Koos and Robby ate sandwiches for hours). Given the synonymity relationship between (30a) and (30q) we could derive (30a) transformationally from (30q) by an optional deletion of the Plural Noun *stukken* (pieces) or *delen* (parts).

However, it appears that (30a) is only partially synonymous to (30q). If we replace *urenlang* by the Durational Adverbial *minutenlang* (for minutes) the interpretation of (30a) does not necessarily include the information that De Machula played pieces or parts from the cello concerto. He most probably played a part from it continuously for the duration of some minutes. This becomes even more clear if we replace *urenlang* by *gedurende vijf seconden* (for five seconds). It would be wrong to use (30q) in that case, whereas (30a) could be used. Apparently, the lexical meaning of the surface structure configuration *stukken uit een concert* (pieces from a concerto) does not correspond to the meaning of its counterpart *uit een concert* (from a concerto) in (30a). *Stuk uit een concert* (piece from a concerto) means 'structured part of a concerto' whereas we need a constituent expressing the meaning '(unspecified) subset of a set of vibrations'. Note also that we cannot paraphrase (30a), whether or not containing *minutenlang* instead of *urenlang*, as:

(30r)   *De Machula speelde urenlang/minutenlang *een stuk (een deel)* *uit het celloconcert van Schumann*.
        *De Machula played *a piece (a part) from Schumann's cello concerto* for hours/for minutes.

because the italicized constituent corresponds to *een boterham* in (28b) and *een Noorse trui* in (29b) rather than to *boterhammen* in (28c) and *Noorse truien* in (29c): the VP *spelen + een stuk uit* ... (play + a piece from ...) is a Nondurative VP like *eten + een boterham* (eat + a sandwich) and *breien + een Noorse trui* (knit + a Norwegian sweater). Sentence (30r) corresponds to (28b) and (29b); (30a) to (28c) and (29c).

In view of the above considerations we can link up with the well-known analysis of pseudo-intransitive Verbs discussed in Chomsky (1964:37–46) and Katz and Postal (1964:79–86) and anticipated in Section 2.3, structure (XIIIc). Chomsky discussed such cases as *His car was stolen*, where the logical subject does not appear in surface structure, and *John is eating*, where the logical object is absent in surface structure, to illustrate an important general condition on transformational grammar. He says:

Each major category has associated with it a "designated element" as a member. This designated element may actually be realized (e.g., *it* for abstract Nouns, *some (one, thing)*), or it may be an abstract "dummy element". It is this designated representative of the category that must appear in the underlying strings for those transformations that do not preserve, in the transform, a specification of the actual terminal representative of the category in question.

In other words, a transformation can delete an element only if this element is the designated representative of a category, or if the structural condition that defines this transformation states that the deleted element is structurally identical to another element of the transformed string. A deleted element is, therefore, always recoverable. (1964:41).

Thus, for example, *John is eating* can be analyzed as *John + is + eating + Δ* where *Δ* is the dummy element. According to Chomsky a sentence like (28d) *Koos en Robby aten urenlang iets* (Koos and Robby were eating something for hours) contains the actualized designated element *iets* (something) of the Direct Object-NP. Katz and Postal (1964:80–4) interpreted the line of thought given in the above quotation by saying that sentences like *John is reading*, etc. "must be derived by deleting one of the pro-forms of a Noun Phrase, in this case either *something* or *it*" (p. 81). Kraak, however, argued that the position that the dummy element is a Pro-form of an Indefinite Pronoun can be questioned. "It implies that in general sentences with indefinite pronouns are synonymous with sentences in which deletion of a deep structure Pro-form has taken place" (1968:151). According to him *M.I.T. papers should be published more often*, being a categorial sentence, is not synonymous with *M.I.T. papers should be published more often by someone*.[5] Kraak proposed that the Pro-form should be replaced by an 'Unspecified' NP, a dummy element which comes close to the meaning of the Indefinite Pronoun but which does not share all syntactic properties of an Indefinite Pronoun. The fact that the Indefinite Pronoun turns out to be non-neutral as to number in some cases, can also be illustrated by the following sentence:

(30s)   De Machula speelde urenlang *iets uit het celloconcert van Schumann.*
          De Machula played *something from Schumann's cello concerto* for hours.

which tends to have a frequency reading rather than a single-event reading. It would appear that the italicized constituent contains a category SPECIFIED, which is not necessarily present in *De Machula speelde urenlang iets* (De Machula played something for hours). In Section 2.4.2 I shall discuss an analogous case which illustrates the difference between *iets* (something) and the 'Unspecified Dummy' more clearly: that is, it is not easy to determine whether *iets* in (30s) refers to a specified subpart of Schumann's cello concerto or not. In the case of Concrete Mass Nouns there is less observational uncertainty as to this point.

---

[5] Recently some other examples illustrating the difference under analysis quite clearly came to my attention in Grinder (1971). A sentence like *Sam ate something$_i$ and it$_i$ was green* cannot be derived from the same underlying structure as *Sam ate and it was green*. The same obtains for *Maxime was told by someone$_i$ that she had to kiss him$_i$* and *Maxime was told that she had to kiss him$_i$*.

It will be clear that Chomsky's quotation with respect to a "designated representative" of a Noun Phrase as well as its amendments immediately apply to sentence (30c). The VP of this sentence can be described in terms of (XIIIc). However, by doing this we would miss an important generalization with regard to structure (XIV). Though we cannot say that (30c) gives information about De Machula's playing music we know that he did temporalize some abstract object having linear structure: he could have played pieces from a comedy, a pantomime act, or the like. Consequently, we could analyze the 'Unspecified NP' inherent to the VP of (30c) as having an internal structure of the form shown in (XVIII).

(XVIII)

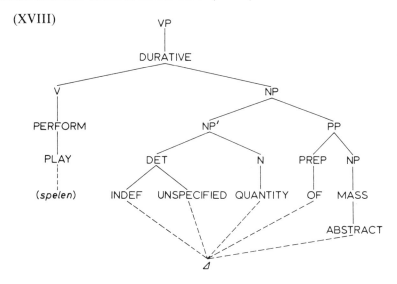

This structure gives us the opportunity to distinguish the underlying Direct Object-NP of the VP in (30c), i.e. the node NP in (XVIII), from its counterpart in sentence (28a) *Koos en Robby aten urenlang* (Koos and Robby ate for hours).

We know from (28a) that the underlying 'Unspecified' NP pertains to something concrete, as we know from (30c) that it refers to something of an abstract nature. Structure (XVIII) accounts for this difference by the presence of the node ABSTRACT. The underlying NP of (28a) would have the same structure as NP_1 in (XVIII) except for the node ABSTRACT, which would be CONCRETE.

The relationship between (30c) and (30a) can be optimally accounted for, if we assume that the latter sentence contains an Unspecified Direct-Object NP of the form given in (XVIII); in this way, we can homogeneously account for the fact that both sentences contain a Durative Aspect. We could represent the VP of (30a) as is shown in (XIX), where NP abbreviates the NP of (XVIII).

In this diagram the Direct Object of *spelen* (play) is NP_1. Its head is the Unspecified Dummy NP, whose sister node PP_1 is taken here as a so-called *Genitivus partitivus*. In the next section I shall discuss alternative representations with the help of structure (XXI) since the sentences under analysis there more overtly posit the problem of whether Prep Phrases with FROM

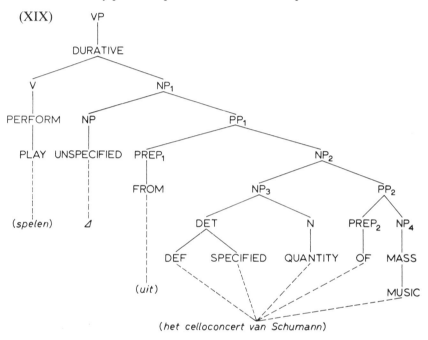

(*het celloconcert van Schumann*)

and Prep Phrases with OF can both be considered partitive genitives. Since PP_1 is taken here as an attributive adjunct, it will be clear that the relationship between V and NP_1 involves the nodes PERFORM and UNSPECIFIED NP rather than any of the nodes dominated by PP_1. The Durative Aspect in sentences like (30a) is composed of information inherent to V and to the unspecified dummy NP of the following configuration:

(33a) $_{VP}[_V[\text{PERFORM}]_V +\ _{NP_1}[_{NP}[\text{UNSPECIFIED QUANTITY}$
       OF $X]_{NP}\ _{PP_1}[\text{FROM}_{NP_2}[X]_{NP_2}]_{PP_1}]_{NP_1}]_{VP}$

where X is a variable.

If (XIX) can be accepted as the correct structural description of the VP *spelen uit het celloconcert van Schumann* (play from Schumann's cello concerto) at a certain pre-lexical stage of the derivation of (30a), then we can account for (XVII) and (XVI) by rules which are operative after (XIX) is generated. A transformational rule deleting the Dummy NP in (XIX), yields structure (XVII) after the application of the convention called *Tree-pruning*, by which a non-branching node, in our case NP_1, can be taken away in derived structure (See Chapter I, footnote 24). Subsequently, (XVI) could, in principle, be derived from (XVII) by a restructuring rule detaching $PREP_1$ from PP_1 and Chomsky-adjoining it to VERB in (XVI); thus, $PREP_1$ would become a sister node of V, just as INTO became a sister-node of GO in (Vc) and (Vd).

However, it remains to be seen whether (XVI) is an adequate representation of any stage of the derivation of the VP in (30a). In relating (XVI) transformationally to (XIX) and (XVII) we face an interesting consequence of Gruber's conception of the lexical attachment component, which I shall briefly discuss in conclusion of point (B). Suppose that our lexicon contains an entry of the form given in (XX), where x represents the lexical

(XX)

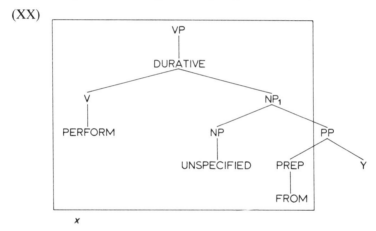

item in question and Y is a variable representing the peripheral environment of (XIX). Then (XVI) can be derived from (XIX) and (XVII) to obtain a transitive Verb x which takes *het celloconcert van Schumann* as its (surface structural) Direct-Object NP. Like *go into* the VERB *spelen uit* (play from) in (XVI) consists of a node V and a node PREP. However, whereas *go into* is synonymous with the transitive Verb *enter*, Dutch does not have a transitive Verb x which is synonymous to *spelen uit* (play from). It is of importance to note that if Dutch were enriched with a Verb synonymous to *spelen uit*, say **deelspelen* (lit: partplay), Gruber's polycategorial lexical attachement component could deal adequately with this addition. The lexical entry for this new Verb x would be (XX), and in the same way (Vd) is obtained by a restructuring rule adjoining PREP to V, structure (XVI) would be derived from structure (XVII).

The structural descriptions (XVIII) and (XIX) prepared the ground for (C), i.e. the question of how to account for the opposition between (30a) and (30c) on the one hand, and (30b) on the other (see page 54) in terms of the distinction between the nodes DURATIVE and NONDURATIVE. Since the answer to this question is implicitly given in our discussion under (A) and (B), I shall give it the form of a brief summary of our findings in so far as these apply to (30a), (30b) and (30c). The Verb Phrases of these sentences are structurally described in (XIX), (XIV) and (XVIII), respectively. The chief points concerning (C) are:

(i) we can restrict ourselves to a single Verb *spelen* only, occurring in all three sentences under analysis; hence we can cut down the number of lexical entries for *spelen*.

(ii) the Nondurative Aspect in (30b) appears to be made up of the semantic categories $_V$[PERFORM]$_V$ and $_{NP}$[SPECIFIED QUANTITY OF X]$_{NP}$, where both V and NP are dominated by the node VP (see 32));

(iii) the Durative Aspect in (30a) and (30c) appears to be composed of the semantic categories $_V$[PERFORM]$_V$ and $_{NP}$[UNSPECIFIED QUANTITY OF X]$_{NP}$, where V and NP are also dominated by the node VP (see (33) and (33a)).

Ockham's razor cuts both ways here. On the one side, the restriction under (i) simplifies our lexicon and accounts for the correspondence between *spelen* in (30a), *spelen* in (30b) and *spelen* in (30c). This correspondence is expressed by the node PERFORM. On the other side (ii) and (iii) also express a restriction: the opposition between the Durative and the Non-durative Aspect concerns the same level of constituency. Both Aspects can homogeneously be assigned to one and the same node.

2.4.2. *TAKE-Verbs and Concrete Nouns*

Consider now the following sentences:

(31a)   Karel dronk urenlang whisky.
         Karel drank whisky for hours.
(31b)   *Karel dronk (urenlang) van whisky.
         *Karel drank from whisky (for hours).
(31c)   *Karel dronk urenlang de whisky.
         *Karel drank the whisky for hours.
(31d)   Karel dronk urenlang van de whisky.
         Karel drank from the whisky for hours.
(35a)   De muis at wekenlang kaas.
         The mouse ate cheese for weeks.
(35b)   *De muis at (wekenlang) van kaas.
         *The mouse ate from cheese (for weeks).

(35c)   *De muis at wekenlang de kaas.
         *The mouse ate the cheese for weeks.
(35d)   De muis at wekenlang van de kaas.
         The mouse ate from the cheese for weeks.

The a-sentences have a single-event reading: Karel's drinking whisky can be considered a durative event. The same obtains for the mouse's eating cheese. The d-sentences also contain a Durative Aspect. The c-sentences can express repetition though they are somewhat "strange" from a pragmatic point of view: a definite portion of whisky c.q. cheese is consumed repeatedly. It appears possible to explain the ungrammaticality of the b-sentences in terms of a general rule operating on the underlying structure of the d-sentences.

Let us, however, first discuss Verbs like *drinken* (drink) and *eten* (eat). Consider the following sentences:

(31e)   *Karel stal van whisky.
         *Karel stole from whisky.
(35e)   *De muis snoepte van kaas.
         *The mouse sneaked from cheese.
(31f)   Karel stal van de whisky.
         Karel stole from the whisky.
(35f)   De muis snoepte van de kaas.
         The mouse sneaked from the cheese.
(31g)   *Karel zag van (de) whisky.
         *Karel saw from (the) whisky.
(35g)   *De muis rook van (de) kaas.
         *The mouse smelt from (the) cheese.

The e- and f-sentences indicate that *stelen* (steal) and *snoepen* (sneak) correspond to *drinken* (drink) and *eten* (eat): all four Verbs can occur with *van de whisky* (from the whisky) but exclude the presence of *van whisky* (from whisky). Note that there are Verbs which can occur with *van whisky* and *van kaas*: *Hij hield van whisky* (He loved whisky); *Hij hield zich verre van whisky* (He kept himself aloof from whisky), etc. On the other hand, there are Verbs like *zien* (see) and *ruiken* (smell) which can neither occur with *van whisky* (from whisky) nor with *van de whisky* (from the whisky). Analogously to the c-sentences we do not find *De muis snoepte wekenlang de kaas* (*The mouse sneaked the cheese for weeks) nor *De dief stal wekenlang het geld* (*The thief stole the money for weeks). Thus we can subcategorize *drinken, eten, stelen, snoepen* with respect to a syntactic property they share: they cannot occur in the b-, c- and e-sentences whereas they appear freely in the a-, d- and f-sentences. Semantically they all contain a category which I shall refer to as TAKE; it can be characterized as presenting the meaning 'separate (a subset S_i of a given set M from its complement S_i' in M). This node is absent in *zien* (see) and *ruiken* (smell). It accounts for the difference between the g-sentences on the one hand, and the d- and f-sentences on the other. As we shall see below, it will also account for the ungrammaticality of the b- and e-sentences. It is of importance to note that the Verb *nemen* (take) itself behaves exactly like *eten* (eat), *drinken* (drink) etc.[6]

(36a)   Johnny nam wekenlang whisky.
         Johnny took whisky for weeks.
(36b)   *Johnny nam wekenlang van whisky.
         *Johnny took from whisky for weeks.
(36c)   *Johnny nam wekenlang de whisky.
         *Johnny took the whisky for weeks.
(36d)   Johnny nam wekenlang van de whisky.
         Johnny took from the whisky for weeks.

In my opinion, this fact confirms the point made in respect of the semantic category inherent to Verbs like *drinken* (drink), *eten* (eat), *stelen* (steal), *snoepen* (sneak), etc. The Verb *nemen* (take) seems to be the least specific Verb with respect to the others: its simultaneous and peripheral environment is contained by the lexical entries of the other Verbs, the difference being that the latter are more fully specified. For example, *drinken* has the same lexical entry as *nemen* (take) except for its simultaneous environment which contains a node CONSUME, and for its richer peripheral environment in which the node FLUID will have to occur. *Nemen* is the more general Verb.

I shall now broach the question of how we should express the fact that the a- and d-sentences above contain a Durative Aspect, as contrasted with the c-sentences which are characterized by the presence of the Nondurative Aspect. The ungrammaticality of the b-sentences provides a clue to the underlying structure of the a- and d-sentences. We do not find:

(31h)   *Karel dronk een slok van whisky.
         *Karel drank a draught from whisky.
(31i)   *Karel dronk iets van whisky.
         *Karel drank something from whisky.
(35h)   *De muis at een stuk van kaas.
         *The mouse ate a piece from cheese.

---

[6] I owe this observation to Jan Luif (personal communication).

(35i)   *De muis at iets van kaas.
        *The mouse ate something from cheese.

whereas the following sentences are grammatical:

(31j)   Karel dronk een slok van de whisky (die hem werd aangeboden).
        lit: Karel drank a draught from the whisky (that was offered to
        him).
        Karel took a draught from the whisky.
(31k)   Karel dronk iets van de whisky (...).
        lit: Karel drank something from the whisky (...).
        Karel drank some of the whisky.
(35j)   De muis at een stuk van de kaas.
        lit: The mouse ate a piece from the cheese.
        The mouse ate away a piece of the cheese.
(35k)   De muis at iets van de kaas.
        lit: The mouse ate something from the cheese.
        The mouse ate away some of the cheese.

The above eight sentences show that Mass Nouns like *whisky* and *water* must
be preceded by a Definite Determiner if the Direct-Object NP contains
Quantity Nouns like *slok* (draught), *stuk* (piece), but also Indefinite Pronouns like *iets*. Note in passing that in the j- and k-sentences it is possible
to have *nemen* (take) instead of *drinken* or *eten*. In fact, it is more normal
to use *nemen* in (31j) if the restrictive clause were dropped; nevertheless
drinken can be used as well.

   Thus there appears to be a rule stating that the DET_2 of the following
underlying structure:

(37) $TAKE + {}_{NP}[{}_{NP}[DET_1 + QUANTITY NOUN]_{NP} + FROM +$
        $DET_2 + MASS NOUN]_{NP}$

should be definite.

   We could analyze the Verb Phrase of the d-sentences analogously to the
VP *spelen uit het concert* (play from the concerto) in structure (XIX), as is
shown by (XXI), where the UNSPECIFIED NP is the head of NP_1 and consequently determines the relationship between V and the rest of the Verb
Phrase.

   If this is correct, the grammaticality of the d-, j- and k-sentences is
homogeneously accounted for in terms of (37). Moreover, this analysis
enables us to predict the ungrammaticality of the b-sentences on the basis
of their violating the rule stating that DET_2 in structures of the form (37)
must be definite.

Analogously to (33a) on page 71 we would now have:

(33b) $_{VP}[_V[TAKE]_V +_{NP_1}[_{NP}[UNSPECIFIED QUANTITY}$
$OF X]_{NP\ PP_1}[FROM_{NP_2}[X]_{NP_2}]_{PP_1}]_{NP_1}]_{VP}$

Consequently, we can account for the Durative Aspect in (31d) and (35d) in the same way as we did in the case of sentence (30a). I have used the same indices for Noun Phrases as in diagram (XIX) to indicate which nodes correspond to each other. The node NP_4 should be understood as referring to the universal set of all whisky-cheese particles scattered over the world.

(XXI)

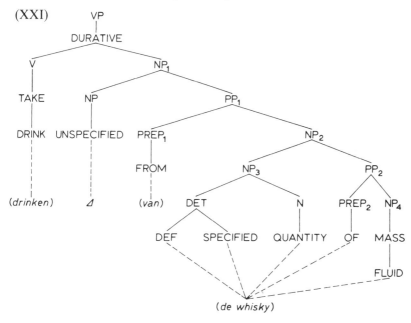

The VP of the a-sentences can be analyzed as shown in diagram (XXII). It will be clear that structure (XXII) fits into our frame (33b). Thus we have uniformly accounted for the Durative Aspect in the a- and d-sentences.

At this point in the present analysis, it is necessary to broach the two unanswered questions raised in the preceding section in connection with the status of the Unspecified Dummy NP. The first concerns the difference in meaning between the Indefinite Pronoun occurring in surface structure and the Dummy NP. The second pertains to the difference between Prep Phrases with FROM and OF.

As I pointed out with respect to (30s) it is not easy, in the case of Abstract Nouns like *concert* (concerto), to determine whether or not *iets* (something) is neutral as to number when occurring with a Prep Phrase containing FROM. By contrast, a sentence like:

(35m)   *De muis at urenlang iets van de kaas.
          lit: The mouse ate something from the cheese for hours.
          *The mouse ate away some of the cheese for hours.

is clearly ungrammatical in a single-event reading. We have already noted
that sentences like (28d) *Koos en Robby aten urenlang iets* (Koos and Robby
ate something for hours) do not necessarily have a frequency reading like
(35m). Apparently *iets van de kaas (eten)* (lit: (eat) something from the
cheese) is different from *iets (eten)* ((eat) something).

(XXII)

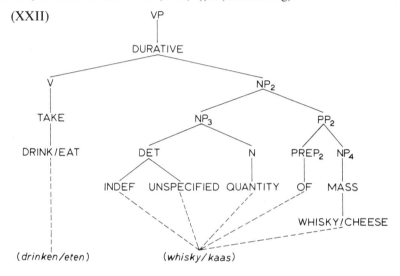

By now we have arrived at the second question, for how do we account
for the fact that *iets* in (28d) and *iets* in (35m) differ from each other? Does
this difference concern *iets* (something) and *iets van de kaas* (lit: something
from the cheese) or *iets eten* (eat something) and *iets van de kaas eten*
(lit: eat something from the cheese)? In the former case, we could consider
van de kaas (lit: from the cheese) an attributive Adjunct, and consequently
the difference in question could be explained by saying that the neutrality
as to number in *iets* (something) is affected by the attributive Prep Phrase
van de kaas (from the cheese). In the latter case we have to assume that *iets*
is modified by *van de kaas eten* (eat from the cheese) and somehow receives
the node SPECIFIED. In both cases, however, a possible explanation for the
difference between *iets* in (28d) and (35m) is that *de kaas* (the cheese) refers
to a specified quantity of cheese particles and we cannot infinitely take
specified quantities of cheese particles from this specified quantity. Note
in this connection that this explanation would also cover the question-
marks with respect to *iets* in (30s). It is, in principle, possible to play

infinitely and continuously specified parts from a concerto (i.e. from a specified quantity of music) owing to the *da capo*-sign. We encounter here a difference between the nouns PERFORM and TAKE.

Our answer to the question of whether it is correct to represent the relationship between NP_2 and NP_1 in structures like (XXI) and (XIX) in the same way as the relationship between NP_4 and NP_2 can now be given, though no particular solution to the descriptive problems will emerge. The question itself is raised for the following reasons. Prep Phrases with OF are generally regarded as sister constituents of Nouns or Noun Phrases at least when occurring in derived structure. In doing this it is possible for us to define the attributive function of these Prep Phrases. Since structures like (XXI) are derived structures (Prep Phrases are transforms as we have seen), and since relatively little is known about Adverbials and attributive Adjuncts, however, it is not easy for us to determine whether the position of PP_1 should necessarily be considered the position of an attributive Adjunct or could equally well be regarded as the place where an Adverbial Prep Phrase can be attached to the tree. I shall discuss some alternative descriptions of the relationship between V, NP and PP_1 in (XXI) so as to show that the main point of the present analysis, namely the compositional nature of the Aspects, remains unaffected.

Traditionally such sentences as:

(35j)   De muis at een stuk *van de kaas*.
          lit: The mouse ate a piece *from the cheese*.
          The mouse ate away a piece of the cheese.
(35n)   De muis zag een stuk *van de kaas*.
          The mouse saw a piece *of the cheese*.

were both analyzed in terms of the *Genitivus partitivus*. Thus, the italicized constituents were considered a partitive Genitive. This position is not at all surprising. Firstly, in several languages the Prepositions corresponding to *van* (FROM and OF) are identical, just as in Dutch; languages like Greek and Latin, using cases rather than Prepositions to relate the Noun Phrases corresponding to *de kaas* and *een stuk* to each other, did not distinguish between the two relationships.[7] Secondly, a logical analysis of (35j) and (35n) reveals that in both sentences there is a relationship between a proper subset of cheese particles P (a piece of cheese) and a finite set of cheese particles C (the cheese itself). The only difference between (35j) and (35n) is that in the former sentence P is separated from its complement P' in C, whereas in (35n) P remains a proper subset of C. The term

---

[7] *Cf.* Kühner (1898:342) and Kühner-Stegmann (1962:423–35).

'Genitivus partitivus' is applied to both (35j) and (35n), apparently because one interpreted the term 'partitive' as pertaining to a relationship between a given set and a proper subset irrespective of whether the latter is still a part of the former.

However understandable the traditional interpretation of the term 'Genitivus partitivus' may be, it appears correct to assume that the differentiation of *van de kaas* into an underlying FROM + NP and an underlying OF + NP should be expressed by different tree configurations. On the other hand we have virtually nothing to go by in the available literature that could provide us with arguments for the view that PP_1 is not a partitive Genitive or for the view that PP_1 is a partitive Genitive but should be attached to the tree structure differently than in (XXI). We need far more insight into the status of Adverbials and Adjuncts, i.e. into their transformational history and their location in derived structures like (XXI).[8]

It will be clear that the present study does not aim at a solution for the problems raised in the preceding paragraphs. I have questioned the correctness of representations like (XXI) on the ground that our analysis of the Aspects could be upset by the results of further research into the partitive Genitive. Let us, for example, suppose that Prep Phrases with FROM cannot be regarded as partitive Genitives because the traditional position proves incorrect, and that they consequently could not be taken as sister constituents of NP in structures like (XXI). Then automatically we are forced to reconsider the validity of our main point about (XXI), i.e. the statement that DURATIVE is composed of the categories given in (33b).

I said earlier that the difference between (35j) and (35n) boils down to a difference between separating *P* from *C* and leaving *P* a proper subset of *C*. This could mean that in (35j) we have to do with a Directional Phrase FROM + NP and that the node TAKE somehow relates to the node MOVEMENT discussed in Section 2.1. Restricting myself now to this not unreasonable correction of the traditional position concerning sentences like (35j) and (35n), we can put forward four possible ways of representing their VP, other than is done in structure (XXI). Three of these are given in (XXIa)–(XXIc); we obtain the fourth by reversing the order of NP and PP_1 in (XXIa).

Both this and (XXIa) itself are highly suspect, since it is not at all clear

---

[8] Chomsky (1965:70*ff*) defined the relation 'is Direct Object of' as a structural relation [NP, VP] thus stating that the NP occurring in $_{VP}[V + NP]_{VP}$ is the Direct Object of the VP. However, we do not find a definition saying that [PP, NP] defines the relationship 'is attributively adjoined to' between PP and a Noun Phrase. Very little is known at yet about Prepositional Phrases and their attributive relationship to Noun Phrases or Nouns. If Prep Phrases do not occur in deep structure it is not even possible to define the relation [PP, NP] as a deep structural function.

(XXIa)

(XXIb)

(XXIc)

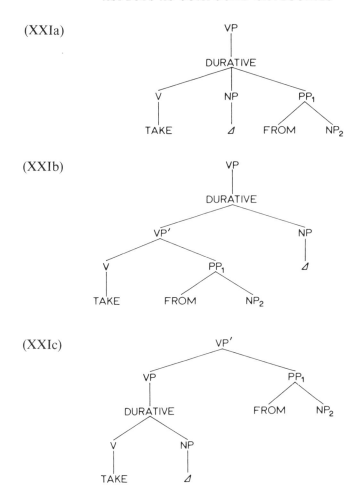

how we are to specify the mutual relationships between the three constituents dominated by VP. Nevertheless, we can apply (33b) to (XXIa) by dropping the NP_1-brackets and thus our position is not affected.

In (XXIb) and (XXIc) PP_1 is taken as an Adverbial rather than as an attributive Adjunct. It appears to correspond closely to Directional Prep Phrases. Given that (XXIa) would have to be rejected, we have the choice between (XXIb) and (XXIc), which is very difficult to make at the moment since we do not know very much about the hierarchy among constituents occurring in the Verb Phrase. The crucial question is whether there is a higher degree of cohesion between V and NP than between V and PP_1. One (weak) argument in favour of (XXIc) is that sentences like ?*Hij dronk iets en wel van de whisky die daar stond (lit: He drank something and (he did) so from the whisky which stood there) are less ungrammatical than **Hij *dronk van de whisky die daar stond en wel iets* (lit: He drank from the whisky and (he did) so something). This could suggest that *iets drinken* (drink something), and in general $V + NP_1$, is a stronger syntactic unit than *van de whisky drinken* (drink from the whisky), in general $V + PP_1$.[9] In Chapter Three section 3.2 structures of the form given in (XXIc) will be under discussion again.

Uncertain though we may be with respect to the relationship between V on the one hand, and PP_1 and NP_1 on the other, in both (XXIb) and (XXIc) the Durative Aspect can be considered a complex category assigned to the VP, which we define here as the node immediately dominating a Direct-Object NP. In the case of (XXIb) we can change (33b) as follows:

(33c) $_{VP}[_{VP'}[_V[TAKE]_V + W]_{VP'} + _{NP}[UNSPECIFIED \ QUANTITY$ $OF \ X]_{NP}]_{VP}$

where W is a variable which may be null. The difference between (35d) *De muis at wekenlang van de kaas* (The mouse ate from the cheese for weeks) and (35j') *De muis at wekenlang een stuk van de kaas* (lit: The mouse ate a piece from the cheese for weeks) can be characterized as a difference between (33b) or (33c) and

(32a) $_{VP}[_V[TAKE]_V + _{NP}[SPECIFIED \ QUANTITY \ OF \ X]_{NP}]_{VP}$

where PP_1 occurs either as W in (33c) or as shown in (33b).

Turning now to the description of the sentences (31c) and (35c) we can follow the lines pegged out in the preceding sections. The VP of (35c) can be represented as is shown in (XXIII).

This structure resembles very much our structural description of the Verb Phrase *een concert spelen* (play a concerto). Analogously to (32) on page 64 we can describe the composition of the Nondurative Aspect in the c-sentences of (31) and (35) as in (32a).

Concluding the present discussion about TAKE-Verbs and their sister constituents I would like to pass on to such sentences as:

---

[9] For an early discussion about this hierarchy in transformational studies see Lakoff (1965) and Kraak (1966). Kraak's proposal, being the more explicit of the two, is stated in terms of the *Aspects*-model. Consequently the rule mechanism involved does not apply any longer to underlying structures occurring in recent studies, apart from those in which Adverbials are generated as deep structural Prep Phrases occurring under the domination of the same category as the VP. Kraak observed that specifying constituents attract the negativeness of the sentence in which they occur. This gives us the opportunity of establishing a hierarchy among specifying constituents (Adverbials). See also Kraak (1967b). As far as diagram (XXIc) is concerned, the node VP' is necessary to express a relationship between the category PP_1 and the syntactic unit VP. The category DURATIVE can be assigned to VP on the basis of schema (33b). However, on the basis of this schema we could also assign DURATIVE to VP'. It appears to be a rather academic problem from the point of view developed in the subsequent chapter.

(28b)   *Koos en Robby aten urenlang een boterham.
         *Koos and Robby ate a sandwich/a slice of bread for hours.
(28g)   Koos en Robby aten urenlang van een boterham.
         Koos and Robby ate from a sandwich/a slice of bread for hours.

(XXIII)

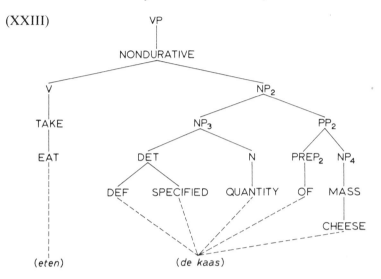

In section 2.3 I proposed that the Verb Phrase *een boterham eten* (eat a sandwich/a slice of bread) occurring in (28b) should be given a structural description as shown in (XIIIa) on page 52. Comparing this structure with e.g. (XXIII) we observe that the nodes making up the category NONDURATIVE in the former structure are dissimilar to those of which this category is composed in the latter. I shall briefly discuss this apparent incongruency.

As far as the node NP in (XIIIa) is concerned, the nodes INDEF and SINGULAR were said on page 51 to be involved in the composition of the category NONDURATIVE. To my mind, however, sentences like (28g) should be analyzed analogously to the d-sentences of (31) and (35). In other words, we can analyze (28g) in terms of the string TAKE+Δ+ FROM+INDEF+SPECIFIED+QUANTITY+OF+BREAD, where *een boterham* (a sandwich/a slice of bread) is analyzed as INDEF+ SPECIFIED+QUANTITY+OF+BREAD. Comparing this string with structure (XIIIa) we see that the present representation expresses the conclusions of our analysis of Noun Phrases like *een concert* and *het concert* on pages 55–61. *Een boterham* refers to a specified quantity of bread just as *een concert* refers to a specified quantity of musical information.

As far as the node AGENTIVE in (XIIIa) is concerned, we observe that Verbs like *eten* (eat) and *drinken* (drink) share the node AGENTIVE with Verbs like *wandelen* (walk), *praten* (talk), etc. The latter two, however, are not TAKE-Verbs. As far as I can see all TAKE-Verbs are AGENTIVE.

On the basis of these considerations we can replace (XIIIa) by structure (XXIV) as a representation of the Verb Phrase *een boterham eten* (eat a sandwich/a slice of bread). As such it is highly provisional. In Chapter Three I shall extensively deal with the category AGENTIVE with the help of sentences like *Arie eet een haring* (Arie ate a herring) and *Wat Arie deed was een haring eten* (What Arie did was to eat a herring). The node AGENTIVE will be replaced by an underlying category DO occupying a different place in the representation.

(XXIV)

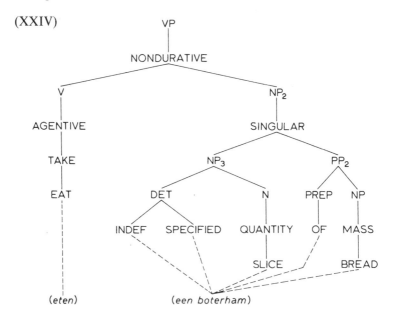

Looking back now at the above formulated proposals for a solution to the descriptive problems raised by the sentences (31a)–(31d) and (35a)–(35d), we can say that the opposition between (32a) and (33b) or (33c) accounts for the differences between the c-sentences on the one hand, and the a- and d-sentences on the other. If the Aspects were assigned to the (surface) Verbs *drinken* and *eten*, we would not be able to describe homogeneously this opposition. Moreover, as far as I can see it is only because we regard Aspects as complex categories that we can account for the ungrammaticality of the b-sentences.

2.4.3. Verbs Occurring with the Accusativus Effectivus

Consider the following sentences:

(29e)   Katinka breide wekenlang aan *een Noorse trui.*
         Katinka knitted at *a Norwegian sweater* for weeks.
         Katinka was knitting *a Norwegian sweater*/was at work on a
         Norwegian sweater for weeks.

(29b)   *Katinka breide wekenlang *een Noorse trui.*
         *Katinka knitted *a Norwegian sweater* for weeks.

(29a)   Katinka breide wekenlang.
         Katinka knitted for weeks.

(38a)   De aannemer bouwt al maandenlang aan *dat huis.*
         lit: The building-contractor builds already for months at
         that house.
         The building-contractor has now been working on the con-
         struction of that house for months.

(38b)   *De aannemer bouwt al maandenlang *dat huis.*
         lit: The building-contractor builds *that house* already for months.
         *The building-contractor has built that house already for months.

(38c)   De aannemer bouwt hier al maandenlang.
         The building-contractor has now been building here for months.

The b-sentences are ungrammatical in the single-event reading. In my dialect, (38b) cannot even express repetition due to the fact that *bouwen* (build) occurs in the Present Tense. Assuming that we should restrict ourselves to one Verb *breien* and one Verb *bouwen* in the above sentences, we can maintain that neither the Verbs nor the italicized constituents in the b-sentences contain the Nondurative Aspect inherently. *Breien* occurs in (29e) and (29a) without causing repetition; the same obtains for *bouwen* in (38a) and (38c). Both *een Noorse trui* (a Norwegian sweater) and *dat huis* (that house) refer to physical objects rather than to temporal entities. The category NONDURATIVE (i.e. TERMINATIVE) in the b-sentences appears to be composed of categories inherent to the Verb and the Direct-Object NP. Thus we are following here the same line of argument as we did in the previous sections. Avoiding duplication of lexical entries for Verbs we leave the position that Aspects are semantic primitives.

The sentences under analysis are equally intriguing and inaccessible to an explicit description, since transformational grammar in none of its variants can, as yet, adequately deal with the existential status of entities referred to by sentences or Noun Phrases. The present subsection should, therefore, be regarded as giving some generalizations which should lead to a formal description at a later stage of the description of the sentences under discussion. In this study, it is my intention to give arguments for the compositional nature of the Aspects and consequently I shall restrict myself to making some suggestions as to how to proceed towards a more explicit description than is possible at this moment. The problem at issue is that the italicized constituent in:

(29f)   Katinka breide *een Noorse trui*.
         Katinka knitted *a Norwegian sweater*.

refers to an object which came into existence as the result of the activity expressed by the Verb. Jacobsohn (1933:297) analyzing German sentences like *Die Maurer bauten das Haus* (The bricklayers built the house) and *Ich schrieb einen Brief* (I wrote a letter) says that in these cases the transitive Verb governs a Direct Object, "das durch den Verbalbegriff erst geschaffen wird: den *Accusativus effectivus*", (which is only created by the meaning of the Verb: *the Acc. effectivus*). In German sentences like *Der Mann schlug den Hund* (The man hit the dog) and *Die Frau wäscht das Kleid* (The woman washes the dress) we find a transitive Verb "das das von ihm abhängige Objekt nur tangiert, affiziert" (which only touches, affects its Object) (*ibidem*). In these sentences the Direct-Object NP is considered an Accusativus affectivus. Our grammar cannot deal adequately with the difference between the Acc. effectivus and the Acc. affectivus at present.

Jacobsohn's opinion is that Verbs taking an Acc. affectivus are Durative Verbs, whereas Verbs occurring with an Acc. effectivus are Perfective (Nondurative). He writes: "Man kann sagen: das Accusativus effectivus macht das Verb perfektiv" (*ibidem*). If we were to accept this position (that the Direct-Object NP renders the Durative Verb Nondurative), we would be forced to call on rules like (17) in section 2.1, which we rejected on (four) good grounds. It is of great importance to bear in mind that it would also be necessary to explain why and how *een Noorse trui* (a Norwegian sweater) in (29f) would have this effect on the Verb. This explanation cannot be given, in my opinion, since *een trui* (a sweater) cannot be specified inherently to contain information that could trigger the rule converting the Durative Verb *breien* (knit) into a Nondurative Verb. *Een Noorse trui* can also occur as an Acc. affectivus after Verbs like *wassen* (wash), *zien* (see), etc. as we see in *Katinka waste een Noorse trui* (Katinka washed a Norwegian sweater). It would be a clumsy solution to the present problem to specify *een Noorse trui* after *breien* differently from *een Noorse trui* after *wassen* so that this inherent specification would trigger the rule changing the inherent specification of the Verb. It depends on the Verb rather than on the NP itself whether or not the NP refers to a complete entity or not. Jacobsohn's circumscription of the notion 'Acc. effectivus' is rather ambivalent. On the one side he contends that the Verb pertains to some activity causing the referent of the Direct-Object NP to come into existence; on the other side he implies that it is precisely this NP which contains a specification converting the Verbal specification DURATIVE into NONDURATIVE.

This incongruency can be eliminated by avoiding rules like (17) and by assuming that Aspects should be assigned to a category dominating the Verb and the Acc. effectivus. The existential status of the referent of the Direct-Object NP can then be dealt with as concerning this category. Thus we say that *een Noorse trui breien* (knit a Norwegian sweater) is Nondurative.

By doing this we face the task of looking for the elementary categories making up the Nondurative Aspect in (29b) and (29f). In section 2.3 I described the composition of the Nondurative Aspect in *een Noorse trui breien* (knit a Norwegian sweater) provisionally as follows:

$$_{VP}[_V[\text{AGENTIVE}]_V + _{NP\ SING}[\text{INDEF. DET} + \text{NOUN}]_{NP\ SING}]_{VP}$$

This description fails to account for the difference between AGENTIVE-Verbs taking an Acc. affectivus such as *oprapen* (pick up), *wassen* (wash), *aanraken* (touch), etc. and AGENTIVE-Verbs like *breien* (knit), *bouwen* (build), *schrijven* (write), etc. which take an Acc. effectivus.

It seems helpful now to introduce the descriptive problems at issue with the help of a logical analysis. As far as I can see the difference between the Acc. affectivus and the Acc. effectivus relates to the distinction between tenseless and tense logic. Sentences like *Katinka waste een trui* (Katinka washed a sweater) are analyzed – in tenseless logic – as:

(39) $(\exists x)$ (x is a sweater and y_1 washed x)

where y_1 abbreviates *Katinka* (Proposition (39) can be read as: there is an x such that x is a sweater and y_1 washes x.). It will be understood that

(29g) $(\exists x)$ (x is a sweater and y_1 knits x)

should be rejected as a correct analysis of sentence (29f). If we take 'x is a sweater' in its normal interpretation, we assume that x is a completed sweater, as in (39). In (29g), however, y_1 knits something which is a completed sweater at the very moment she stops knitting. We cannot identify the predicates 'is a sweater' in (39) and (29g).

In tenseless logic the predicate 'is a sweater' in propositions like (39) and (29g) is taken as tenseless: its truth value is not relative to time. In tense logic the proposition 'there is an x such that x is a sweater' can only be true for those entities x which are sweaters at this moment, i.e. at the moment this proposition is being used. Thus, when Katinka started to knit, it was not true that there was an x such that x was a sweater at that moment.

Tense logic analyzes propositions containing such expressions as 'it was the case that' and 'it will be the case that'. In formal systems recently developed these expressions are taken as sentential operators (see e.g. Massey, 1970:404–13). The proposition 'P (there is an x such that x is a sweater)' means 'it was the case at some moment that there was an x such that x was a sweater', where P is the Past-tense operator. The Future-tense operator F ($=$ "it will be the case that ...") can be prefixed analogously.

Sentence (29f) can now be analyzed as follows:

(29h) $(\exists x)$ P [y_1 was knitting/worked on x & F (x is completed & x is a sweater)]

which should be read as: there is an x such that is was the case that y_1 worked on x and that it was the case that it would be the case that both x were completed and x would be a sweater. Notice that the expression 'y_1 was knitting at/worked on x' pertains to *Katinka breide aan een trui*, that is, to what is expressed by the VP of sentence (29e). If (29h) is a correct analysis of (29f) it would follow that *breien aan een trui* (work on a sweater) covers part of the meaning of *een trui breien* (knit a sweater).

In terms of the Time axis we could reformulate the above analysis. Consider the following representation:

(XXV)

where $t_i < t_j < t_o$ ('$<$' is the relation 'earlier than'), and where t_o is the point of speech. The point of time t_j is the point at which x is a completed sweater; t_i is the point at which y_1 starts knitting. Relating (29h) to (XXV) we see that y_1 is knitting at/works on x' pertains to the interval (t_i, t_j), whereas the conjunction following the future-tense operator pertains to t_j.

We have now obtained a sufficiently elaborate framework to be able to pass on to analysis. What I aim to determine is the relationship between such Verbs as *breien* (knit), *bouwen* (build), *schrijven* (write), etc. and MOVEMENT-Verbs like *wandelen* (walk), *rijden* (drive), etc. on the other. The rather intricate structure of Verb Phrases like those occurring in the sentences (29f) and (29e) appears to correspond partly to the structure oı Verb Phrases containing MOVEMENT-Verbs. I shall try to show that the former relate to the latter in that they can be analyzed in terms of co-occurrence with categories inherent to Directional Phrases, i.e. in terms of FROM ... TO. If this relationship indeed holds we are in a position to make a generalization with respect to the composition of the Aspects.

Let us first consider the Preposition *aan* in (29e) and (38a). It appears to correspond to *aan* in constructions like *werken aan* (work on) and *bezig zijn aan* (lit: be busy at/on; be at work on). Sentences like:

(29i)   Katinka was wekenlang bezig aan een Noorse trui.
         Katinka was at work on a Norwegian sweater for weeks.
(38d)   De aannemer werkte maandenlang aan dat huis.
         The building-contractor worked on that house for months.

are partially synonymous with (29e) and (38a), respectively, the difference being that the latter sentences give more specific information about the technique of construction having been applied. Compare also: *Jopie borduurde aan een wandkleed* (lit: Jopie embroidered at a tapestry) with *Jopie werkte aan een wandkleed* (Jopie worked on a tapestry) and *Hans schilderde aan een stilleven* (lit: Hans painted at a still life) with *Hans werkte aan een stilleven* (Hans worked on a still life). *Borduren* (embroider) and *schilderen* (paint) contain only extra information about the technique being used to create the objects in question.

Let us tentatively assume that the underlying structure of the Verbs under discussion contains a semantic category CONSTRUCT accounting for the fact that in all cases we know that the logical subjects of these Verbs pertain to living beings creating something. This category might be analyzed further in terms of a partitive. To construct something is to add something to an object (concrete or abstract) until it is completed. Thus knitting a sweater at t_m is an activity consisting of adding parts to an object which can be referred to as an incomplete sweater at t_m. There is some evidence that sentences like (29e) and (38a) can be analyzed in terms of a partitive. In Finnish e.g., sentences like *Hän rakensi taloa* (Hij bouwde aan een huis; he was building at/worked on a house) contain a Partitive case, *taloa* (house). By contrast, *talon* (house) in *Hän rakensi talon* (Hij bouwde een huis; he built a house) is a Genitive, which is identical to the Accusative. Compare also: *Hän luki kirjaa* (Hij las uit het boek; hij was het boek aan het lezen; he was reading the book) where *kirjaa* (book) is a Partitive, with *Hän luki kirjan* (Hij las het boek; he read the book), where *kirjan* is a Genitive (Accusative). Thus it appears that in languages having cases the difference between sentences corresponding to (29e) and (29g) can manifest itself as a contrast between the Partitive and some other case, here the Genitive or Accusative.[10]

On the other hand, sentences like:

(29j)   Katinka breide wekenlang stukken aan een Noorse trui.
         Katinka knitted parts/pieces on to a Norwegian sweater for weeks.

(38e)   De aannemer bouwde maandenlang delen aan dat huis.
         The building-contractor built parts on to that house for months.

are not even partially synonymous with (29e) and (38a). Both sentences assert that something was added to an object that had already been completed. Thus the result of Katinka's activity in (29j) is a sweater with extra parts on it. The same holds for sentences like:

(38f)   *De aannemer bouwde maandenlang iets aan dat huis.
         *The building-contractor built something on to that house for months.

To me, this sentence is ungrammatical as well as incomprehensible unless we take *bouwen* (build) as *verbouwen* (alter, rebuild) (Cf. (30q), (30s) and (35m)).

The last three examples suggest that *breien aan* and *bouwen aan* cannot directly be connected with underlying nodes like ADD TO such that *breien* corresponds to ADD and *aan* to TO. By contrast, *eten van* and *drinken van* were analyzed in terms of the (reverse) nodes TAKE FROM, where *van* is the surface reflection of the underlying FROM. We could simply leave out of consideration the information that ADD TO concerns something incomplete, and that TAKE FROM pertains to objects which already existed in their completed form. However, there are some indications that we can analyze (29e) and (38a) indirectly in terms of ADD TO and thus in terms of an underlying Dummy NP representing the information UNSPECIFIED QUANTITY OF X, though ADD TO does not have the same status as TAKE FROM; that is, whereas FROM directly corresponds to the surface constituent *van*, TO does not correspond to *aan*. The nodes ADD TO are part of a rather complicated internal structure. Consider the following sentences:

(29k)   Katinka breide een stuk verder aan die trui.
         lit: Katinka knitted a bit further at that sweater.
         Katinka went on knitting that sweater.

---

[10] *Cf.* Jacobsohn (1933:301). In this connection it is of interest to note that such Verbs as *rakastaa* (love), *vihata* (haten), *ajathella* (think), etc. take a Partitive Object. See example (30d) in Section 2.4.1.

(38g)   De aannemer bouwde iets verder aan dat huis.
        lit: The building-contractor built somewhat further at that
        house.
        The building-contractor went on building that house.

(29m)   Katinka breide verder aan die trui.
        lit: Katinka knitted further at that sweater.
        Katinka went on knitting that sweater.

(38h)   De aannemer bouwde verder aan dat huis.
        lit: The building-contractor built further at that house.
        The building-contractor went on building that house.

Sentence (29k) is nearly synonymous with (29m), if we take *een stuk* (a bit, a piece) in its most neutral sense, i.e. without any stress on it. (We can use (29k) for expressing that Katinka brought the completion of that sweater *considerably* nearer to its termination. In that case *een stuk* receives stress. The same holds, *mutatis mutandis*, for the relationship between (38g) and (38h)). Sentence (29k) is logically equivalent to (29m) and (38g) to (38h) if we take *een stuk* (a bit) and *iets* (something/what) without emphasis. In all four cases we know that objects referred to have not yet been completed and that they are on their way to being completed. Notice also that *breien* and *bouwen* occurring as in (29a) and (38c) can take *(een stuk) verder* as well: *Katinka breide een stuk verder* (Katinka knitted a bith further); *De aannemer bouwde verder* (The building-contractor built further). The following sentences:

(40)   *Hij *belde haar* een stuk verder *op*.
        *He *called her* a bit further.

(41)   *Marijke *werd* een stuk verder *geboren*.
        *Marijke *was born* a bit further.

are ungrammatical because the italicized constituents are momentaneous, i.e. pertain to just one moment. They can never occur with *een stuk verder* in a way corresponding to (29k) and (38g).
        Sentences like

(26a)   ?Luns heeft die verklaring over Nieuw-Guinea een stuk verder
        afgelegd.
        lit: Luns made that declaration about New Guinea a bit further.

(42)   ?Zij vertelde Joanne dat verhaal een stuk verder.
        lit: She told Joanne that story a bit further.

containing Terminative Verb Phrases can be interpreted analogously to (29k) and (38g) if we take *dat verhaal* (that story) as pertaining to a serial story and *die verklaring* (that declaration) as a serial declaration. Notice also that such sentences as:

(39a)   ?Zij waste haar trui een stuk verder.
          lit: She washed her sweater a bit further.
(43)   ?Zij deed haar kleren een stuk verder uit.
          lit: She took off her garments a bit further.

can only be interpreted as implying that she went on with an activity which necessarily led to an end. Sentence (39a) is strange because it implies that she was washing her sweater as it were linearly: she had already washed some parts of her sweater and now she went on with remaining parts. Sentence (43) would most probably be a report of a striptease-girl's activities. The reverse situation sketched by the sentence:

(43a)   ?Zij deed haar kleren een stuk verder aan.
          lit: She put on her garments a bit further.

implies an initial point (her being naked) as well as a terminal point (her being dressed).

The ungrammaticality of (40) and (41) as well as the restrictions put on the interpretation of the other sentences under analysis, strongly suggest that *een stuk verder* (a bit further) can only occur with constituents pertaining to linearly experienced events which have not yet been terminated. The sentences (40) and (41) indicate that *een stuk verder* requires that a certain stretch (of time) be given by the italicized constituents; the sentences with question-marks reveal that terminative constituents are not the most natural partners for *een stuk verder*. It is only constituents pertaining to non-bounded stretches (of time), i.e. durative constituents like *wandelen* (walk), *rijden* (drive), *breien* (knit) *breien aan X* (knit at X), *bouwen* (build), *bouwen aan X* (build at X) etc., that can occur freely with *een stuk verder*.

In this connection I would like to make an additional observation. The constituent *een eind door* (lit: a piece on) containing the quantifying constituent *een eind* (a piece) has similar co-occurrence restrictions with Momentaneous and Terminative Verb Phrases as *een stuk verder* (a bit further). I shall restrict myself here to giving some examples which clearly show that Terminative VP's cannot occur with *een eind door* at all:

(43b)   *Zij deed haar kleren een eind door aan.
          *She put on her garments a piece on.
(39b)   *Zij waste haar trui (een eind) door.
          *She washed her sweater (a piece) on.

Both sentences are ungrammatical and cannot even be interpreted analogously to (43a) and (39a).

The possibility for such constituents as *wandelen, rijden, breien (aan X)*, *bouwen (aan X)*, etc. to occur with *(een stuk) verder* and *(een eind) door* is a property not inherent to all Durative Verb Phrases. Beside (29k) and (38g) we do find:

(29n)   Katinka breide (een eind) door aan die trui.
         lit: Katinka knitted on (a bit) at that sweater.
         She went on knitting at that sweater.
(44)   Jan reed een eind door.
         lit: Jan drove on a piece.
         Jan drove on a bit further.

but the following sentences containing Durative VP's are ungrammatical:

(45)   *Boumibol regeerde een stuk verder.
         *Boumibol governed a bit further.
(46)   *Die steen lag een eind door.
         *That stone lay on a piece.

Regeren (govern) and *liggen* (lie) are Statives (Vendler, 1957:151; Lakoff, 1966). However, not that *drijven* (float) being Stative according to Lakoff can take *een stuk verder* since it contains a category MOVEMENT.

Summarizing the above observations we can say that *breien* (knit), *breien aan X* (knit at X), *bouwen* (build), *bouwen aan X* (build at X), etc. and *wandelen* (walk), *rijden* (drive) have in common that they all can take constituents like *verder* (further), *door* (on), *een stuk verder* (a bit further), *een eind door* (lit: a piece on). As far as *verder* and *door* are concerned they imply movement along a line in the direction of a terminal point which has not yet been reached. In terms of (XXV) we could say that (29k) and (29m) should be analyzed as stating that Katinka's activity is as it were a movement from the direction of t_i in the direction of t_j, just like Jan's driving in (44) can be considered a movement from a given point in the direction of a terminal point which is only implicitly given. We can only have sentences like (29k), (29m) and (44) because t_j has not yet been reached. Thus, the presence of *verder* and *door* indicate that the linearly experienced activity pertains to a stretch between two points, in (XXV) between t_i and t_j.

As far as *een stuk* and *een eind* are concerned we can say the following: given that the view is correct that our grammar has to express the correspondence between such constituents as *breien (aan X)*, *bouwen (aan X)*, etc. and Verb Phrases containing overt MOVEMENT-Verbs, we shall more

closely examine these Verbs in their relationship to Quantifying Constituents. Consider such sentences as:

(1m)   Greetje wandelde een kilometer.
        Greetje walked a kilometre.
(1n)   Greetje is naar het strand gewandeld.
        Greetje walked to the beach.
(1o)   Greetje is van de Munt naar de Dam gewandeld.
        Greetje walked from the Mint to the Dam.

All three sentences contain a Terminative Verb Phrase. As far as I can see
all Verbs taking Quantifying Complements like *een stuk* (a bit), *een kilometer* (a kilometre), i.e. pertaining to one-dimensional measuring units,
can take Directional Phrases, and vice versa. To my mind, the above con-
·siderations provide some reasons for analyzing the Nondurative Aspect in
(1m) in terms of the following scheme:

(47) $_{VP}[_V[MOVEMENT]_V + _{QC}[SPECIFIED \ QUANTITY \ OF$
        $DISTANCE \ MEASURING \ UNITS]_{QC}]_{VP}$

This scheme would account for the ungrammaticality of the single-event
reading of sentence (1b) *Greetje wandelde urenlang een kilometer* (*Greetje
walked a kilometre for hours). It will be clear that if (47) can be accepted
as a proper account of the composition of the Nondurative Aspect in (1m)
and (1b), we have obtained a generalization applying to all cases that have
been under analysis up to now. Scheme (47) closely resembles such schemata
as (32) and (32a).

I would propose that we should also analyze (1n) and (1o) with the help
of (47). The distance between an initial point, implied as in sentence (1n)
or explicitly given as in (1o), and a terminal point can be taken as a specified
quantity of distance measuring units in the sense described above.

One further step is to analyze the Durative Aspect in sentence (1a)
Greetje wandelde urenlang (Greetje walked for hours) as follows:

(48) $_{VP}[_V[MOVEMENT]_V + _{QC}[UNSPECIFIED \ QUANTITY \ OF$
        $DISTANCE \ MEASURING \ UNITS]_{QC}]_{VP}$

where QC appears as a Dummy element '*Δ*' in surface structure.

Notice that (47) and (48) also account for the Nondurative and Durative
Aspects in:

(44a)   *Jan reed urenlang een eind door. (Nondurative)
        *Jan drove on a piece for hours.
(44b)   Jan reed urenlang door. (Durative)
        Jan drove on for hours.

In (44a) QC is realized as *een eind* (lit: a piece); in (44b) as a Dummy element. In both (44) and (44b) we can ask *Hoe ver is hij doorgereden?* (How far did he drive on?). By assuming the presence of a Dummy QC in the under-lying structure of sentences like (44b) and (1a) we can account for the fact that these sentences closely relate to questions with *How far? How many kilometres?* etc.

Overt MOVEMENT-Verbs take Quantifying Complements pertaining to locative measuring units. Since these units, however, are of a linear nature they can be related to the Time axis. Returning now to *breien (aan X)*, *bouwen (aan X)* etc., we can see that (47) and (48) cannot directly be applied to these constituents, since the linear "movement" they express does not involve locative measuring units nor any movement of the logical subject of the sentence in which they appear. Referring back to the category CONSTRUCT introduced provisionally and tentatively as a label for a complicated set of more elementary categories, I venture to say that schemes like (47) and (48) can at least be regarded as belonging to this category or as translatable into its more elementary categories. That is, all constituents pertaining to the activity of constructing something contain the categorial configuration MOVEMENT + QC in their underlying structure, or a con-figuration of categories which closely resembles schemes like (47) and (48). It will be clear that QC in the underlying structure of constituents like *breien (aan X)*, etc. should be taken as more neutral with respect to the nature of the measuring units involved. Whereas QC in (47) and (48) pertains to loca-tive units, QC in the underlying structure of *breien aan X*, etc. pertains to linear ordering. Likewise the node MOVEMENT might primarily pertain to activities involving locative notions. We can reasonably well expect that the node MOVEMENT can be broken down into more elementary categories which also occur in the underlying structure of CONSTRUCT-constituents.

Speculating further on the possibility of relating MOVEMENT + QC to the node CONSTRUCT we could say that the predicate 'ADD TO' is of great relevance to both categories. If we say at some moment t_m, where $t_i < t_m < t_j$, that Katinka is constructing something, we could equally well say that she is adding something to what has been constructed during the interval (t_i, t_{m-1}). One can only say *Katinka breit nu aan die trui* (Katinka is working now at that sweater) if she had already begun knitting. It is not possible to say this sentence at t_i: something must have resulted from Katinka's knitting before we can use *breien aan* (work on). As far as MOVEMENT + QC is concerned, we could say that moving from some point P_i to another point P_j, where the distance between P_i and P_j is the inter-val (P_i, P_j), can also be conceived in terms of the predicate 'ADD TO'.

If someone is walking at P_m, where $P_m \in (P_i, P_j)$ such that $P_i < P_m < P_j$ and where '$\in$' symbolizes the relation 'is an element of' and '$<$' the relation 'is between', we can say that he is adding some distance measuring units to the interval (P_i, P_{m-1}). It is not possible to use the sentence *Hij wandelt nu* (He is walking now) if he is at P_i.

As I have said before I do not aim to give a formal description of the underlying structure of such constituents like *breien aan X, bouwen aan X*, etc. since their underlying structure is far too complicated with regard to the principal point being made in the present chapter. What I have been doing here is to make some generalizations which reveal that the line of argument followed in the previous sections can be extended. The fact that sentences like (29e), (29b), (38a), (38c) can be related to schemata like (47) and (48) indicates that the Nondurative and Durative Aspects in these sentences can be accounted for in terms of configurations like SPECIFIED QUANTITY OF X or UNSPECIFIED QUANTITY OF X and by some preceding Verbal category.

2.5. CONCLUSION

Concluding this chapter we can summarize the results set out as follows:

(a) the Durative Aspect in the sentences under discussion appears to be composed of elementary semantic categories one of which is a Verbal subcategorial node such as MOVEMENT, AGENTIVE, PERFORM, TAKE, ADD, the other one a Nominal node dominating categories containing quantificational information. The general scheme on which the composition of the Durative Aspect proceeds is

$$(49) \qquad _{VP}[_V[\text{VERB}]_V + _{NP}[\text{UNSPECIFIED QUANTITY OF X}]_{NP}]_{VP}$$

where VERB is one of the above given subcategorial nodes, and where NP also stands for QC in schemata like (47).

(b) the Nondurative Aspect in the sentences under discussion appears to be composed of elementary categories on the basis of the following scheme:

$$(50) \qquad _{VP}[_V[\text{VERB}]_V + _{NP}[\text{SPECIFIED QUANTITY OF X}]_{NP}]_{VP}$$

Thus the difference between the categories DURATIVE and NONDURATIVE can be explained in terms of set theoretical notions. It has become clear that the semantic information 'UNSPECIFIED QUANTITY OF X' or 'SPECIFIED QUANTITY OF X' pertains directly or indirectly to the Time axis. That is, the quantities of X involved are expressible in terms of linearly ordered sets of temporal entities. The subcategorial node VERB in the cases under discussion appears to express change rather than state, at any rate in the cases fitting into the Nondurative scheme (50).

The main issue of this chapter has been to make clear that the Aspects should not be regarded as unanalyzable categories inherent to Verbs.

CHAPTER III

THE UPPER BOUND OF THE ASPECTS

3.0. INTRODUCTION

In the preceding chapter I tried to support my statement that Aspects cannot be taken as semantic primitives assigned to Verbs by showing that the term 'Aspects' appears to be applicable to *configurations* of certain categories generated by the base. The mechanism underlying the composition of the Aspects seems relatively clear: a certain fundamental subcategory of an underlying V is combined with a complex set of categories of a nominal nature and pertaining to quantity.

Up to now I have been restricting myself to discussing the opposition between the two Aspects in terms of generalizations made with respect to the VP so as to be able to demonstrate the principle involved in its most simple form. In Section 3.1 I shall give some evidence that the term 'Aspects' also applies to configurations of underlying categories some of which are dominated by the Subject-NP. The Indirect Object also appears to be involved in the composition of the Aspects under the appropriate conditions. In view of these facts it is necessary to determine the upper bound of the Aspects. This amounts to locating the lowest node dominating categories which make up configurations to which the term 'Aspects' applies. It can be expected that this node is involved in the restrictions between Durational Adverbials and the Nondurative Aspect.

In Section 3.2 it is shown that it is possible to regard the Nondurative scheme as a *constraint* on the application of a transformational rule, called *Adverbialization*, developed in Klooster and Verkuyl (1971). This constraint can not only be formulated so as to block the single-event reading in the case of Nondurativity, it can also account for the frequency reading. In Klooster and Verkuyl it is argued that there is a transformational relationship between sentences containing the Verb *duren* (last) and those containing Duration-Measuring Adverbials, i.e. Durational Adverbials having an Indefinite Determiner. This proposal rests upon the assumption that Duration-Measuring Adverbials are Predications over events. A distinction can be made between Durative events and Nondurative events because Duration-Measuring Adverbials may or may not occur as the VP of an underlying S whose embedded sentential Subject refers to events.

In trying to locate the upper bound of the Aspects we have to deal with the problems of hierarchy among Adverbials because it can safely be stated that those constituents which are located "higher" than Durational Adverbials will not be involved in the relationship between Durational Adverbials and constituents to which the labels 'Durative' and 'Nondurative' can be assigned.

In Section 3.3 the criterion for VP-constituency stated by Lakoff and Ross (1966) will be under discussion. In their paper attention was given to the question of how to determine the mutual relations between the constituents dominated by the category *Predicate Phrase* in Chomsky (1965). They proposed a transformational rule, *Do so-replacement*, which was intended to make explicit a criterion determining which constituents were to be located inside the VP and which outside. According to this criterion Durational Adverbials were, in contrast with Chomsky's claim, generated outside the VP. Their *do so*-rule showed that the degree of cohesion between V and Durational Adverbials is not as strong as between V and constituents dominated by VP, e.g. the Direct-Object NP.

As far as I can see, there is no serious proposal available in recent literature stating that the node *Predicate Phrase* is a deep structural entity. At best we can consider it a category developed during the transformational derivation. This very fact renders the *do so*-rule inadequate and as a matter of consequence we need to re-state the generalization made in Lakoff and Ross (1966).

The re-formulation of the *do so*-analysis by Lakoff and Ross, which amounts to describing the underlying structure of "action sentences" (i.e. sentences containing Nonstatives), makes it possible to determine which constituents form an event-S. It is exactly this S which can be considered the upper bound of the Aspects. The necessity of describing the underlying structure of "action sentences" in a study of the Aspects can easily be understood against the background of the discussion mentioned in Section 1.1. The more suggestive (German) term 'Aktionsarten' is often used as synonymous with the term 'Aspects': it is the temporal structure of actions which is under analysis (*Cf.* Streitberg (1889), Behaghel (1924), Poutsma (1926)).

Much attention will be given to the relationship between "normal" declarative sentences containing *doen* (do) as in *Arie at een haring en Piet deed dat ook* (Arie ate a herring and Piet did so too) and pseudo-cleft sentences pertaining to their first half such as *Wat Arie deed was een haring eten* (What Arie did was to eat a herring), *Wat Arie at was een haring* (What Arie ate was a herring), and *Degene die een haring at was Arie* (The one who ate a herring was Arie). It will be shown that these sentences can be accounted for in terms of one common underlying structure setting aside different topicalization elements.

The pseudo-cleft paradigm '*Wat* + *Arie* + X + *doen, zijn* + Verb + Y' (What + Arie + X + do, be + Verb + Y), where X and Y are variables, gives us the opportunity to determine which constituents occur in the S which is taken to be the upper bound of the Aspects. The referent of the S whose surface structural reflection occurs as 'Verb + Y' in this paradigm can be said to constitute an 'event-unit'. However, there are constituents which can both occur as Y as well as X in this paradigm. This fact makes it necessary to determine the notion 'minimal event'.

In Section 3.4 I shall compare the present analysis with proposals made by logicians like Reichenbach (1966) and Davidson (1967) concerning the logical structure of action sentences, who also argued for the necessity to determine the basic structural properties of events. It will be shown that the introduction of variables ranging over temporal entities into the linguistic description of action sentences in Section 3.3 not only narrows the gap between logic and linguistics but also might contribute to developing more refined analytical tools.

The notion 'minimal event' will be developed syntactically. Thus we can determine the event-unit necessary to account for the frequency in sentences fitting into our Nondurative schema as well as for other predications over events.

3.1. THE ROLE OF THE SUBJECT AND THE INDIRECT OBJECT IN THE COMPOSITION OF THE ASPECTS

In Verkuyl (1969b; 1970) it was suggested that the upper bound of the Aspects could be located at the level of the Verb Phrase. Accordingly, a distinction was made between Durative and Nondurative (Terminative and Momentaneous) Verb Phrases. No arguments leading to the necessity of locating the Aspects higher than the VP were available at that time because the mechanism involved in their composition was not yet fully known. However, it was already clear that the term 'Aspects' could apply to configurations of categories occurring as part of V and of the Subject, as we can easily see in:

(30t) **Het celloconcert van Schumann werd* urenlang *gespeeld* door De Machula.
       *Schumann's cello concerto was olayed by De Machula for hours.

(30u) *Er werd* urenlang door De Machula *uit het celloconcert van Schumann* gespeeld.
       lit: *There was played* for hours by De Machula *from Schumann's cello concerto.*

The Aspects can be located in the italicized constituents according to the same principles as we were able to sketch with respect to sentences (30b) and (30a), respectively (see Section 2.4.1). The Subject-NP and the Verb are involved in the composition of the Aspects in these passive sentences in the same way as the Direct Object-NP and the Verb in the corresponding active sentences.

This fact need not, however, be seen as a refutation of the view that Aspects are a matter of Verb Phrase constituency as long as there are reasons to believe that (30t) and (30u) transformationally relate to (30b) and (30a), respectively. As the Aspects are relevant to deep structure rather than to derived structure, there are no reasons to consider (30t) and (30u) counter-arguments to the contention that their domain is restricted to the VP, given the correctness of the view that these sentences are transforms of active sentences.

In Verkuyl (1971) the following sentences were given as evidence for the view that the Subject of a sentence can also be involved in the composition of the Aspects:[1]

(51a)   Er stroomt urenlang water uit die rots.
         There has been water streaming out of that rock for hours.
(51b)   *Er stroomt urenlang een liter water uit die rots.
         *There has been a litre of water streaming out of that rock for
         hours.

Sentence (51b) is ungrammatical for exactly the same reason that the b-sentences of (1)–(5) in Chapter I were considered ungrammatical. It cannot be interpreted as asserting that a litre of water is continuously streaming from that rock for hours. At best it could be taken in a frequency reading: several portions of water (each portion being a litre) are being excreted by that rock. It is rather unlikely that (51a) and (51b) are passive

---

[1] Overdiep (1937), building on Jacobsohn (1926; 1933), and after him Van Es (to appear) considers the Aspects (stilistic) functions of the sentence (*Cf.* also footnote 7 in Chapter I). Overdiep maintains that the Aspects are characterized not only by "syntactic-grammatical forms" but also by intonation, tempo and rhythm (1937:57). Following Overdiep and many others, Van Es considers the aspectual function as expressing the point of view of the speaker who presents events, etc. in relation to time. However, neither Overdiep nor Van Es analyze the aspectual function any further. They restrict themselves to discussing the Aspects in terms of the classifications exemplified in Section 1.1. On the other hand, if we translate Van Es' framework into a framework that accepts the distinction between deep structure and surface structure, we could say that Van Es' so-called *phase-aspects* (among which durative, momentaneous, durative-perfective) by large and coincide with underlying S-nodes. Van Es does not recognize an upper bound for these Aspects. In Miller (1970:502) where the Aspects are analyzed in terms of features, some consideration is given to the possibility that aspectual features like 'stative' are "features of the sentence rather than of the verb". It is not clear, however, whether or not Miller would assign them to the highest S. He does not elaborate this point in detail.

transforms of underlying structures where *water* and *een liter water* appear as Direct Objects. As a matter of fact the examples below will clearly exclude this possibility. There can be few doubts as to the nature of the Verb *stromen* (stream); like *wandelen* (walk), *drijven* (float), *dansen* (dance), *rijden* (drive) etc., it can be classified as a MOVEMENT-Verb. Consequently, we can represent the composition of the Durative Aspect in (51a) analogously to our schemata in Chapter II, as follows:

$$(52a) \quad _{NP}[\text{UNSPECIFIED QUANTITY OF X}]_{NP} + _{VP}[_V[\text{MOVE-MENT}]_V + Y]_{VP}$$

where Y is a variable for constituents occurring as part of the VP. The composition of the Nondurative Aspect in (51b) can be analyzed in terms of the following schema:

$$(52b) \quad _{NP}[\text{SPECIFIED QUANTITY OF X}]_{NP} + _{VP}[_V[\text{MOVEMENT}]_V + Y]_{VP}$$

The above material can be extended. There are sentences like:

(53a)   *Maandenlang overleed de patiënt aan geelzucht.
        *The patient died of jaundice for months.

(53b)   *Maandenlang overleed een patiënt hier aan geelzucht.
        *A patient here died of jaundice for months.

(53c)   *Maandenlang overleden deze twee patiënten aan geelzucht.
        *These two patients died of jaundice for months.

(53d)   Maandenlang overleden er patiënten aan geelzucht.
        lit: For months there were dying patients of jaundice.

(53e)   Maandenlang overleden de patiënten hier aan geelzucht.
        For months the patients here died of jaundice.

The ungrammatical sentences can only be interpreted if we assume that the patients involved were given the opportunity to rise from the dead each time they departed this life.[2] In (53d) and (53e) we do not have repetition: for an unspecified class of patients it is said that each member of this class died of jaundice, just once.

The five sentences above cannot be accounted for in terms of schemata of the form given in Chapter II. The Verb *overlijden* (die) occurs in all five sentences and consequently it cannot be held responsible for the difference between (53a)–(53c) on the one hand, and (53d) and (53e) on the other. It is rather the difference between the constituents occurring as Subject of the sentences which seems to be the relevant factor here. In (53a)–(53c) the italicized constituents all refer to specified quantities of patients.

---

[2] Recall that the Dutch Verb *overlijden* unlike the English *die* can only pertain to Momentaneous events. *Cf.* footnote 20 to Chapter I.

In (53d) as well as in (53e) unspecified quantities of patients are referred to. It is of importance to notice that the NP *de patiënten hier* (the patients here), though containing a Definite Article, in fact refers to an unspecified class of patients, where the term 'unspecified' should be taken in the sense developed in Chapter II. The exact interpretation of (53e) runs as follows: for whoever was a patient here and died it held that he died of jaundice. Compare:

(53f)   De patiënten hier zijn gisteravond overleden aan geelzucht.
        The patients here died of jaundice last night.

which has the following interpretation: for all members of the class of persons who were patient here (last night) it holds that they died of jaundice last night. Notice that sentence

(53g)   *De patiënten hier zijn gisteravond urenlang aan geelzucht overleden.
        *The patients here died of jaundice for hours last night.

is ungrammatical for the same reason that (53a)–(53c) are ungrammatical.

The above sentences give sufficient evidence for the view that the composition of the Aspects involves information about the Subject. Since this information appears to be of the same kind as the information contained by our schemata in Chapter II, we can represent the composition of the Durative and the Nondurative Aspects in the sentences under discussion as follows:

(54a) $_{NP}[\text{UNSPECIFIED QUANTITY OF X}]_{NP} +$
        $_{VP}[_V[\text{TRANSITION}]_V + Y]_{VP}$

and:

(54b) $_{NP}[\text{SPECIFIED QUANTITY OF X}]_{NP} +$
        $_{VP}[_V[\text{TRANSITION}]_V + Y]_{VP}$

where Y is a variable.

As far as the category TRANSITION (which can be considered a subcategory of MOVEMENT) is concerned, we can say that this node, tentatively, represents the fact that *overlijden* (die) pertains to change, transition. In this connection it cannot be a matter of coincidence that *overlijden* can be paraphrased by more or less colloquial expressions such as *dood gaan, kapot gaan, de pijp uitgaan, het hoekje omgaan*, etc., meaning 'to die', 'to peg out', 'to kick the bucket', 'to go west', etc. in which the Verb *gaan* (go) occurs. This Verb closely relates to the category TRANSITION.[3]

---

[3] Etymologically *-lijden* in *overlijden* means 'gaan' (go). In Middle Dutch *overlijden* meant 'pass into another state'. A similar meaning can be found in the English *pass away*. Note also that the circumscriptions given here, when taken literally, are all Nondurative, e.g. *De postbode ging tot twaalf uur de hoek om* (*The postman turned the corner till twelve o'clock).

As far as Y is concerned, it might be the case that *overlijden* should be analyzed as a VP of a more complex structure than we can perceive in surface structure, e.g. dominating an underlying V-category as well as a quantifying complement of the sort occurring in our schemata of Chapter II. I shall leave this possibility out of consideration here, since it does not concern the main issue of this chapter.

It will be clear that the above facts force us to extend the schemata given in Chapter II. I shall give one example with the help of the following sentences:

(55a)   Er liepen urenlang agenten van de Munt naar de Dam.
         There have been policemen walking from the Mint to the Dam
         for hours.
(55b)   *Er liepen urenlang twee agenten van de Munt naar de Dam.
         *There have been two policemen walking from the Mint to the
         Dam for hours.

Sentence (55b) cannot be taken in a single-event reading. At best the two policemen can have been walking repeatedly from the Mint to the Dam. By contrast, we know from (55a) that no policeman necessarily covered the distance between the Mint to the Dam more than once. The NP *agenten* refers to an unspecified quantity of policemen.

In Chapter II the Nondurative Aspect in sentence (1k) *Greetje wandelde urenlang van de Munt naar de Dam* (Greetje walked from the Mint to the Dam for hours) was analyzed as being restricted to the VP. It was said that the term 'Aspects' applied to a subcategory MOVEMENT and to the FROM ... TO-Phrase which was analyzed as SPECIFIED QUANTITY OF X (a specified quantity of distance units between the Mint to the Dam). It will have become clear now that the Subject-NP *Greetje* cannot be left out of consideration. The Subject-NP of sentence (55a), which refers to an unspecified quantity of policemen determines that *urenlang* can occur without restrictions. Consequently, we can say that the Proper NP *Greetje* can also be analyzed in terms of a configuration of categories having the form $_{NP}$[SPECIFIED QUANTITY OF X]$_{NP}$ since (1k) behaves exactly like sentence (55b) where *twee politie-agenten* has this form.

In view of the above considerations we can say that the Durative Aspect in (55a) can be analyzed in terms of the following configuration of categories:

(56a) $_S$[$_{NP}$[UNSPECIFIED QUANTITY OF X]$_{NP}$ +
         $_{VP}$[$_V$[MOVEMENT]$_V$ + $_{QC}$[SPECIFIED QUANTITY
         OF X]$_{QC}$]$_{VP}$]$_S$

The Nondurative Aspect of (55b) and (1k) can be represented with the help of the following schema:

(56b) $_S[_{NP}$[SPECIFIED QUANTITY OF X]$_{NP}$ + $_{VP}[_V$[MOVE-
MENT]$_V$ + $_{QC}$[SPECIFIED QUANTITY OF X]$_{QC}]_{VP}]_S$

It appears that under the appropriate conditions the Indirect Object can also contribute to the composition of the Aspects. Consider the following sentence:

(57a)   *Den Uyl overhandigde een uur lang het PVDA-speldje aan een
          congresganger.
          *Den Uyl handed out the Labour Party badge to a congress-goer
          for an hour.

(57b)   Den Uyl overhandigde een uur lang PVDA-speldjes aan een
          congresganger.
          For an hour Den Uyl handed out Labour Party badges to a
          congress-goer.

(57c)   Den Uyl overhandigde een uur lang het PVDA-speldje aan
          congresgangers.
          For an hour Den Uyl handed out the Labour Party badge to
          congress-goers.

(57d)   Den Uyl overhandigde een uur lang PVDA-speldjes aan congres-
          gangers.
          For an hour Den Uyl handed out Labour Party badges to
          congress-goers.

Sentence (57a) is ungrammatical in a single-event reading, (57b) is grammatical on account of schemata like (49): the Direct-Object NP *PVDA-speldjes* (Labour Party badges) refers to an unspecified quantity of badges. Sentence (57b) says that Den Uyl handed out Labour badges to a congress-goer and that this activity of giving Labour Party badges to this person went on for an hour. The said activity is considered one event as we can see from (57d) where Den Uyl occupies himself with giving badges to people. It is his giving badges rather than his giving just one badge which is taken as the event-unit in question. In other words, we can analyze both (57b) and (57d) in terms of the expression 'there was an event such that this event was Den Uyl's handing out badges to a congress-goer/congress-goers and this event had the duration of an hour'.

Now, the contribution of the Indirect Object to the composition of the Aspects can be illustrated with the help of (57c), which is perfectly grammatical. Note in passing that this sentence does not concern one physical object, the Labour Party badge, but rather samples of some abstract entity, a design.[4] The important thing, however, is that (57c) differs from (57a) because the Indirect Object in (57c) is specified as UNSPECIFIED QUANTITY OF X. This specification eliminates Nondurativity in (57c).

I shall not go any further into the problem of describing exactly the conditions under which the Indirect Object may contribute to the composition of the Aspects since this would take us too far away from the main line of argument. It is sufficient to have shown that the term 'Aspects' can also apply to a configuration of categories some of which are dominated by the Indirect Object.

We can extend the schemata closing off the preceding chapter as follows.

The general schema on which the composition of the Durative Aspect proceeds in the cases under analysis is:

(49a) $_S[_{NP_1}[(UN)SPECIFIED\ QUANTITY\ OF\ X]_{NP_1} + _{VP}[_V[VERB]_V +$
$[(UN)SPECIFIED\ QUANTITY\ OF\ X]_{NP_2\ (or\ QC)} +$
$_{NP_3}[(UN)SPECIFIED\ QUANTITY\ OF\ X]_{NP_3}]_{VP}]_S$

> *Condition:* at least one of the categories NP_1, NP_2 (or QC) and NP_3 must be UNSPECIFIED.

NP_1 is the Subject of S, NP_2 is a Direct Object, QC is a Quantifying Complement or a Directional Prep Phrase, and NP_3 is an Indirect Object.

The Nondurative Aspect in the sentences under discussion up to now appears to be composed of elementary categories on the basis of the following schema:

(50a) $_S[_{NP_1}[SPECIFIED\ QUANTITY\ OF\ X]_{NP_1} + _{VP}[_V[VERB]_V +$
$[SPECIFIED\ QUANTITY\ OF\ X]_{NP_2\ (or\ QC)} +$
$_{NP_3}[SPECIFIED\ QUANTITY\ OF\ X]_{NP_3}]_{VP}]_S$

> *Conditions:*
> (i) VERB must stand for subcategorial nodes discussed above such as MOVEMENT, PERFORM, TAKE, ADD TO, CHANGE, DO, etc.
> (ii) (50a) does not apply to negative sentences.

It will be understood that both (49a) and (50a) abbreviate configurations discussed above such as $NP_1 + V + NP_2 + NP_3$ in the sentences (57), $NP_1 + V + NP_2$ (or QC) in (56a) and (56b), and perhaps even $NP_1 + V$ in (52a), (52b), (54a) and (54b). That is NP_3 (and perhaps NP_2) are optional.

---

[4] An analogous case can be found in: *Deze architect heeft dat huis vijftien keer gebouwd* (This architect built that house fifteen times) which must be taken as saying that he made fifteen houses (tokens) on the basis of one design (type).

As to condition (ii) in (50a) it can be observed that the opposition between the Durative and Nondurative (i.e. Terminative and Momentaneous) Aspects is neutralized by the Negation element *Neg*. This can be demonstrated with the help of the following sentences, discussed in Verkuyl (1970), where the differentiation into Durative, Terminative and Momentaneous Aspects was related to the meaning of the Setting Preposition *tijdens* (during).[5]

(58a)   Tijdens de wandeling *hadden Piet en Teun het over schaatsen.* (Durative)
        During the walk *Piet and Teun had a discussion about skating.*

(59a)   Tijdens de wandeling *hield Karel een korte toespraak.* (Terminative)
        During the walk *Karel gave a short speech.*

(60a)   Tijdens de wandeling heeft Albert zijn been gebroken. (Momentaneous)
        During the walk Albert broke his leg.

The Setting Preposition *tijdens* (during) can be considered a two-place Predicate whose arguments are events. For example, in (59a), Karel's giving a speech is a Terminative event relating to the event 'the walk'. If we represent 'the walk' in (58a)–(60a) as an interval (A, B) and the events referred to by the italicized constituents in (58a) and (59a) as (C, D), then we can say that (t_A, t_B) and (t_C, t_D) are the images of (A, B) and (C, D) in T, respectively, where T is the Time axis. We can say that the image of the Terminative event in T, i.e. the interval (t_{C_i}, t_{D_i}), is a proper subset of (t_A, t_B) in (59a). Thus, we find the following situation: $t_A < t_{C_i} < t_{D_i} < t_B$, where '$<$' represents the relation 'earlier than'. In (58a), the interval (t_{C_j}, t_{D_j}), being the image of the Durative event 'Piet and Teun' discussion about skating' in T, is a subset of (t_A, t_B): Piet and Teun can, but need not, have had a discussion about skating throughout the walk. In (60a) there is a relationship between one moment t_C, which is the image of the momentaneous event 'Albert's breaking his leg' in T, and (t_A, t_B). Thus we see that Adverbials with *tijdens* (during) can take constituents referring to Durative, Terminative and Momentaneous events. The meaning of *tijdens* (during) can be described in terms of the existential quantifier '$(\exists t)$' viz. as 'there is at least a t (in t_A, t_B) such that t ...'. That is, saying that *tijdens* has a meaning corresponding to the existential quantifier amounts to analyzing it as a two-place predicate allowing for the three types of relation discussed here. (*Cf.* (1c)–(3d) on pag. 8).

The Setting Preposition *gedurende* (for (the duration of)) in Duration-

---

[5] To simplify the present exposition I have sowewhat changed the examples in question.

Dating Adverbials (i.e. in Durational Adverbials having a definite Determiner) can accordingly be analyzed in terms of the universal quantifier '(∀t)' viz. as 'for all t in (t_A, t_B) it is the case that ...'. If we replace *tijdens* in (58a) by *gedurende* we are forced to interpret this sentence as saying that Piet and Teun had a discussion about skating throughout the walk. As we have seen it is not possible to substitute *gedurende* for *tijdens* (during) in sentences like (59a) and (60a), since these fit into our Nondurative schema (50a).

Now, the crucial point is that if the a-sentences are put under negation, the meaning of *tijdens* (during) can no longer be described in terms of the existential quantifier; it appears to correspond to the universal quantifier. Consider the following sentences:

(58b)   Tijdens de wandeling hadden Piet en Teun het niet over schaat-sen.
        During the walk Piet and Teun did not have a discussion about skating.
(59b)   Tijdens de wandeling hield Karel geen toespraak.
        During the walk Karel did not give a speech.
(60b)   Tijdens de wandeling heeft Albert zijn been niet gebroken.
        During the walk Albert did not break his leg.

All b-sentences can be paraphrased as 'for all moments of the walk it was the case that ...'. It is said that the Durative, Terminative and Momentaneous events did not take place. The fact that it is denied that certain events took place during the time that the walk took place, makes it possible for Momentaneous and Terminative constituents to occur with the existential quantifier under negation which expresses duration just as the universal quantifier. Note in this connection the following logical equivalence

$$\sim (\exists t)\, P(t) \equiv (\forall t) \sim P(t)$$

which shows that expressions containing the existential quantifier under negation are logically equivalent to expressions containing the universal quantifier. Compare now:

(61a)   *Arthur is een week lang over die tak gestruikeld.
        *Arthur stumbled over that branch for a week.

which cannot be taken in a single-event reading since the Nondurative Aspect is incompatible with the Durational Adverbial *een week lang* (for a week), with

(61b)   Arthur is een week lang niet over die tak gestruikeld.
        Arthur did not stumble over that branch for a week.

Then it can easily be seen that the incompatibility of the Nondurative Aspect with *een week lang* in (61a) is eliminated by the element *Neg* in (61b).

Assuming that schemata (49a) and (50a) are essentially correct, we shall go into the question of whether or not the mechanism involved in the composition of the Aspects is operative upon larger configurations than those under discussion up to now. We shall claim that the upper bound of the Aspects is formed by an S dominating the Subject-NP and the VP in schemata like (49a) and (50a). This claim means that the upper bound is located at a relatively low S in underlying structure as I shall illustrate in the subsequent sections. Our hypothesis can be falsified by sentences containing constituents that have not yet been under consideration, e.g. Instrumental Adverbials, Manner Adverbials, Adverbials of Reason, Circumstance, etc. I shall restrict myself to giving examples pertaining to the first group. Sentences like:

(62a)   *Carla schreef die brief een half uur met potlood.
        *Carla wrote that letter with a pencil for half an hour.
(62b)   *Carla schreef die brief een half uur met potloden.
        *Carla wrote that letter with pencils for half an hour.

are both ungrammatical for the same reason, viz. the ungrammaticality of *Carla schreef die brief een half uur* (Carla wrote that letter for half an hour). There is no difference between the Singular *met dat potlood* (with that pencil) and the Plural *met potloden* (with pencils). Consider also:

(63a)   *Brutus doodde Caesar een kwartier lang met een mes.
        *Brutus killed Caesar for a quarter of an hour with a knife.
(63b)   *Brutus doodde Caesar een kwartier lang met messen.
        *Brutus killed Caesar for a quarter of an hour with knives.

where it is shown that no difference can be found between (63a) and (63b) as to the relationship between the Instrumental Adverbials and the configurations of categories to which the term 'Nondurative Aspect' applies. Thus we can observe that Instrumental Adverbials are not involved in the composition of Aspects. This fact could be taken as an indication of the relatively high position of Instrumental Adverbials with respect to the upper bound of the Aspects. That is, Instrumental Adverbials seem to be located higher than the S dominating those categories which make up the Aspects.

3.2. THE LOCATION OF DURATIONAL ADVERBIALS AND THE UPPER BOUND OF THE ASPECTS

Rather than giving an arbitrary number of examples showing the correctness of the above made claim, I shall discuss another way of determining the upper bound of the Aspects. It will be clear by now that the distinction between the Durative and Nondurative Aspects primarily concerns the possibility for sentences to contain Durational Adverbials in a single-event reading. Durational Adverbials when occurring in sentences do not themselves contribute to the composition of the Durative Aspect. As we have already seen, the possibility for Durational Adverbials to occur in sentences depends on selectional restrictions. Consequently, we can say that it is not possible for constituents located higher than Durational Adverbials to contribute to the nature of the Aspects. If follows then, that the location of Durational Adverbials with respect to those constituents with which they have selectional restrictions, can give a clue to the determination of the upper bound of the Aspects. Consider diagrams (XXVIa, b and c).

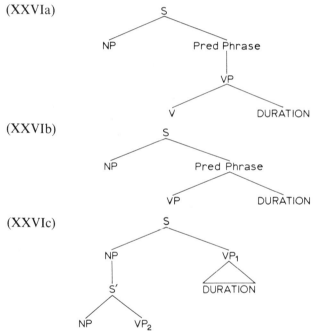

(XXVIa)

(XXVIb)

(XXVIc)

Structure (XXVIa) represents the Chomskyan position discussed in Chapter I, where Durational Adverbials were considered sister constituents of V. In Chapter II this position was left in favour of the view that Aspects are compositionally made up of categories dominated by the category VP. As a matter of consequence Durational Adverbials were to be taken as sister constituents of the VP. As far as selection is concerned, it became necessary to develop selectional rules differentiating into several types of Verb Phrase. This position was held in Verkuyl (1969b; 1970) where a distinction was made between different types of Verb Phrase (Durative, Terminative and

Momentaneous Verb Phrases) accounting for generalizations at a relatively early stage of transformational derivation.

Structure (XXVIb) represents the position held in the preceding chapter and in Verkuyl (1969b; 1970). It appears to be a derived structure, however, as follows from Section 3.1 and from Klooster and Verkuyl (1971) where it was shown that in the case of so-called Duration-Measuring Adverbials (i.e. Durational Adverbials whose Determiners are Indefinite) structures like (XXVIb) are descriptively inadequate since they fail to account for the transformational relationship between such sentences as:[6]

(64a)   Het platliggen van Lex duurde een week.
         Lex's lying flat on his back lasted a week.
(64b)   Lex lag plat gedurende een week.
         Lex lay flat on his back for a week.

Structure (XXVIc) roughly represents the position held by Klooster and Verkuyl. There is strong evidence that (64a) and (64b) should be described as relating to each other transformationally. The adoption of Gruber's principle of polycategorial lexical attachment makes it possible to derive both sentences from one underlying structure. I shall briefly sketch this structure as well as the relevant transformations necessary to obtain the differences between (64a) and (64b) so as to make clear that our Nondurative schema (50a) can be taken as a condition on a transformational rule. I would refer to Klooster and Verkuyl (1971) for the arguments and the relevant details.

Verbs like *duren* belong to the category of the so-called semicopulas, like *wegen* (weigh), *kosten* (cost), *betekenen* (mean), *bedragen* (amount), etc. They have obligatory complements specifying the duration, weight, price,

---

[6] In Verkuyl (1969b; 1970) a distinction was made between Duration-Measuring Adverbials (e.g. *gedurende een week* (for a week)) and Duration-Dating Adverbials (e.g. *gedurende die week* (for the duration of that week, during that week)). The latter are characterized by the presence of a definite Determiner. There are a great many differences between DMA's and DDA's as shown in Verkuyl (*ibidem*) and in Klooster and Verkuyl (1971). For example, DMA's can take Quantifying constituents such as *ongeveer* (about), *iets meer dan* (a little more than), and *ruim* (a good) as in *ruim een half uur* (for a good half an hour), whereas DDA's cannot take them: **ruim dat half uur* (*a good that half an hour). Further we do not find **Gedurende drie jaar gevangenisstraf was hij ziek* (*For three years of imprisonment he was ill) against *Gedurende die drie jaar gevangenisstraf was hij ziek* (During those three years of imprisonment he was ill).

DDA's should be considered closely akin to Adverbials of Time like *gisteren* (yesterday), *in 1966, tijdens die vergadering* (during that conference) whose function is to date events, the difference being that the latter can be analyzed in terms of the existential quantifier, whereas the former are analyzable in terms of the universal quantifier (Verkuyl 1969b; 1970). Though I shall restrict myself in this chapter to DMA's the analysis to follow covers DDA's as well. The difference between DDA's and DMA's can be explained in logical terms as a difference between the types of variable involved. In the case of DDA's we are concerned with the quantification of moments constituting an identified (dated) interval, in the case of DMA's it is the quantification of units of measurement, e.g. 'hour', 'week', etc.

meaning, amount, etc. The Measure Phrase *een week* (a week) is called a 'Specifying Complement' (Klooster, 1971a; 1971b; Klooster *et al.*, 1969:50–2; Verkuyl, 1969b:42–50). Klooster has named these Verbs 'semicopulas' because they do not only share many syntactic properties with copulas but they can also be paraphrased in terms of copulas. Sentences with semicopulas are synonymous to sentences containing copulas and Measure Phrases as well as to sentences containing the Verb *hebben* (have) plus a Noun pertaining to the Measuring parameter in question. The following three sentences are synonymous:

(65a)   Hij *is* 80 kilo.
         lit: He *weighs* 80 kilo.
(65b)   Hij *weegt* 80 kilo.
         lit: He *weighs* 80 kilo.
(65c)   Hij *heeft een gewicht* van 80 kilo.
         lit: He *has a weight* of 80 kilo.

Klooster proposes that we describe these sentences in terms of one underlying structure, which roughly has the following form as far as thè italicized constituents are concerned: BE + WITH + WEIGHT. The lexical item *hebben* (have) in (65c) is attached to BE + WITH, *gewicht* to WEIGHT. In (65b) *wegen* is attached to BE + WITH + WEIGHT. In (65a) *zijn* (be) is attached to BE. The categories WITH + WEIGHT do not lexicalize in this case, but they do in sentences like *Hij is 80 kilo zwaarder dan zijn vrouw* (He is 80 kilos heavier than his wife) and *Hoe zwaar is hij?* (How heavy is he?).

The relationship between *hebben* (have) and *zijn met* (be with) can be illustrated with cases like *Een man die een gewicht heeft van 80 kilo* (lit: A man who has a weight of 80 kilos) as against *Een man met een gewicht van 80 kilo* (lit: A man with a weight of 80 kilos). We can account for the relationship of synonymity between these two Noun Phrases in a simple way by deriving the latter from the former with the help of the *Relative Clause Reduction*-transformation, deleting the Relativum (in this case *die* (who)) and the Copula *zijn* (be), assuming that *die een gewicht heeft* (lit: who has a weight) should be analyzed in terms of an underlying string WHO + BE + WITH + WEIGHT. *Met een gewicht* in the second NP is the realization of the underlying (remaining) string WITH + WEIGHT. Thus, the domain of the *Relative Clause Reduction* can be extended in a natural way.

In the case of *duren* a similar analysis can be applied, although it should be said that the underlying structure of this Verb is more complicated than that of *wegen*. Klooster (1971a) argues that *duren* should be analyzed as having an underlying structure of the form BE + WITH + DURATION + WITH + LENGTH. Sentences with *duren* contain not one but two

underlying WITH-strings. As far as BE + WITH + DURATION is concerned, it can be observed that sentences like *Dat concert duurt een uur*
(That concert lasts an hour) and *Dat concert heeft de duur van een uur*
(That concert has the duration of an hour) are synonymous. The string
WITH + LENGTH accounts for an underlying parameter in the meaning
of *duren*. In *Dat duurde uren lang* (lit: That lasted hours long), *Dat duurde
langer dan ik dacht* (That lasted longer than I thought) WITH + LENGTH
appears in surface structure.

Given the correctness of Klooster's analysis of *duren* and given the correctness of all arguments favouring the position that (64a) and (64b) relate
transformationally to each other, we can say that structure (XXVId)
– which is an extension of (XXVIc) – underlies both sentences.

(XXVId)

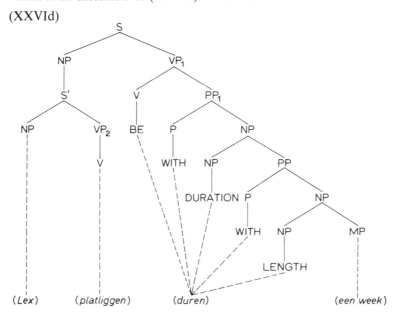

To derive (64a) it is necessary to apply the well-known *Nominalization*-
transformation, operating on S′. Thus we obtain the nominalized Noun
Phrase *Het platliggen van Lex* (Lex' lying flat on his back) which is the Subject-NP of (64a). The lexical entry of *duren* consists of the categorial structure
corresponding to the categorial string BE + WITH + DURATION +
WITH + LENGTH.

For sentence (64b) to be derived it is necessary to apply a new transformation called *Adverbialization*. Its effect is the deletion of BE in (XXVId)
and the adjunction of PP₁ to VP₂. The transformation has the following
form:

(66)   *Adverbialization.*

S.D. $X_{-NP[S'}[NP\text{-}VP_2]_{S'}]_{NP\ VP_1}[BE\text{-}PP]_{VP_1} - Y$
　　　　　 1　　　2　　3　　　　　4　　5　　　　6　OPT
S.C.   　1　　　2　　3+5　　　∅　　∅　　　6　⇒

The result of this rule is structure (XXVIe), which closely resembles structure

(XXVIe)

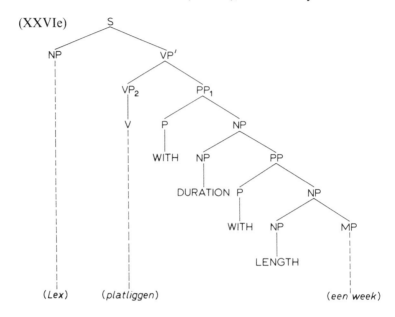

(XXVIb). The node VP′ is in fact the node *Predicate Phrase* of Chomsky's "Illustrative Fragment" in *Aspects* (1965). Thus we can say that *Adverbialization* is a transformation having as its output a derived structure which was taken as a deep structure in Chomsky (1965). The Durational Adverbial PP$_1$ is a sister constituent of VP$_2$ in derived structure, i.e. as the result of the application of a transformational rule. See in this connection footnote 14 to Chapter I and structure III on page 25.

The lexical entry of *gedurende* (for, during) consists of a simultaneous environment closely akin to the simultaneous environment of *duren* (last), the difference being that the latter contains a Tense-carrier BE whereas the former occurs without this category, as shown in (XXVIf).

The peripheral environment of this entry contains the appropriate selectional information. In view of the fact that *gedurende* can only occur with Temporal Nouns expressing Duration, the Measure Phrase must contain nodes involved in the selection (*Cf.* Chapter I, pages 15 and 38). As far as the other part of its peripheral environment is concerned, it is clear that the non-null variable *W* does not contain a categorial node DURATIVE as was provisionally suggested in Chapter I, page 38, when we were discussing the Aspects as entities assigned to V.

The preposition *gedurende* (for) is to be attached to derived structure, i.e. after the application of *Adverbialization*. In other words, *gedurende* cannot be attached if *Adverbialization* does not take place. This fact opens some perspectives for the present analysis (See for a slightly modified description of (XXVId)–(XXVIf) Klooster, 1971b).

(XXVIf)

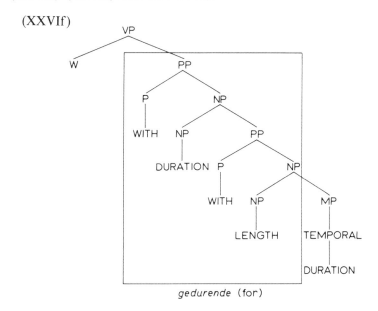

gedurende (for)

If we were to mark the peripheral environment of (XXVIf) as DURATIVE, we would be forced to extend this entry so as to include S' and consequently BE, since – as we have seen – the Durative Aspect is assigned to an S. In that case *gedurende* would have to be attached to (XXVId) rather than to (XXVIe). This solution, however, would force us to state a condition under which this lexical attachment could take place: BE in (XXVId) must be deleted in case *gedurende* is attached for we do not find **Het platliggen van Lex was gedurende een week* (*Lex's lying flat was for a week). It is obvious, however, that a condition on lexical attachment should not interfere with the application of a pre-lexical rule like (66).

We can, instead, formulate a condition under which *Adverbialization* may operate. This condition can be taken as a constraint preventing structures like (XXVIe) from being derived in case structures like (XXVId) contain S' dominating a set of categories to which our Nondurative scheme (50a) applies. This constraint can be formulated as follows:

(66a)   *Adverbialization* cannot apply so as to obtain Durational Adverbials if S' dominates a set of categories fitting into the Nondurative scheme (50a).

It blocks the single-event reading of sentences having a Nondurative Aspect and containing Durational Adverbials. Notice that we need not any rule or condition to account for the relationship between Durational Adverbials and S', when we have sentences containing a Durative Aspect. *Adverbialization* correctly derives these sentences.

In our introductory chapter the distinction between the Durative and Nondurative Aspects was illustrated with the help of sentences (1)–(5). The b-sentences, characterized by the presence of a Nondurative Aspect, systematically tend to allow for an interpretation in which frequency is expressed. It will be understood that it is necessary for any grammar to account for this fact. At least we can slacken our constraint on (66) so as to let through all sentences fitting into (50a) and expressing frequency. This alteration of (66a) should amount to stating that a Nondurative S' must be marked somehow as pluralized, e.g. $S'_{n>1}$ (If a Nondurative S' refers to a single event we can account for this by the index $n = 1$). The index $n > 1$ roughly represents the presence of an underlying Frequency Adverbial which does not lexicalize in the case of e.g. sentence (2b) *De jager bereikte drie weken die berghut* (*The hunter reached that mountain-hut for three weeks). As I already said in section 1.1 most native speakers of Dutch would prefer to insert Frequency Adverbials like *een paar keer* (several times) or *telkens* (repeatedly) into (2b); they would prefer to lexicalize the Frequency Adverbial rather than to prevent it from occurring in surface structure.

In view of these considerations we can reformulate (66a) as follows:

(66b)   If *Adverbialization* applies to structures whose PP_1 dominates the string WITH + DURATION + WITH + LENGTH, and if S' dominates a set of categories fitting into the Nondurative scheme (50a), then it must be the case that $S'_{n>1}$. If $S'_{n=1}$ and S' is Nondurative, then *Adverbialization* blocks.

In Verkuyl (1969b:60–70) and Klooster *et al.* (1969:68) Frequency Adverbials were regarded as adjuncts to Predicates expressing the number of times Durative and Nondurative events take place. The function of Frequency Adverbials can be compared with the function of Numerical elements in Noun Phrases.[7] This point is demonstrated by the correspondences

---

[7] A similar position is held in McCawley (1968a:162).

between the italicized constituents in the a- and b-sentences of the following
examples:

(67a)   *Onze laatste drie vergaderingen* was Eddy voorzitter.
         (*For*) *our last three meetings* Eddy was chairman.
(67b)   *De laatste drie keer dat we vergaderden* was Eddy voorzitter.
         The last three times we had a meeting Eddy was chairman.
(68a)   *?*Sinds zijn drie jeugden* was hij erg verlegen.
         *?*Ever since his three youths* he was very shy.
(68b)   *?*Sinds hij drie keer jong was*, was hij erg verlegen.
         *?*Ever since he was young three times*, he was very shy.

Sentence (67a) is synonymous with (67b). If we derive them from one underlying structure, this structure must express that three similar events are
referred to, in other words we must quantify over events. I shall represent
this information here in terms of S_n where n ranges over numerical values. In
(67a) and (67b) $n = 3$. This means that $S_{n=1}$ is taken as the event-unit with
respect to which $S_{n>1}$ can be considered a Plural.[8]

Sentences (68a) and (68b) are ungrammatical (or strange in our world) for
exactly the same reasons (see McCawley, 1968a:129*ff*). As said earlier on
page 61 *jeugd* (youth) is traditionally classed as a Non-Count Noun: it does
not take an Indefinite Article (**een jeugd*) nor can it occur in Plural
(Kraak and Klooster, 1968). Note that both (68a) and (68b) allow for an interpretation: if we presume that he has been born three times he can have
grown up three times. In both cases we find exactly the same interpretation.
That is, the restriction on **zijn drie jeugden* (his three youths) is not
different from the restriction on **Hij was drie keer jong* (He was young
three times). We can account for this by assuming that the S-node dominating the sentence *Hij was jong* (He was young) is inherently specified as for
a numerical value $n = 1$, and that the Noun Phrase *zijn jeugd* (his youth)
relates transformationally to this S. The incompatibility between the Fre-

---

[8] In Verkuyl (1969b) an element EVENT where n ranges over numerical values was postulated
in the underlying structure of both sentences containing Frequency Adverbials and sentences
in which syntactic frequency occurs. The term 'syntactic frequency' applies to sentences like
Zij wachtten avondenlang (They waited for evenings), *In het weekeind zeilde hij op de Loos-
drechtse plassen* (At the weekend he sailed on the lakes of Loosdrecht) and **Greetje wandelde
urenlang een kilometer* (*Greetje walked a kilometre for hours). The necessity for having an
index $n = 1$ (i.e. for giving an account of single-event readings as opposed to frequency) can be
shown in cases like *Heb je nu gerookt?* (Did you smoke nów?) which cannot question a habit,
but must pertain to a single act of smoking something. The same applies to imperative sentences
like *Geef hier die fiets* (Give that bike here). This command can only be taken as pertaining to
just one act of giving that bike, (I owe this example to Klooster (personal communication)).
Note also the difference between *In het weekend bezocht hij zijn oom* (At the weekend he used
to visit his uncle) against *In het weekend heeft hij zijn oom bezocht* (At the weekend he visited
his uncle; last weekend he visited his uncle).

quency Adverbial *drie keer* (three times) and *Hij was jong* (He was young) and between the Numerical element *drie* (three) and *zijn jeugd* (his youth) can now be explained uniformly. Both *drie keer* and *drie* require that the S be specified as $n = 3$, whereas this S in fact is inherently specified as $n = 1$.

The crucial point emerging from the present analysis is that the question of where the upper bound of the Aspects should be located does not differ very much from the question of which S-nodes should be assigned numerical values to the effect of pluralizing them. If we can determine the internal structure of $S_{n=1}$, we can automatically account for its Plural $S_{n>1}$. For only if we can determine the unit of quantification, can we quantify.

Returning now to (66b) we could say that determining the internal structure of $S'_{n=1}$ amounts to specifying the notion 'event unit'. If it is correct to assume that (66b) applies to quantification over Nondurative events, we must know what a Nondurative event is.

It will be understood that the internal structure of S' in (XXVId) is determined by the presence of constituents which occur in it: or more precisely, by the absence of constituents which cannot occur in it. What we need is a syntactic means for determining which constituents occur outside, and which constituents occur inside S'.

3.3. A CRITERION FOR VERB PHRASE CONSTITUENCY?

In this section I shall extensively deal with the proposal by Lakoff and Ross (1966) concerning Verb Phrase constituency since its purpose -to determine a certain syntactically significant constituent on the basis of a strong degree of cohesion between its members – runs concurrently with the aim set in the preceding section, viz. to determine the internal structure of S'.

Lakoff and Ross claimed that there are syntactic means to determine which constituents are dominated by the node VP and which are not. The latter occur outside VP in the rest of the Predicate Phrase. However, recent developments in linguistic theory tend to show that Chomsky's "Illustrative Fragment" in *Aspects* (1965) can at best be regarded as providing for some generalizations of derived structure. There is no such node as *Predicate Phrase* in deep structure and it can even be questioned whether there is a deep structural category VP.[9] Therefore it is necessary to re-interpret the proposal by Lakoff and Ross and to reformulate a criterion separating

---

[9] In generative semantics rules like (i) $S \rightarrow NP_1$ VP and (ii) $VP \rightarrow V \ NP_2$ are replaced by (iii) $S \rightarrow V \ NP_1 \ NP_2$, where V is taken as a logical predicate holding between two arguments. There is a rule called *Subject-Raising* which transforms $_S[V \ NP_1 \ NP_2]_S$ into $_S[NP_1 \ _{VP}[V \ NP_2]_{VP}]_S$. See McCawley (1970); Lakoff (1970). To simplify the exposition I shall present the description of the sentences under analysis in terms of the rules (i) and (ii) since it does not affect the argument.

constituents with a certain degree of cohesion in underlying structure from those which are transformationally introduced into what develops into the surface Predicate Phrase. This criterion appears to determine a minimal S dominating a relatively simple pattern of categories. It is this S which turns out to be the upper bound of the Aspects.

There are several reasons for discussing the Lakoff-Ross proposal in detail. Firstly, its reformulation and extension lead to a description of sentences in terms of events which can be quantified. Secondly, it enables us to gain more insight into the exact nature of such primitive Verbal categories as PERFORM, TAKE, MOVE, ADD TO, discussed in Chapter II, since the related node DO will extensively be analyzed. Finally, the relationship between "normal" declarative sentences and pseudo-cleft sentences can be specified more adequately.

The attempt by Lakoff and Ross to formulate a criterion for Verb Phrase constituency with the help of a transformational rule called *do so*-replacement will be under discussion in this section mainly in terms of the Dutch equivalent version of this rule, the *doen dat*-replacement (See: Kraak and Klooster, 1968:208*ff.*; Klooster *et al.*, 1969:42*ff.*; Verkuyl, 1969b:11–7). I shall argue that the claim that *doen dat* (do so) is a Pro-VP substituting for a VP generated by the base rules is wrong. There are reasons to assume that *doen* (do) can be generated by the base rules and that *dat* (so; that) is a category occurring as the sister constituent of *doen*.

3.3.1. *Doen dat (do so)-replacement*

Lakoff and Ross claim that *doen dat* (do so) occurs as a Pro-VP replacing 'all of the constituents of the verb phrase and only these'. They argue that a sentence like

(69a)   Arie at een haring en Piet deed dat ook.
         Arie ate a herring and Piet did so too.

should be derived from an underlying string corresponding to sentences like:

(69b)   Arie at een haring en Piet at ook een haring.
         Arie ate a herring and Piet ate a herring too.

Both (69a) and (69b) are derived from a structure as given in diagram (XXVII).

For (69a) to be generated it is necessary that VP_1 in S_b is replaced by *doen dat*. The following rule relates (69a) to (XXVII) and consequently to (69b):

(XXVII)

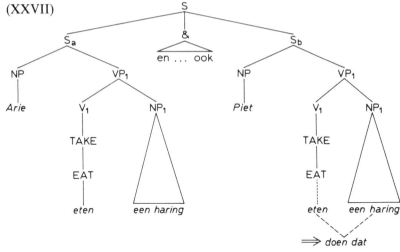

(70)   *Doen dat-replacement*

S.D.	X	-	VP	-	Y	-	VP	-	Z	
	1		2		3		4		5	OPT
S.C.	1		2		3		*doen dat*		5	⇒

> *Condition:*
> (i) 2=4
> (ii) 2 begins with a Nonstative Verb.

where X, Y and Z are variables. Condition (ii) is necessary in view of the ungrammaticality of sentences like:

(69c)   *Arie zag een haring en Piet deed dat ook.
        *Arie saw a herring and Piet did so too.

Doen dat (do so) cannot replace the stative Verb *zien* (see) (see in this connection Lakoff, 1966). Condition (i) reveals that rule (70) can be taken as the pendant of a rule called *Pronominalization*, which has essentially the same structural index as (70), as we will see on page 135. Condition (i) states that structurally and lexically the two Verb Phrases be identical and that they are also referentially identical. We can say that *doen dat* anaphorically refers back to the VP labelled 2.

The claim that the Pro-VP *doen dat* replaces all of the constituents of the VP receives support from the fact that sentences like:

(69d)   *Arie at een haring en Piet deed dat ook een haring.
        *Arie ate a herring and Piet did so too a herring.

are ungrammatical. If *deed dat* (did so) were to refer back to the Verb *eten* (eat) alone, then it would be possible to generate *een haring* in the second part of (69d). We find the same situation in sentences like:

(71)   *Greetje wandelde naar het strand en Jan deed dat naar het bos.
         *Greetje walked to the beach and Jan did so to the woods.

Apparently, *doen dat* cannot only replace the Verb. There appears to be a certain degree of cohesion (see Chomsky, 1965:101) between the Verb and a Direct Object or a Directional Prep Phrase, which requires that any combination [Verb + Direct Object] or [Verb + Directional Prep Phrase] be taken as an elementary unit with respect to a Pro-form. Lakoff and Ross called these units Verb Phrases and considered *doen dat* a Pro-VP just as *hij* in:

(69e)   Gisteren at Arie een haring en vandaag deed hij hetzelfde.
         Arie ate a herring yesterday and to-day he did the same (thing).

is a Pro-NP with respect to the NP *Arie*. Note in passing that *hetzelfde doen* (do the same) just like *dat doen* (do so) anaphorically refers back to the VP *een haring eten* (eat a herring), and that this constituent indeed must be identical to what is replaced by *hetzelfde doen*, as we can see from the lexical meaning of *hetzelfde*. Note also that *hetzelfde doen* does not replace *een haring eten gisteren* (eat a herring yesterday), since this would mean that Arie to-day ate a herring yesterday, which is absurd.

Lakoff and Ross claim that *doen dat* replaces *only* constituents belonging to the Verb Phrase. In Section 3.3 I shall argue that the "*only*-claim" is wrong since the referential power of *doen dat* is much greater than suggested by Lakoff and Ross.

I shall now set out some arguments for the view that the proposal by Lakoff and Ross in so far as it results into rule (70) should be regarded as both incomplete and inadequate. Consider the following sentences:

(71a)   Greetje wandelde naar het strand en Jan deed dat ook.
         Greetje walked to the beach and Jan did so too.
(71b)   *Wat Greetje *naar het strand* deed was *wandelen*.
         *What Greetje did *to the beach* was *to walk*.
(71c)   Wat Greetje deed was *naar het strand wandelen*.
         What Greetje did was *to walk to the beach*.
and

(69f)   *Wat Arie *een haring* deed was *eten*.
         *What Arie did *a herring* was *to eat*.
(69g)   Wat Arie deed was *een haring eten*.
         What Arie did was *to eat a herring*.

We can say that in any grammatical construction of the form:

$$(72) \quad \left[\left[\begin{array}{c} Wat \\ What \end{array} + \text{Subject} + X + \begin{array}{c} doen \\ do \end{array} \right]_{S} \right]_{NF} \quad {}_{NP} {}_{VP}\left[\begin{array}{c} zijn \\ be \end{array} + {}_{PN}[\text{Verb} + Y]_{PN} \right]_{VP}$$

all constituents necessarily occurring as Y in the Predicate Nominal fall inside the scope of reference of *doen wat* in exactly the same way constituents necessarily fall inside the scope of *doen dat*. In other words, sentences like (71b) and (69f) are ungrammatical for exactly the same reason that (71) and (69d) are ungrammatical. 'Verb + Y' constitutes a unit with respect to *wat doen*, at some stage of the derivation of sentences like (71c) and (69g).

The proposal by Lakoff and Ross is incomplete because they restricted themselves to coordinated (and subordinated) structures like e.g. (XXVII) where the Pro-VP *replaces* a Verb Phrase. Since sentences like (71c) and (69g) do not contain two VP's, we cannot use the term 'replace'. It is unlikely that *wat doen* and *dat doen* are different Pro-forms, because *wat* (what) can be analyzed as $[PRO_1 + [WH + PRO_2]]$ (= that which), where PRO_1 is a category from which the Pronoun *dat* (that) can be developed. (See for a detailed analysis Section 3.3.4, diagrams (XXXVIII) and (XXXIX)). Therefore, if Lakoff and Ross are right in stating that *doen dat* is a Pro-VP, then it follows that *wat doen* should also be regarded as a Pro-VP. However, there is no rule accounting for sentences like (71c) and (69g).

Let us first try to continue the line of argument followed by Lakoff and Ross to see what kind of rule will be necessary to render their proposal complete. This step is also motivated by the fact that pseudo-cleft constructions like (71c) and (69g) appear to give a clue to a better understanding of the nature of constituents like *doen dat*. I think that the proposal by Lakoff and Ross can be extended so as to cover cases like (69g) by saying that structure (XXVIIa), which corresponds to the sentence:

(XXVIIa)

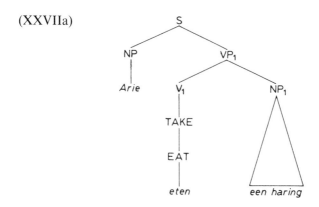

(69h)   Arie at een haring.
         Arie ate a herring.

(XXVIII)

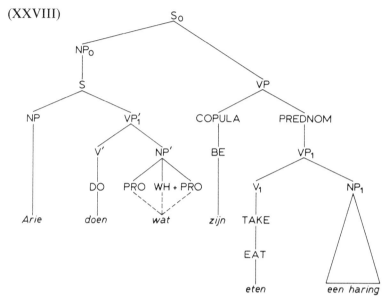

, transformationally relates to structure (XXVIII) which is generated after the application of a *Pseudo-Cleft*-transformation. Structure (XXVIIa) seems to be (part of) the input to this transformation.

It should be noticed here that we might use the expression that VP_1' *replaces* VP_1. As such, VP_1' could be considered the pro-VP of VP_1, which occurs in a nominal form itself. In short, we would need rules moving VP_1 from its original position to the Predicate Nominal and substituting the Pro-VP for the place left by VP_1. If these rules were available, the proposal by Lakoff and Ross could be said to cover cases like (69g). In Chomsky (1968a) an attempt was made to develop such rules. Later on, I shall discuss his proposal in some detail rejecting it on the ground that it is descriptively inadequate (see page 148).

At any rate, it appears possible, in principle, to cover cases like (69g) thus extending the point made by Lakoff and Ross that the Pro-VP *doen dat* (do so) provides for a criterion for Verb Phrase constituency.

3.3.2. *On the Underlying Category DO*

I shall now set to describe the relationship between sentences like (69a) *Arie at een haring en Piet deed dat ook* (Arie ate a herring and Piet did so too) and its first part (69h) on the one hand, and corresponding pseudo-cleft sentences like (69g) *Wat Arie deed was een haring eten*. For this to be done adequately we should be able to account uniformly for the presence of *doen* in both (69a) and (69g). Since I shall propose that (69h) *Arie at een haring* and (69g) are derived from one underlying source (setting aside the presence of topicalization elements) it is necessary to account satisfactorily for the presence of *doen* in (69g) and for its absence in (69h). I shall argue that *doen* need not be introduced transformationally.

We closed off the preceding section by giving a more or less satisfactory account of the derivation of sentences like (69g). The only disadvantage seems to be that *doen* + PRO must be introduced into derived structure, via two different transformational rules, namely rule (70) and a *Pseudo-Cleft* rule converting (XXVIIa) or the structure containing (XXVIIa) into (XXVIII).

There are some other reasons why we should reject the proposal by Lakoff and Ross even in its extended domain. Both (69g) and (69h) are proper answers to the question:

(73)   Wat deed Arie?
        What did Arie do?

Staal (1967), discussing the relation between declarative sentences and questions, described the structure of sentences like (73) as diagrammed in (XXIX).

(XXIX)

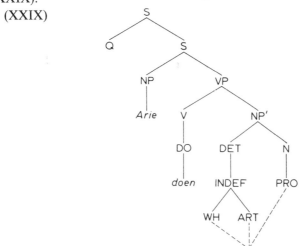

In both (69g) and (69h) the comment given on Arie is that he ate a herring, if these sentences answer question (73).

Staal defines the notion 'comment-of' as follows: "The comment of a sentoid S with Phrase-marker P is the relation $[P, P']$ between P and another Phrase-marker P', such that P and P' differ as follows. If NP in P dominates a lexical item *l*, the corresponding NP' in P' dominates an occurrence of *wh*. This is also expressed by saying that *l* is the comment of S. (The notion of 'correspondence' can be defined without difficulty in terms of grammatical relations.)" (1967:77–8).[10] This definition rests upon the position held by Katz and Postal (1964:105*ff*.) that it is mostly Noun Phrases that can be questioned. "Hence Noun-phrases are both the constituents which can be questioned and the constituents which can be the comment of the sentence. This has interesting consequences. It may seem peculiar that Verbs or Verb-phrases cannot be questioned. It might in fact be asked whether there are natural languages in which they can be questioned" (Staal, 1967:79).

According to Staal, structures like (XXVIIa) do not contain an NP corresponding to NP' in structures like (XXIX). That is, there is no comment of S in (XXVIIa) with respect to structure (XXIX). (NP₁ in (XXVIIa) is the comment of S with respect to the question *Wat eet Arie* (lit: What eats Arie; What is Arie eating)). Now, one of the possibilities of accounting for the relation between (69h) and (73) is to introduce DO into every VP. Slightly modified, Staal's proposal with respect to a structural description of sentences like (69h) can be represented as in diagram (XXX):

(XXX)

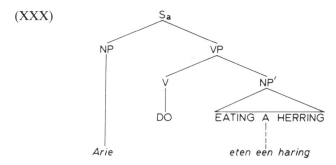

In English such a structure underlies partly *Arie eats a herring, Arie is eating a herring, Arie does eat a herring, Arie doesn't eat a herring, Arie isn't eating a herring, Does Arie eat a herring? Is Arie eating a herring?* As far as the status of DO is concerned, Staal treats it as a "purely grammatical formative". It may even be so that V in (XXX) dominates a dummy symbol for which *do, be* and perhaps other grammatical formatives can be substituted. Staal does not elaborate this possibility any further (1967:82)[10a].

---

[10] Later on in his paper Staal extends this definition of 'comment of' so as to cover sentoids with multiple comments. This extension is not relevant to the present argument.

[10a] While this book was in print I discovered that J. R. Ross independently arrived at the conclusion that DO is a part of the underlying structure of action sentences (J. R. Ross, 'Act', in D. Davidson and G. Harman, *Semantics of Natural Language*, Dordrecht 1972). Some of Ross' ten arguments are also given in the present section. Though Ross relates his analysis to Da-

Staal's proposal has the merit of accounting for questions and their relation to declarative sentences, but also for negative and emphasized sentences as we were able to see from the English examples above. I think his proposal should be extended so as to cover also the relationship between sentences like (69h) and (69g). The basic assumption underlying this extension is that *wat* (what) in (69g) is not essentially different from *wat* (what) in (73) as far as reference is concerned. We might say that there is a relation between the underlying structure of the pseudo-cleft sentence (69g) as (provisionally) represented in (XXVIII) and the underlying structure of (73) which can be accounted for in terms of the relation 'comment-of' just as there is a similar relationship between the underlying structure of (73) represented in (XXIX) and the underlying structure of (69h) if represented as in (XXX). For (69h) to contain a constituent which is its comment with respect to structure (XXIX), it is necessary to assume that (XXX) rather than (XXVIIa) is the essentially correct representation of its underlying structure. If this is indeed the case, we obtain the opportunity to account for the relationship between (67g) and (67h).

I shall argue that Staal's proposal should be accepted as far as its main points are concerned. It seems correct to generate an underlying category DO together with a constituent of a nominal nature, so that this latter one can be questioned.

However, it appears desirable to assume that NP' in (XXX) is an S, as is shown in (XXXI).

Putting off the question of how to account for the Subject-NP of S_1 until Section 3.3.3, I shall now discuss the relationship between NP' in (XXXI) and NP' in (XXVIII). If it is true that these nodes are corresponding nodes with respect to the relation 'comment-of' then we may conclude that VP_1 in (XXVIII) is a derived constituent. Thus, NP' in (XXVIII) does not occupy the place of VP_1 but rather the place of a node comparable to S_1 in (XXXI). In other words, VP_1 in (XXVIII) can be considered a transform derived by the application of a transformational rule deleting a Subject-NP.

---

vidson's proposal about the logical form of action sentences, he does not discuss the internal structure of the complement of DO in detail. That is, he does not investigate into the internal structure of the event-argument involved in the action predicates. Staal's proposal appears to provide a proper perspective for such an analysis. It is the purpose of the present section to relate pseudo-cleft action sentences to "normal" declarative action sentences with a view to a better understanding of the nature of the Aspects. The point at issue is clear: the terminative aspect in (69h) *Arie at een haring* (Arie ate a herring) is identical to the aspect in (69g) *Wat Arie deed was een haring eten* (What Arie did was to eat a herring). Both *Arie at urenlang een haring* (*Arie ate a herring for hours) and *Wat Arie urenlang deed was een haring eten* (*What Arie did for hours was to eat a herring) are ungrammatical in the same way as (1b)–(4b) in Chapter I. The category DO plays a crucial role in the account of the transformational relationship between sentences like (69h) and (69g).

(XXXI)

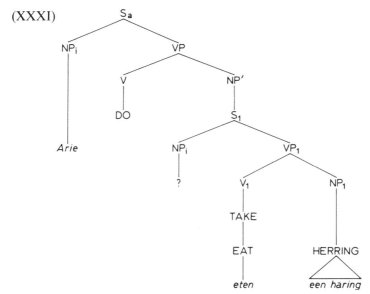

Before giving a formal description of the derivation of sentences like (69g) and (69h) by which the above position will become clear, I shall give some arguments for the view that the unit 'Verb + Y' in (72), and hence VP₁ in (XXVIII), is only part of an underlying sentential structure.

First of all, we find sentences like:

(74)   Wat je echt niet kunt doen is dat je de commissie gaat vertellen hoe Polletje zich gedragen heeft.
         lit: What you really cannot do is that you are going to tell the committee how Polletje behaved.

(75)   Wat hij beter had kunnen doen in die omstandigheden is dat hij mij had gezegd waar het geld lag.
         lit: What he should have done under those circumstances is that he had told me where the money was hidden.

which indicates that *zijn* (be) in pseudo-cleft constructions like (72) can be followed by clauses preceded by the Complementizer *dat* (that). For *dat* to be generated as a Complementizer it is necessary that there is an S containing a Subject as well as Tense elements. We might say that *dat*-Placement is an alternative to the placement of an Infinitival marker as in sentences like (69g). Admittedly, there are some restrictions on *dat*-Placement. Not all of my informants consider (74) and (75) acceptable. And we cannot have *dat*-Placement in cases like (69g) as shown by:

(69i)   *Wat Arie deed is dat hij een haring at.
         *What Arie did is that he ate a herring.

On the other hand, there are many people, including myself, who accept sentences like (74) and (75) without any problem at all. Given this fact, we can say that the occurrence of *dat*-Placement in Pseudo-cleft-constructions with *Wat + Subject + doen*, *+ zijn + ···* (What + Subject + do, + be + ···) strongly suggests that *wat* (what) refers to an S rather than to a VP.[11] It would be rather undesirable to assume that the reference of PRO in cases like (74) and (75) is essentially different from the reference of PRO in cases like (69g).

Secondly, consider the following dialogue:

(76) (a) Arie heeft iets gevaarlijks gedaan.
         Arie has done something dangerous.
     (b) Wat heeft hij dan gedaan?
         What has he done then?
     (c) (Wat Arie heeft gedaan?)   Een haring gegeten.
         (What Arie has done?)   Eaten a herring.

Following Staal's analysis there is a relation between *iets* (something) in (76a) and *wat* (what) in (76b): *iets* is questioned by *wat*. Sentence (76c) is an answer to (76b) if we look away from the question in parentheses. That is *een haring gegeten* (lit: eaten a herring) can immediately be given as an answer to sentence (76b). Note that the question in (76c) echoes (76b). *Een haring gegeten* (lit: Eaten a herring) in (76c) is an answer to both (76b) and the question in (76c).

Now the point is that the answer in (76c) must contain a Perfect Tense element. Combinations like:

(76d)   Wat heeft hij dan gedaan?   *Een haring eten.
        What has he done then?   *To eat a herring.
(76e)   Wat Arie heeft gedaan?   *Een haring eten.
        What Arie has done?   *To eat a herring.

are not possible. Apparently, the infinitival construction in (76d) and in (76e) cannot be taken as a construction which is indifferent as to Tense. This fact might be taken as an indication that *een haring eten* (eat a herring) in

(69j)   Wat Arie gedaan heeft, was een haring eten.
        What Arie has done, was to eat a herring.

[11] I follow here the Rosenbaum (1967) – analysis of Complementizers. They are regarded as being introduced transformationally into derived structure. An alternative proposal is the introduction of Complementizers directly into the base component, as argued by Bresnan (1970). However, the point made here does not depend on the correctness of the Rosenbaum-proposal. The Complementizer *dat* (that) always requires that the Subject and Tense be generated. As to the difference between (74) and (75) on the one hand, and (69i) on the other, I cannot explain why *Complementizer-placement* is blocked in the latter case. Perhaps the *irrealis* in (74) and (75) may be held responsible for their acceptability.

should also be taken as being derived from a sentential structure. For the relation between the two parts of sentence (76c) and the corresponding parts in (69j) cannot be essentially different as far as the reference of *wat* is concerned: it is rather unlikely that *wat* in (76c) would refer to a sentential structure, and in (69j) to a VP.

Thirdly, a theory of reference based upon our linguistic theory needs to uphold the position that it is only Noun Phrases and Sentences (or more precisely: propositions) which can refer to the world. (*Cf.* Reichenbach, 1966:4–9). It is worth remembering that one of the implications of regarding *doen dat* as a Pro-VP is that a VP can refer to some entity in the world. Condition (i) on rule (70) requires that the two VP's occurring in its Structural Description be referentially identical. A logical notation of the structural representation of sentences like (69h) *Arie at een haring* (Arie ate a herring) may elucidate the point at issue. The expression

(69k) $(\exists y)\, E\, (x_1, y)$

can be read as 'there is a y such that x_1 (= Arie) ate y'. Both x_1 and y, being arguments, correspond to Noun Phrases. They refer to entities in the world, more precisely, in our Universe of Discourse. However, the whole expression being a proposition does also refer to entities, events, facts, situations. It is only well-formed expressions that can refer. To say that a Verb Phrase refers to something similarly to (69k) or to its two arguments, would mean that the ill-formed expression

(69k') $(\exists y)\, E\, (\ \ , y)$

can refer to some entity in our Universe of Discourse. To my mind, any theory should avoid this situation, since the distinction between *reference* and *meaning* of certain constituents can apply only to constituents which have a meaning. Ill-formed expressions like (69k') do not have a meaning and consequently we should not use the term 'reference' to relate them to the world.

After having given some arguments for the sentential nature of the structure underlying the constituent 'Verb + Y' in the pseudo-cleft construction (72), I shall now proceed with describing the relationship between (69g), (69h) and (69a). It will be shown that rule (70) as well as a possible *Pseudo-Cleft*-rule introducing *doen dat* into derived structure are not necessary. In re-describing structures like (XXVII) in terms of structures like (XXXI) it is my intention to provide for a solid base upon which the criterion for separating Adverbials from other parts of the surface Predicate Phrase can be founded.

Sentence (69h) and consequently the first part of sentence (69a) can be derived from structure (XXXI) as follows. I propose that the entry for the Verb *eten* has a form as is shown in diagram (XXXII).[12]

(XXXII)

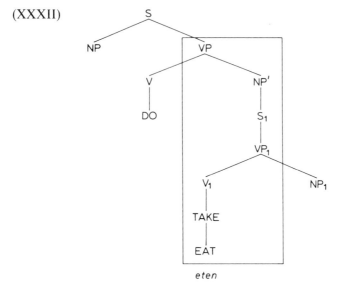

The lexical item *eten* can be attached to (XXXI) after the rule deleting the Subject of S_1 has been applied. This rule will be under discussion below. The simultaneous environment of (XXXII) contains lexical information part of which was discussed in Section 2.4.2. To account for the fact that *eten* is a Nonstative, the category DO occurs in the peripheral environment of entry (XXXII). In other words, Nonstatives can uniformly be characterized in terms of entries like (XXXII) because they can only be attached to structures in which DO has been generated. This accounts for the fact that sentences containing Nonstatives can be questioned with sentences containing *doen* in their surface structure as e.g. (73), whereas sentences containing Statives cannot be questioned by such sentences. Statives do not contain DO in their peripheral environment but rather categories like BE. This would explain why Statives cannot be attached to structures like (XXXI).

As far as DO is concerned there seem to be two possibilities. Either it

[12] The relationship between Tree pruning (i.e. taking away non-branching nodes in derived structure) and the rules of lexical attachment is not sufficiently known. One might consider the possibility of including the Subject-NP of S_1 into (XXXII). There are, however, no arguments as yet for or against this inclusion. If DO were included into the simultaneous environment of (XXXII) we would be able to account properly for the fact that DO does not occur in surface structure in (69h) *Arie at een haring* (Arie ate a herring), at the cost of accounting for the lexicalization of DO in (69g) *Wat Arie deed was een haring eten* (What Arie did was to eat a herring). See, hoewever, diagram (XXXIIa) on page 154.

can be generated directly by base rules or it can be introduced into derived structure by transformational rules. Staal does not elaborate this alternative further. As to the transformational solution of accounting for DO he suggests that it can substitute for a dummy symbol for which BE could be substituted as well, under the appropriate conditions (1967:83).

Whatever the right choice may be, in both cases we have to account for the question of why *doen* can be attached to certain structures to the exclusion of other ones. It appears as if the following lexical entry for *doen*

(XXXIII)

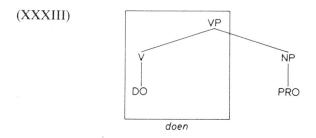

can account for the fact that DO lexicalizes in sentences like (69a) and (69g) and that DO doesn't occur in surface structure in sentence (69h).[13] Diagram (XXXIII) incorporates the claim that *doen* can only be attached

(XXXIV)

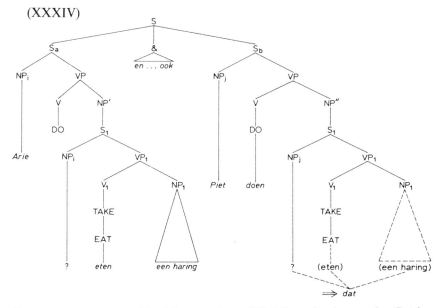

[13] Overdiep (1937:168) considered *doen* as an "empty" Verb for performing an action (Dutch: "werking") as such, the most neutral Verb apart from the Copula *zijn* (be). A similar position is held by Gruber (1967:56–7).

to a categorial tree if this tree contains a PRO-element. If PRO does not
occur, as in the case of sentence (69h) and in structure (XXXI), then *doen*
cannot be lexicalized. Consider diagram (XXXIV), which (provisionally)
represents the structure underlying sentence (69a) *Arie at een haring en
Piet deed dat ook* (Arie ate a herring and Piet did so too). Structure S_a is
identical to (XXXI) and underlies sentence (69h). The italicized constituents of S_a are lexicalized as described above. A transformational rule substituting PRO for S_1 in S_b would yield the input to the rule lexicalizing
DO, since for DO to occur in surface structure it is necessary that the categorial tree contains a category PRO.

In the case of sentence (69g) *Wat Arie deed was een haring eten* (What Arie
did was to eat a herring) *doen* can also be attached to the underlying structure, i.e. to (XXVIII) on account of the presence of PRO+[WH+PRO].

I shall now first focus the attention on the peripheral environment of entry
(XXXIII) assuming that lexicalization of *doen* is dependent on the presence
of PRO in the categorial tree. The rules accounting for PRO in the categorial tree will be discussed in 3.3.3 and 3.3.4.

Lexical entries like (XXXIII), in combination with (XXXII), might
account for such cases as:

(69m)   Arie at een haring en daarna deed hij iets anders.
        Arie ate a herring and then he did something else.

(69n)   *Arie zag een haring en daarna deed hij iets anders.
        *Arie saw a herring and then he did something else.

Sentence (69n) suggests that there is a general condition on conjoined structures requiring that *doen* in the second part only occur if the first part
contains a Nonstative. Sentence (69m) cannot be generated via rule (70)
since the constituent *doen iets anders* (do something else) violates condition
(i) which states that replacement of a VP can only take place if the Pro-VP
is identical to the VP being replaced. In (69m) Arie must have done something, but what he was doing was something quite different from what he did
before, eating a herring. If we accept the present analysis leading to entries
like (XXXIII), we can automatically account for (69m) because *iets anders*
(something else) is a PRO. Accordingly *doen* can be attached to DO in
the second part of (69m). Note that (69m) can be used (as a whole) for ans-
wering question (73) *Wat deed Arie?* (What did Arie do?)

Though we may say that *doen* normally occurs only if accompanied by a
Pronoun, the lexicalization of *doen* is not as straightforward as might have
been suggested. The following sentences show that *doen* can also occur with
NP's which do not contain a category PRO:

(77)   Marie deed de kamer met boenwas.
          Marie did the room with beeswax.
(78)   Wim doet vaak de afwas.
          Wim often does the dishes.
(79)   Ik doe die muur met grijs.
          I shall do that wall with grey.

In (77) *doen* is synonymous to the Verb *schoonmaken* (clean), in (79) to the
Verb *verven* (paint). It can be doubted whether we have to do here with the
same Verb *doen* as in (69a), (69g), (69m), etc. If *schoonmaken* and *verven*,
however, have lexical entries of the form given in diagram (XXXII), then we
could say that lexical attachment of these Verbs need not take place and
that if they are not attached, DO will lexicalize. I shall not occupy myself
with this question here. Sentences (77)–(79) are not real counterexamples
to the present analysis of the Verb *doen*, in either of the alternatives.
    It is of some interest to discuss such sentences as:

(80)   Ik moet nog *iets* doen vanavond.
          I must do *something* tonight.
(81)   Ik heb *veel* te doen vanavond.
          I have *many things* to do tonight.
(82)   Ik heb *drie dingen* te doen vanavond.
          I have *three things* to do tonight.

since the relationship between *dat* (that), *iets* (something), *veel* (much;
many things), and *drie dingen* (three things) brings us back to the analysis
of Pronouns like *iets* in Chapter II.
    In Sections 2.4.1 and 2.4.2 the Pronoun *iets* (something) was analyzed as
having an underlying structure of the form $_{NP}$[SPECIFIED QUANTITY
OF X]$_{NP}$. In sentences like (35m) *De muis at urenlang iets van de kaas*
(lit: The mouse ate something from the cheese for hours) we know that *iets*
(something) must refer to a specified portion of the cheese since the sentence
can be interpreted only in a frequency reading. The same analysis applies to
sentence (30s) on page 69.
    Since the referents of *iets* in such sentences as (35m), (30s) and also (80)
are specified quantities of something, it stands to reason to assume that
iets (something) can be "pluralized". That is, there should be constituents
which refer to more than one specified quantity of X. *Drie dingen* (three
things) in (82) and *veel* (many things) in one of its senses in sentence (81)
can be considered the "Plural" of *iets*. We cannot use (80) to give the same
information as (82): the information of (80) applies to (82) three times.
    In English the Pronoun *something* reveals in surface structure its status
as "Singular" with respect to *three things*. In French we find *quelque chose*

as against *trois choses*. Likewise (81) can be interpreted as asserting that its speaker has to do many things (Its other reading is that I have to do something which will take a long time).

On the basis of these considerations we could replace PRO in diagram (XXXIII) by some other category which covers both Pronouns as well as Numerical elements like *veel* and constituents like *drie dingen*. It will be understood in view of the above sketched relationship between *iets* and *veel* or *drie dingen*, that postulating this category certainly cannot be regarded as an *ad hoc*-solution to the problem of whether (81) and (82) should be considered counterexamples to entries like (XXXIII).

As far as I can see both (XXXIII) and (XXXIV) render rules like (70) superfluous. *Doen* need not be introduced transformationally by substituting for constituents, as was held by Lakoff and Ross. DO can immediately be generated as an underlying category. Whether or not lexicalization of DO takes place depends on the application of certain pre-lexical transformations as well as on the arrangement of the relevant lexical entries.

3.3.3. *Concerning the Condition of Strict Identity on Coreferentiality*

In this section I shall deal with some problems concerning anaphoric reference arising by the assumption that DO occurs with sentential complements whose Subject is coreferential with the surface Subject of Nonstatives (which is the underlying Subject of DO). The point at issue is that we need not extend our transformational apparatus if we drop rule (70). We can account for sentences like (69a) *Arie at een haring en Piet deed dat ook* (Arie ate a herring and Piet did so too) in terms of generalizations with respect to pronominal reference.

By assuming that (XXXI) is an essentially correct representation of the structure underlying (69h) *Arie at een haring* (Arie ate a herring) and the first half of (69a) and by claiming that *doen* results from the lexicalization of an underlying category DO which is not introduced transformationally into the categorial tree, we can account for *dat* in (69a) in terms of a rule called *S-Pronominalization*.

The domain of *S-Pronominalization* is restricted by a condition on coreferentiality. This condition has been under heavy fire several times. There seems to be, however, a solution to some of the difficulties met by those who regard pronominalization as a matter of transformational rules. The condition of strict identity can be dropped in favour of a condition of identity stated in terms of the so-called *lambda*-function used in mathematics. This makes it possible to describe sentence (69a) in terms of the transformational rule *S-Pronominalization* and to deal with the relationship between (69a), (69h) and (69g). The present analysis hinges upon the correctness of the Bach-McCawley analysis of Noun Phrases.

In recent literature much attention has been given to the account of pronominalization in grammar (See e.g. Lees and Klima, 1963, Lakoff, 1967; Langacker, 1969; Ross, 1969; Dougherty, 1969; Postal, 1970; McCawley, 1967, 1968d). The status of this rule is very much under discussion at present, notably with respect to the question of whether there is a transformational rule called *Pronominalization* substituting Pronouns for Noun Phrases (or S's) if these are identical to other Noun Phrases (or S's). For example, McCawley (1968d) regards Pronouns as elements replacing indices in a semantic representation to which no corresponding NP can be attached and dispenses with *Pronominalization*. Dougherty claims that Pronouns "are inserted into the deep structure phrase marker by the lexical insertion rule" (1969:492).

In view of the main theme of this chapter, which is the structural description of the category referring to events coming under the opposition 'Durative vs. Nondurative', I shall only obliquely discuss pronominalization. The sentences under analysis seem to make it possible to contribute to a better understanding of the rules necessary to account for pronominalization.

Consider the following rule:

(83)   *NP-Pronominalization*

S.D.	X	-	NP	-	Y	-	NP	-	Z	
			[−PRO]				[−PRO]			
	1		2		3		4		5	OBL
S.C.	1		2		3		4		5	⇒
							[+PRO]			

$$Condition: 2 = 4$$

where X, Y and Z are variables. This rule introduces Pronouns into derived structure and represents the view that they are not generated by base rules. I ignore here the so-called *Backward Pronominalization* since this does not play any role in the argument (See: Ross, 1969).

Rule (83) applies e.g. to sentence (69m) whose underlying structure corresponds to the string *Arie + at + een haring + & + Arie + doen + iets anders + daarna (Arie + ate + a herring + & + Arie + do + something else + then)*. The first occurrence of *Arie* corresponds to number 2 in the Structural Description of (83), its second occurrence to number 4. The second *Arie* must be replaced by a Pronoun, giving (69m).

The domain of rule (83) is too narrow, because Pronominalization does not restrict itself to Noun Phrases. S's can also be pronominalized, as we have seen. Notice that (83) cannot be extended so as to cover S's because it is an obligatory rule: *S-Pronominalization* is optional. We find sentences like (69b) *Arie at een haring en Piet at ook een haring* (Arie ate a herring and Piet ate a herring too). Therefore, to account for (69a) and (69b) we could think of the following rule:

(83a)   *S-Pronominalization*

S.D.   X - S - Y -   S   - Z
         1   2   3   4   5   OPT
S.C.   1   2   3   NP   5 $\Rightarrow$
                           [PRO]

Condition: 2=4

which rests upon exactly the same principle as rule (83).

It should be noticed that rule (83a) might be required for the description of discourse. The variable Y corresponding to the index-number 3 may contain a sentence boundary as we can see from:

(69o)   Arie heeft een haring gegeten. Wanneer heeft hij dat gedaan?
         Arie ate a herring. When did he do that?

The list of transformations of M.I.T.-course 1967 contains a rule, called *S-deletion*, which has the following form: [14]

(83b)   *S-Deletion*

S.D.   X - S - Y - $_{NP}$[IT - S]$_{NP}$ - Z
         1   2   3   4   5   6   OPT
S.C.   1   2   3   4 $\emptyset$ 6 $\Rightarrow$

Condition: 2=5

This rule having the same effect as (83a), however, primarily relies on the correctness of the Rosenbaum (1967)-analysis (See for an alternative account of *it* McCawley (1968d)). In this section the condition on (83a) and (83b) will be under discussion; in the subsequent section it will become clear that (83b) in its modified version should be preferred to (83a).

The condition on (83a) and (83b) gives us the opportunity to discuss the Subject-NP of sentences like (69h) and (69a). I have made use of question-marks to indicate that a lot of descriptive problems are involved in the description of structures like (XXXI) and (XXXIV) with respect to the

---

[14] Grinder and P. M. Postal (1971:110–2) refer to a pre-cyclical rule *Sentence Pronominalization* developed in an unpublished paper by Lakoff written in 1966. As far as I can see this rule is identical to rule (83b). It will be clear that *S-deletion* in this version primarily relies on the correctness of the Rosenbaum (1967) – analysis allowing for base rules like NP→IT S so as to account for *Extraposition*.

question of whether the Subject of S_1 should be identical to the Subject of the next higher S. If we followed a rather general view upon such structures, we could replace the question-marks by *Arie* in (XXXI) and by *Arie* and *Piet* in (XXXIV). The rule of *Equi-NP-deletion* obligatorily removes NP_i of S_1, thus resulting into a structure which is the input to the lexical attachment rule attaching *eten* to the categorial tree (see: Rosenbaum, 1967; Lakoff, 1965; Chomsky, 1968a; McCawley, 1968b; Postal, 1970).

However, suppose that the underlying string corresponding to (XXXIV) has the following form:

(84) $_{S_a}$[Arie - DO - $_{S_1}$[Arie eten een haring]$_{S_1}$]$_{S_a}$ &
        $_{S_b}$[Piet - DO - $_{S_1}$[Piet eten een haring]$_{S_1}$]$_{S_b}$

which would be the consequence of the above position, then it will become clear that the condition on (83a) does not meet the constraint imposed on Pronominalization-transformations which requires that number 2 and 4 in (83) and (83a) be strictly identical. "Strict identity requires that the portion of the phrase marker dominated by NP_x be identical to the portion of the phrase marker dominated by NP_y both structurally and lexically, and that the referential items dominated by NP_x bear the same indices as the referential items dominated by NP_y," (Dougherty, 1969:489). This quotation applies also to (83a) and (83b). Now, S_1 of S_b cannot be strictly identical to S_1 of S_a. Though *dat* (that; so) substitutes for S_1 of S_b on the grounds that the S being replaced is identical to another S, we can clearly see that the referents of these sentences cannot be identical: Arie and Piet are different persons and they did not consume the same herring. Apparently, if we say that Piet did the same thing as Arie we say that he did something which was similar to what Arie was doing.[15] Likewise the postman in the first part of a sentence like

(85)   De postbode bezorgde gisteren een pakje en vandaag bracht hij
        een brief.
        The postman delivered a parcel yesterday and today he brought
        a letter.

need not be the same person as the one referred to by *hij* (he). It is the function, the profession of the person delivering the parcel which must be identical to the function or profession of the person delivering the letter. Consider also:

(85a)   Sinds ik in Amsterdam woon is er al acht keer een fiets van me
        gestolen en daarom zet ik hem nu maar in een stalling.

---

[15] For some other counterexamples to the condition of strict identity see Bach (1970) and Dougherty (1969).

> Since I have been living in Amsterdam a bike of mine has already been stolen eight times and therefore I now put it in a bike garage.

where *hem* (it) is a Pronoun referring to my present bike, not to my former ones. In referring to my ninth bike I can use a Pronoun, thus pronominalizing on other grounds than identity of the referents. There are some x and these x are or were my bike and for eight of these x it is the case that they were stolen, for the remaining x (my present bike) the Predicate 'being stolen' does not hold. Thus it appears that the condition of identity concerns some Predicate (in this case 'being my bike') *in its relation to the argument* 'I' rather than the entity taking the value of x.

Following Bach (1968) and McCawley (1968a) we can analyze *de postbode* in sentence (85) as 'the y such that y is a postman' or 'the y who is a postman'. By separating the NP-description ('such that y is a postman' or 'who is a postman') from an operator-like part ('the y'), we can obtain a better position for formulating a more adequate condition on (83) and (83a) than before. For in the case of (85) there may be a z who is a postman and who delivered a letter. For *Pronominalization* to apply it is not necessary that y and z are identical.

I shall illustrate this point with the help of the following sentences:

(69p)   Arie probeerde een haring te eten en Piet probeerde *dat* ook.
Arie tried to eat a herring and Piet tried *the same* too.

(69q)   Arie probeerde een haring te eten en Piet probeerde ook een haring te eten.
Arie tried to eat a herring and Piet tried to eat a herring too.

with respect to which there is consensus of opinion as far as the status of the Subject-NP's is concerned. In recent studies sentences with *proberen* (try) are generally taken as consisting of a V plus a sentential complement whose Subject is identical to the Subject of the whole sentence, as shown in diagram (XXXV).

(XXXV)

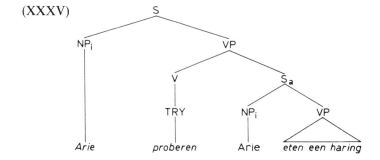

This structure is said to underlie the first part of sentence (69p) because it accounts for the fact that *Arie* is its logical subject with respect to *eten een haring* (eat a herring) (See: Rosenbaum, 1967; Perlmutter, 1968; Lakoff, 1965; Chomsky, 1968b; Postal, 1970).

It will be understood that what Piet tried to do in sentence (69p) cannot be the activity referred to by S_a in (XXXV). Sentence (69p) is derived from (69q) and hence we know that *dat* corresponds to a sentence whose logical subject is *Piet*. Nevertheless *dat* can refer back to something of a propositional form.

Let us suppose now that the Bach-McCawley idea of separating the NP-description from operator-like constituents is essentially correct and that we can analyze *Arie* in (XXXV) as 'the *x* who is Arie'. Then we can represent the underlying structure of (69p) as shown in (XXXVI).

(XXXVI)

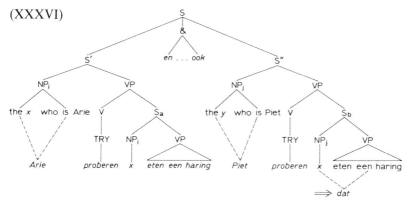

The Subject-NP of S' is described along the lines suggested by Bach (1968:115) who proposed that the underlying structure of a sentence like *the man is working* corresponds to a string of the form *the one who is a man is working*. Thus, the Noun Phrase *the man* is analyzed analogously to what is done in logical analysis, particularly in the theory of description. (See: Reichenbach, 1966:256*ff.*; Quine, 1965:146*ff.*; Quine, 1960:183*ff.*) If we abbreviate the property of being a man as 'M', then the Noun Phrase *the man* is analyzed as '(ιx) M (x)', which means 'the entity x such that x is a man', more precisely 'the unique entity x such that x is a man'. The operator '(ιx)' is called the *iota*-operator. It binds the variable of the propositional function 'M (x)'. Evading the logical idiom relating the operator and its description, we can rephrase 'the entity x such that x is a man' as 'the x who is a man'. In the following section I shall give a more accurate description of the Subject-NP of S' than is done in diagram (XXXVI).

Let us abbreviate the propositional function S_a in S' of (XXXVI) as 'H (x)', where 'H' represents the VP 'eat a herring', to simplify our exposition. Now, the crucial point of our argument is that the variable x in S_a is not "affected" by the information 'who is Arie'. Logically spoken, the variable x in S_a is a free variable. This opens the possibility for rule (71a) to apply to structure (XXXVI) on the ground of a relationship of identity between two "unaffected" propositional functions, viz. S_a and S_b. Hence we can evade a condition stating that the indexical numbers 2 and 4 in (71a) be strictly identical.

I shall elaborate this point in some detail here. The point is that the relation described by 'H (x)' can be considered a function applied to the descriptional part of the NP *Arie* in which it is said that x is Arie. This function is called a *lambda*-function consisting of the abstraction-operator '(λx)' and the formula 'H (x)'.[16] In the case of

(73) $((\lambda x) H(x))$ $((\iota x) \text{Arie}(x))$

the abstraction-operator '(λx)' is applied to the formula 'H(x)' resulting into a propositional function '$((\lambda x) H(x))$'. In (73) this function operates on an object 'the unique x such that x is Arie', which gives:

(73a) $H((\iota x) \text{Arie}(x))$

Since

(73b) $(\iota x) \text{Arie}(x) = \text{Arie}$

we may apply the rule of substitution to (73a), which gives:

(73c)   H (Arie)

to be read as (69h) *Arie at een haring* (Arie ate a herring).

Before showing the relevance of an analysis in terms of the lambda-function with respect to sentence (69a) *Arie at een haring en Piet deed dat ook* (Arie ate a herring and Piet did so too), I shall illustrate its application with the help of some other examples. Consider first:

(73d) $((\lambda x) x^2) 3 = 9$

We say then that '$((\lambda x) x^2)$' is a lambda-function applied to 3. The equation should be interpreted as follows: we can substitute 3 for x such that we obtain 3^2, which is 9. The lambda-function '$((\lambda x) x^2)$' applied to 5 is 25. $((\lambda x) x^2)$ is a function associating numbers to numbers. Consider also:

(73e) $((\lambda x) (x > 2)) 4 = 4 > 2$

where we can say that the abstraction-operator '(λx)' associates the pro-

---

[16] See e.g. Quine (1965:226*ff.*). I am very much indebted to D. van Dalen for the discussion which led to this result.

position '4 > 2' to the propositional function '$(x > 2)$'. Analogously we can say that in:

(73f) $((\lambda x)\, H(x))\, \text{Arie} = H(\text{Arie})$

where the lefthand side of the equation is identical to (73), the abstraction-operator, associates the proposition 'H(Arie)' to the propositional function '$((\lambda x)\, H(x))$'. That is, we may substitute 'Arie' for 'x' in the propositional function 'H(x)', thus obtaining the proposition (73c).

We can now interpret structure (XXXVI) in terms of an identical lambda-function applied to different descriptional parts of the Subject Noun Phrases of S' and S″, as we see in

(73g) $((\lambda x)\, H(x))\, \text{Arie} \,\&\, ((\lambda x)\, H(x))\, \text{Piet}$

That is, an identical lambda-function is applied to Arie and Piet, respectively. Thus pronominalization, or more generally, anaphoric reference of *dat* to an S-node of a preceding conjoined sentence, seems to take place on the basis of identical lambda-functions applied to the descriptional parts of Noun Phrases. Hence we can avoid complications inherent to analyses leading to structures like (XXXV).

It seems that pronominalization on the basis of the mathematical principle just sketched can avert some of the criticisms levelled against the transformational treatment of pronominalization. In the subsequent section I shall propose that the transformational approach to pronominalization should not consist of inserting PRO into derived structure as suggested by

(XXXIa)

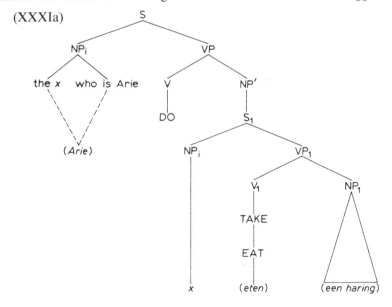

diagram (XXXVI), but should rather be taken as deleting descriptional constituents on the basis of identity of lambda-functions. In terms of rule (83b) this amounts to claiming that IT be replaced by PRO and that the S whose index number is 5 can be considered the descriptional part of the NP.

Returning now to structure (XXXI) we can modify it as shown in structure (XXXIa), which is also the structure of S_a in diagram (XXXIV). It will be clear that (XXXIa) contains a coreferential complement Subject in the same way as (XXXVI).

It should be stressed here that the correctness of (XXXIa) does not entirely depend on the present analysis of pronominalization. However, if pronominalization can be accounted for as suggested here, the relationship between (69a), (69h) and (69g) can be described more adequately.

3.3.4. *The Underlying Structure of Action Sentences*

In this Section I shall discuss the derivation of sentences like (69g) *Wat Arie deed was een haring eten* (What Arie did was to eat a herring) as well as pursue the description of sentences like (69h) *Arie at een haring*. It is my purpose to show that these two sentences can be derived from one common underlying structure, their difference being caused by the application of transformational rules. Of course, it may be the case that this structure contains some topicalization elements if the pseudo-cleft sentence (69g) is to be derived. However, since little is known about these things I shall identify here the term 'one common underlying structure' with 'one partly identical underlying structure'.

To my knowledge no explicit proposal concerning the underlying structure of pseudo-cleft sentences is available.[17] In Rosenbaum (1967) the term 'pseudo-cleft sentence' applied to examples like *What was demonstrated by Columbus was that the world is not flat*, which are said to be derived from *Columbus demonstrated that the world is not flat* by a set of transformations among which the *Pseudo-Cleft* transformation. However, in Jacobs and Rosenbaum (1968: 39) the term '*cleft-sentence* transformation' applies to a rule (introduced non-formally) converting the sentence *the frog jumped into the soup* into either *what jumped into the soup was the frog* or *what the frog jumped into was the soup*. In Dutch this rule is operative as well. Thus we find:

---

[17] While closing off the present section in its final version Akmajian (1970) came to my notice. As is suggested by the title of his paper he makes a clear distinction between pseudo-cleft and cleft sentences. He argues that the cleft sentence *It was Agnew who Nixon chose* should be derived from an underlying structure of the form $_S[[it\ [Nixon\ chose\ one]]\ was\ Agnew]_S$, which corresponds to the pseudo-cleft sentence *Who Nixon chose was Agnew*. He does not account for the presence of *be* in the latter sentence. Perhaps this account can be found in a paper announced in his bibliography, called 'Toward a Theory of Pseudo-Cleft Sentences'.

(69r)   Wat Arie at was een haring.
         What Arie ate was a herring.

Jacobs and Rosenbaum state that there are restrictions on its application:
if the NP is specified as HUMAN, the rule cannot work as is shown by *Wie
een haring at was Arie (*Who ate a herring was Arie). However, this only
a superficial restriction since we do find:

(69s)   Degene die een haring at was Arie.
         The one who ate a herring was Arie.

as was pointed out to me by Els Elffers (personal communication). Note also
that we find Wie wèl een haring at was Arie (Who certainly ate a herring was
Arie).

I shall now try to account for the derivation of (69r), (69s) and (69g)
Wat Arie deed was een haring eten (What Arie did was eat a herring) by
showing that they can be derived from one underlying structure on the basis
of one and the same principle. I shall argue that the three sentences under
analysis are derived by a Pseudo-Cleft rule and that their differences are
due to the different places of application of this rule. The proposal to be
made seems to account properly for the presence of the Copula in pseudo-
cleft sentences by making use of the Bach-McCawley analysis of Noun
Phrases already discussed in the preceding section. The Copula in (69r), (69s)
and (69g) can be regarded as the lexicalized Copula of the descriptional part
of the Noun Phrase.[18] I shall demonstrate that it is possible to relate the
proposals by Bach (1968) and McCawley (1967; 1968d) to the Gruberian
framework. In its extended form it can cover their nonformalized positions.

Following Bach (1968:115) the NP een haring (a herring) can be given an
underlying structure divided into an operator-like part and a descriptional
part, as we have already done in the case of the NP Arie in (XXXVI) and
(XXXIa). Let us also follow Bach by using the symbol 'TERM' to refer to a
Noun Phrase when occurring in deep structure, or in other words to an NP
in its most abstract representation. Let us also use the symbol 'NP' to refer
to Noun Phrases at a less abstract stage of their development. Finally, let
us assume that Pronouns, when occurring in surface structure, are reflections
of the operator-like part of a term.

We can visualize Bach's proposal as shown in (XXXVII).

The lowest categories of this structure roughly correspond to strings of
the form some + z + such + that + z + is + a herring, or some + z + which +
is + a herring, or something + that + is + a herring. The symbol 'HERRING'

---

[18] I am very much indebted to Jan Luif for the discussion leading to the view that it is the
Copula of the descriptional part of a Noun Phrase which is lexicalized in Pseudo-Cleft sentences.

(XXXVII)

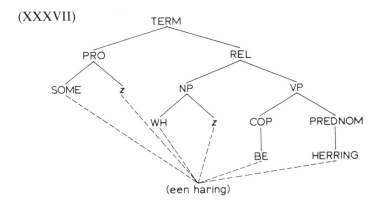

(een haring)

is equivalent to the symbol 'H' in the logical expression '$(\exists z)\,H\,(z)$', which can be read as 'there is a z such that z is a herring'. In other words, 'HERRING' is a logical predicate (*Cf.* Bach *id.*: 115). The bound variable z in the Relative Clause REL is preceded by *WH* (either introduced transformationally or directly into the base). The constituent $WH + z$ develops into a Relative Pronoun *wat* (which) or *dat* (that), the constituent SOME $+ z$ can emerge as the Pronoun *dat* (that) or *iets* (something).

Structures like (XXXVII) are closely akin to some of the structures under discussion in the previous chapter and in Section 3.1 under the assumption that the symbol PRO abbreviates quantificational information. It is worth remembering here our analysis of sentences such as (30s), (31i), (35k), (35m), and (80)–(82). It was argued that the element PRO should sometimes be analyzed in terms of configurations of categories giving information about quantity, viz. [SPECIFIED QUANTITY OF X]. Recall also our analysis of the Proper NP *Greetje* in sentence (1k) on page 104. The description of *Greetje* in terms of the configuration [SPECIFIED QUANTITY OF X] seems to relate to the Bach-representation demonstrated in (XXXVII) in a quite natural way: *the one who is Greetje,* where *the one* gives information about quantity. Thus we link up the symbolization of Chapter II and Section 3.1 with the descriptional device employed in the present section.

Bach's proposal to describe a Noun Phrase in terms of an operator-like part and a descriptional part should be taken as an attempt to connect the linguistic description of Noun Phrases with logical insights into their underlying structure. Diagrams like (XXXVII) are, in fact, visualized representations of logical expressions from the first order predicate calculus containing operators, bound variables and predicates. Now, the present analysis relating the structures under discussion in Chapter II and Section 3.1 to structures like (XXXVII) suggests very strongly that *the internal struc-*

ture of operators should receive far more attention than till thusfar, particularly with respect to the quantificational information contained by them. In view of the main argument of this section I shall continue to represent the structural descriptions of the sentences under analysis in terms of structures like (XXXVII).

Let us first consider what happens if *Relative Clause Reduction* does not apply to (XXXVII). Then it follows that $WH + z$ as well as BE must occur in surface structure. This brings us to the description of (67g), (69r), and (69s). Consider diagram (XXXVIII) which provisionally represents the underlying structure of these sentences as well as the structure underlying (69h) *Arie at een haring* (Arie ate a herring).

(XXXVIII)

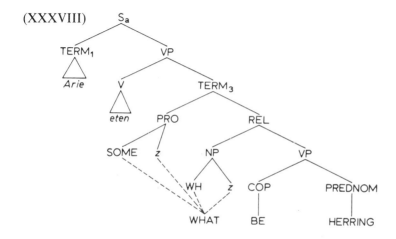

This structure demonstrates the point to be made with respect to the derivation of sentence (69r) *Wat Arie at was een haring* (What Arie ate was a herring). Hence it is only the underlying structure of TERM$_3$, on which the *Pseudo-Cleft* transformation operates, that will be scrutinized now.

In (XXXVIII) the operator PRO and the Relativum $wh + z$ are united so as to constitute the complex Pronoun *wat* (what) in (69r). The Pronoun *wat* is analyzed as consisting of two constituents, earlier referred to as [PRO + [WH + PRO]], as becomes clear by its paraphrases *dat wat* (that which), *datgene dat* (that which), *iets wat* (something which), etc. This Pronoun *wat* differs from the Pronoun *wat* in sentences like *Jan at wat* (Jan ate something).

What we need now is a rule transposing the complex Pronoun *wat* (what) in front of the sentence and transferring BE + HERRING to a place outside the S$_a$-node, as is shown in diagram (XXXVIIIa). This rule is the *Pseudo-*

Cleft rule operating upon TERM$_3$ in structure (XXXVIII) and having the following form:

(86)   *Pseudo-Cleft*

S.D. $[_S \text{X} - [_{TERM} \text{PRO} - [_{REL} \text{WH} + [_{VAR} \quad] - [_{VP} \text{COP PREDNOM}]]_{VP}]_{REL}]_{TERM} - \text{Y}]_S$

    1   2   3   4   5

                              $\Rightarrow$

S.C. 2   3 + 1   ∅   5   4

To my knowledge, there are no transformational rules containing variables for the (bound) variables of the type occurring in logical expressions such as *the x such that x is Arie* and *some z such that z is a herring*. I have used an empty place whose labelled brackets indicate that WH is adjoined to a variable of the predicate calculus, in the case of (XXXVIII) to *z*.

The application of rule (86) to (XXXVIII) will yield structure (XXXVIIIa).

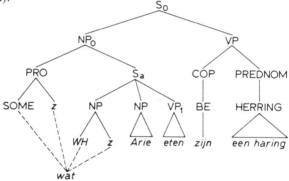

Pseudo-Cleft is a rule most probably triggered by the presence of topicalization elements. For example, the presence of such an element in TERM$_3$ will obligatorily trigger rule (86). Since the presence of a topicalization element in TERM$_3$ implies the absence of this element in TERM$_2$ and TERM$_1$, rule (86) cannot apply to these constituents. It seems quite natural to regard iota-operators as topicalization elements triggering *Pseudo-Cleft* in (86). In that case SOME in (XXXVIII) and (XXXVIIIa) must be replaced by THE. See also footnote 20 to page 152. The crucial point expressed by (86), however, is that the descriptional information contained by COP + PREDNOM is separated from the PRO and the Relativum.

It will be clear that the same analysis can be applied to sentence (69s). In this case *Pseudo-Cleft* must operate on TERM$_1$ in (XXXVIII), the difference being that [[THE + x] + [WH + x]] does not lexicalize as *wie* (who) but rather as *degene die* (the one who). Note that X in (86) is null in this case.

Let us finally consider the derivation of sentence (69g) *Wat Arie deed was een haring eten* (What Arie did was to eat a herring). If we assume that DO occurs with a TERM containing a PRO (i.e. an operator-like part) and a REL (i.e. a descriptional part) we can extend (XXXVIII) so as to obtain an underlying structure which is the input to the *Pseudo-Cleft* rule operating upon this TERM$_2$. Consider diagram (XXXIX).

(XXXIX)

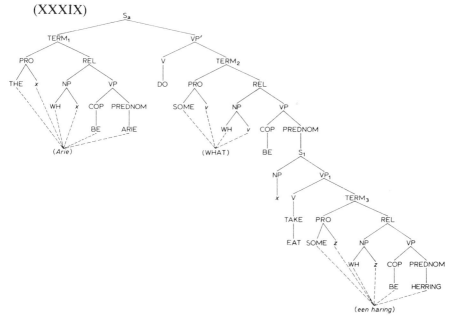

Its lower categories correspond to a string of the form *Arie + doet + iets + wat + een haring eten + is* (Arie + does + something + which + is + eating a herring). The variable v ranges over temporal entities. Structure (XXXIX) can be related to the paraphrase 'there is an event v such that Arie relates as an agent to v'. The predicate 'relating as an agent to' is represented by DO. The node S$_1$ is taken as describing the event v.

The *Pseudo-Cleft* rule operating on TERM$_2$ to generate (69g) must transpose VP$_1$ to a place located higher than S$_a$, as was sketched in (XXXVIIIa). As a result those constituents which form WHAT will be lexicalized after having been put in front of the sentence. Thus we obtain paradigm (72):

(72) $_{NP}[_S[Wat + Subject + X + doen]_S]_{NP}$ $_{VP}[zijn + _{PN}[Verb + Y]_{PN}]_{VP}$

where Verb corresponds to *eten* (eat) and Y to *een haring* (a herring), the NP of S$_1$ being deleted obligatorily.

To my mind, the present analysis should be preferred to Chomsky's proposal in *Remarks on Nominalization* (1968a) concerning the base structure underlying such sentences as *What John did was read a book about himself* and *What John read was a book about himself*, which correspond to (69g) and (69r), respectively. Chomsky's proposal amounts to saying that both (69g) and (69r) should be derived from an underlying structure of roughly the form (XXVIIIa) where the Copula "serves as a kind of existential operator" (*ibid.*:198), and where Δ represents an unspecified Predicate which can be replaced by constituents dominated by NP$_0$.

(XXVIIIa)

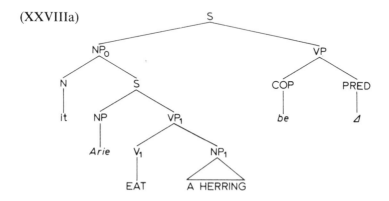

Sentence (69r) *Wat Arie at was een haring* (What Arie ate was a herring) would be derived as follows. "A new substitution transformation replaces the unspecified predicate Δ of (XXVIIIa) by the object of the embedded sentence [*een haring*], leaving a 'pro-form' in its place". This gives *it - Arie past* EAT *it - past be -* A HERRING. "Relativization and other familiar rules, supplemented by a rule that replaces *it that* by *what*, give (69r)" (*ibid.*:209).

Sentence (69g) *Wat Arie deed was een haring eten* (What Arie did was to eat a herring) can be derived by applying "the new substitution transformation so that it replaces the unspecified predicate not by the object of the embedded sentence but by its whole verb phrase, which is replaced by a 'pro-form'" (*ibid.*:209). That is, VP$_1$ is replaced by DO IT. This gives *it - Arie past* DO *it - past be -* EAT A HERRING. It can easily be seen that this string corresponds to structure (XXVIII) on page 123. It follows that all objections raised to (XXVIII) apply to Chomsky's analysis.

However, there are several other weak spots in Chomsky's proposal as it stands now, which I shall briefly discuss here since the repudiation of (XXVIIIa) automatically lends support to the analysis leading to (XXXIX). First of all, the only motivation for postulating a dummy Predicate Nominal are sentences like *The question is whether John should leave* and Noun Phrases like *The question whether John should leave*. Chomsky argues that if the latter were derived from the former we would not be able to explain the ungrammaticality of *The question whether John should leave is why Bill stayed "since there is no reason why [this sentence] should be ruled out". (ibid.:198) Its ungrammaticality would be explained by assuming that *the question is whether John should leave* is derived from a structure incorporating *The question whether John should leave*. According to Chomsky the former sentence is derived from an underlying structure of the form $_{NP}$[Det N Comp]$_{NP}$ *be* $_{Pred}$[Δ]$_{Pred}$, where the NP is *The question whether John should leave* (ibid.:198). *Whether John should leave* substitutes for Δ.

To my mind, the argument put forward here is rather superficial. At least we could consider *whether John should leave* a sentential Subject and *the question* the Predicate Nominal as in *Whether John should leave is the question*. Comparing English with Dutch we see that there are some arguments supporting this view. Consider the following sentences:

(87a)   De vraag is of John zou moeten weggaan.
         The question is whether John should leave.
(87b)   Of John zou moeten weggaan is *zeer* de vraag.
         Whether John should leave is *very much* the question.
         Whether John should leave is *highly* questionable.

Sentence (87b) shows that we can insert an Adverbial of Degree into the Phrase *de vraag* (the question). If this phrase were a Noun Phrase in the Subject position this insertion would not be possible. We can, however, insert Adverbials into Predicate Nominals. Note in passing that the phrase *very much the question* in the English version of (87b) can easily be replaced by the Predicate Nominal *highly questionable*. Note also that (87a) is synonymous to (87b) apart from the adverbial *zeer* (very much; highly). Therefore, since *of John zou moeten weggaan* (whether John should leave) is the sentential Subject of (87b), we may give serious consideration to the possibility of having a sentential Subject in (87a) too. There are some arguments for this position. Consider:

(87c)   *De vraag is dat.
         *The question is that.
(87d)   Dat is de vraag.
         That is the question.

If we replace *of John zou moeten weggaan* (whether John should leave) in (87a) by *dat* (that), we obtain the ungrammatical result (87c) unless we put the Pronoun in the Subject-position. Furthermore, we find in Dutch sentences like:

(87e)   Het is de vraag *of John zou moeten weggaan.*
         lit: It is the question *whether John should leave.*

resulting from the application of the *Extraposition*-transformation (*Cf.* Rosenbaum, 1967). Note that we can explain the ungrammaticality of *The question whether John should leave is why Bill stayed* by the simple fact that *the question* and *why Bill stayed* cannot both occur as the Predicate Nominal of the same sentence.

Secondly, structure (XXVIIIa) requires that new substitution transformations be developed. Chomsky optimistically speaks of one substitution rule; however, he needs two of them, and if we wanted to derive (69s), three. These rules are not independently motivated and therefore they are *ad hoc*-solutions. The *Pseudo-Cleft* rule (86) necessary to derive (69g), (69r) or (69s) can be stated just once since the TERMS upon which it operates all have identical underlying structures; by contrast Chomsky's substitution rules have different Structural Descriptions.

Thirdly, we need substitute "pro-forms" like IT, SO, DO IT and DO SO for the places left by the constituents replacing the Dummy Predicate Nominal. The analysis leading to (XXXIX) is much simpler since no rules of this sort are required.

Summarizing now we can say that Chomsky's analysis of sentences like (69g) and (69r) is descriptively inadequate. His proposal is unsatisfactory since his structure (XXVIIIa) is based upon the implicit assumption that the Copula in sentences like (87a) is identical to the Copula in pseudo-cleft sentences like (69g) and (69r). This assumption is wrong, which is also shown by the following sentences:

(87f)   De vraag blijft of John zou moeten weggaan.
         The question remains whether John should leave.
(69g')   *Wat Arie deed bleef een haring eten.
         *What Arie did remained to eat a herring.

The Copula *blijven* (remain) can substitute for *zijn* (be) in (87f) whereas this is excluded in the case of (69g'). The analysis leading to (XXXIX) accounts properly for this difference by making explicit that these two Copula's are not identical.

Structure (XXXIX) can also be considered the structure underlying sentence (69h) *Arie at een haring* (Arie ate a herring). The three pseudo-cleft sentences discussed above could only be derived because *Relative Clause Reduction* did not operate on the TERM which was the input to *Pseudo-Cleft*. Suppose now that *Relative Clause Reduction* applies to TERM$_3$, TERM$_2$ and

TERM$_1$ in (XXXIX). Then *Pseudo-Cleft* cannot be applied at all. In that case we can derive (69h).[19] I shall demonstrate this point with the help of (XXXVII), i.e. TERM$_3$ in (XXXIX).

Relative Clause Reduction, which takes away the Relativum 'Wh + z' and the Copula 'BE', would result in (XXXVIIa) where REL and VP are put between brackets to indicate that they are pruned.

(XXXVIIa)

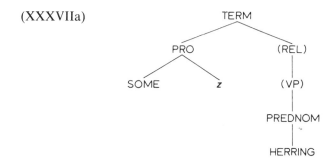

We can now think of a transformational rule, which I shall call *PRO-replacement*, substituting PREDNOM for PRO, thus deriving the Noun Phrase *een haring* (a herring) after the application of lexical attachment rules. *PRO-replacement* prevents the lexicalization of the category PRO in structures like (XXXIX). It should be borne in mind that particularly the category 'HERRING' in (XXXVIIa) should be considered an abbreviation. It represents a very complicated set of categories including some information about the definiteness or indefiniteness of the surface Noun Phrase.

I feel justified in restricting myself to presenting an outline of how the description of Noun Phrases proceed. There are too many areas about which very little is known, such as the relationship between the Determiner and Numerical elements, the deep structural status of the Determiner, etc. which makes it impossible to account for the correct lexicalization of *een haring* (a herring) on the basis of rules operating on (XXXVIIa).

[19] *Relative Clause Reduction* is an optional rule applying cyclically. Suppose that it operates on TERM$_2$ only. Then we obtain a sentence like (i) *?Degene die at wat een haring was, was Arie* (?The one who ate what was a herring was Arie) which is a grammatical sentence, though ugly and rather wordy and therefore unacceptable. If *Relative Clause Reduction* operates on TERM$_1$ only, we obtain (ii) *?Wat Arie deed was eten wat een haring was* (?What Arie did was to eat what was a herring). If it applies to TERM$_3$ we obtain (iii) *?Wat degene die Arie was deed, was een haring eten* (?What the one who Arie was did, was to eat a herring). These facts may indicate that the structures underlying (69g), (69r) and (69s) though very much alike may differ as to the presence of topicalization elements. The unacceptability of (i)–(iii) can certainly be explained by constraints on topicalization (e.g. the number of possible focusses).

(XL)

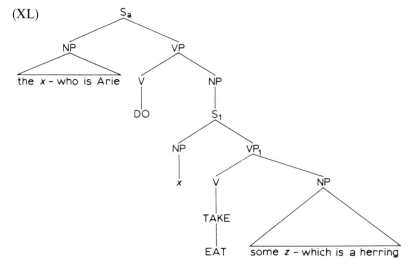

However, the general idea seems correct, since it accounts satisfactorily for the relationship between (69g), (69r), (69s) and (69h).[20]

Focussing on TERM$_2$ in (XXXIX), we can derive structure (XL) by substituting REL, i.e. its remaining part after the application of the *Relative Clause Reduction* for PRO. That is, the propositional function S$_1$ substitutes for the operator SOME + v.

---

[20] In this connection I refer to Seuren (to appear) who dealt with the same problem of accounting for the relation between operators and their descriptions in his paper on Comparatives. He assumed an optional rule *Relative Raising* of essentially the following form 'the $x(...x...)$ Copula + NP⇒...NP...'. I shall illustrate this with the help of (69h) *Arie ate a herring*. According to Seuren this sentence can be derived from a structure corresponding to 'the z (Arie ate z) BE a hérring' by *Relative Raising* if *herring* carries stress. In terms of diagrams:

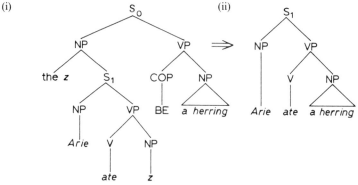

Relative Raising has the same effect as *PRO-replacement*. The difference between Seuren's analysis and mine is that BE in (i) is deleted by *Relative Clause Reduction* in the latter and by *Relative Raising* in the former. Another difference concerns the operator. Seuren assumes a definite operator *the z* in the underlying structure of the Indefinite NP *a herring*, whereas TERM$_3$ in (XXXVII) contains an indefinite one. *Cf.* my remarks on topicalization with respect to *Pseudo-Cleft* on page 146.

Structure (XL) is the input to an obligatory rule deleting the Subject-NP of S_1. This rule is a new version of the *Equi-NP-deletion* transformation which in its original form removed the lower *Arie* in structure (XXXV). In its present version the (bound) variable of the embedded propositional function will be obligatorily deleted. The resulting categorial tree contains the lexical environment of the lexical entry for *eten* (eat) in (XXXII) on page 130. Since non-branching nodes can be pruned there will be a derived structure of the form given in (XLI) after the rules of the lexical attachment component have been applied.

(XLI)

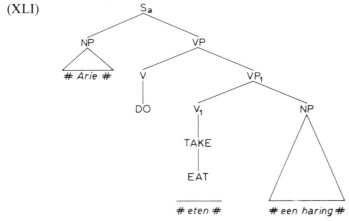

As far as the category DO is concerned there are some possibilities which I shall briefly discuss here.

First of all there might be a convention stating that non-lexicalized categories are obligatorily deleted after the lexical attachment component.

Secondly, we could Chomsky-adjoin V_1 to the left branch of VP. For this to be possible we need a convention stating that remaining V-nodes should

(XLII)

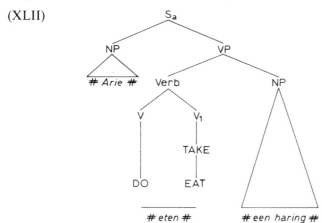

be collected under the surface label *Verb*, as is shown in structure (XLII).

The transformational rule necessary for transforming (XLI) into (XLII) is the post-lexical version of the pre-lexical rule called *Predicate Raising* (See McCawley, 1968b; De Rijk, 1968; Lakoff, 1970).

Finally, we can account for DO in (XLI) by following a suggestion made by Gruber (personal communication) with respect to lexical entry (XXXII).[21] We could specify DO "as an optional part of the simultaneous environment while always a part of the environment as a whole". There are many such cases, Gruber observes, and he proposes that a notation might be developed to express it in a simple manner. Thus we could revise (XXXII) as is shown in diagram (XXXIIa).

(XXXIIa)

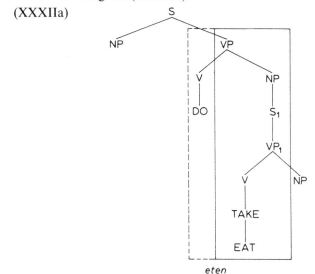

eten

If DO lexicalizes, *eten* (eat) will be attached to that part of the categorial tree which corresponds to the smallest simultaneous environment. If, however, S_1 in (XXXIX) substitutes for PRO, *eten* will also cover those categories that correspond to the categories contained by the dotted lines.

I do not know which solution should be preferred to the other two. The final choice depends upon further insights into the generality of the solution in question.

As a final remark on the present analysis I would draw the attention to its consequences for *S-Pronominalization*. Rule (83a) clearly fails to account properly for the facts presented and it should accordingly be brought in line with the descriptional apparatus developed here. The rule called

---

[21] This suggestion was made with respect to an analogous case discussed in Klooster (1971) and Klooster and Verkuyl (1971) namely the necessity of having two entries for *duren* (last) one being a proper subset of the other.

S-deletion given in (83b) appears to be essentially correct if we adjust it to structures like (XXXIX). Thus, (83b) would become:

(83c)   *S-Pronominalization*

S.D.   X - S - Y - $_{\text{TERM}}$[PRO - S]$_{\text{TERM}}$ - Z
       1 2 3   4   5   6 OPT

S.C.   1 2 3   4   ∅   6 ⇒

Hence, *S-Pronominalization* can be conceived of as a rule deleting the descriptional information and leaving the operator-like part of a TERM, i.e. PRO, behind for lexicalization. As far as I can see the same obtains for *NP-Pronominalization*.

3.3.5. *Conclusion*

I would conclude this section by summarizing the results of the present analysis as well as its implications. Lakoff and Ross assumed the existence of a rule, called *Do so-replacement* operating on deep structures generated by a grammar developed in Chomsky (1965). This 'Pro-VP' was said to replace a deep structural category VP, generated by a rule '*Predicate Phrase* → VP + X', where X is a variable standing for constituents located outside the VP. Recent work in generative semantics done by Gruber, McCawley, Lakoff, Ross, Postal, etc. tends to show that there is no such node as the VP at the most abstract level of representation of underlying structure. It follows that rule (70) in fact applies to derived structure.

I have tried to point out that (70) also fails to account for the relationship between (69a) *Arie at een haring en Piet deed dat ook* (Arie ate a herring and Piet did so too) and (69g) *Wat Arie deed was een haring eten* (What Arie did was to eat a herring). It appears possible to relate these sentences transformationally to each other by arguing that (69g) and (69h) *Arie at een haring* (Arie ate a herring) can be derived from one underlying source (presumably from a partly identical underlying structure if we take into account the presence of topicalization elements).

The structural description of (69a) and (69g) was necessary to account for the fact that both can be used as a paradigm to separate Adverbials among which Durational Adverbials from constituents which have a certain strong degree of cohesion at some relatively early stage of the transformational derivation, perhaps even in the most remote underlying structure. It was also necessary to provide for an adequate descriptive apparatus necessary to specify the relationship between S-nodes pertaining to events and Durational Adverbials. Particularly the presence of variables pertaining to temporal entities seems to be of crucial importance to a better understanding of sentences fitting into our Nondurative schema (50a). We have now obtained the position in which we can define the notion 'event-unit'.

3.4. EVENT-UNITS AND MINIMAL EVENTS

In this Section I shall try to show that we can use the pseudo-cleft paradigm (72) to delimit a certain constituent of the form 'Verb + Y' (where Y is a variable which may be null). It appears that there are constituents which must occur as Y, that there are constituents which cannot occur as Y and that there are constituents which can occur both as Y and X in this paradigm. The constituents dominated by S' in structure (XXVId) on page 113, i.e. by the S constituting the upper bound of the Aspects, belong to the first category, Durational Adverbials to the last. Thus paradigm (72) seems to enable us to define a minimal scope of reference of S_1 in structures like (XXXIX), i.e. the sentential node occurring in structures described in the preceding section. This minimal scope determines the notion 'minimal event'. This notion applies to the referents of S's falling under the minimal scope of reference of S_1. Hence we can determine the notion 'event-unit' which is necessary to account for the frequency reading in sentences fitting into our Nondurative scheme and containing Durational Adverbials: minimal events can be taken as units of quantification. We shall see, however, that the notion 'event-unit' is wider than the notion 'minimal event'.

The description of the structure underlying action sentences like (69h) and (69g) given in the preceding section relates to some recent logical analyses concerning their logical structure. Logicians like Reichenbach (1966) and Davidson (1967) analyzed these sentences in terms of existential quantifications over events and consequently they met the problem of how to determine what is being quantified. Since the proposal by Lakoff and Ross (1966) can be re-interpreted as an attempt to provide for a criterion for determining the linguistic object corresponding to an event, I shall discuss their claim that *do so* replaces all and only constituents belonging to the (surface) VP in Section 3.4.2. Finally, I shall amplify, in Section 3.4.3, the statement that paradigm (72) can be used to obtain a tripartition among constituents occurring as its variables.

3.4.1. *On the Logical Structure of Action Sentences*

The present linguistic analysis leading to structures like (XXXIX) appears to relate closely to recent proposals concerning the logical form of action sentences, in logical analysis the equivalent of sentences containing Nonstatives. At any rate both (69h) *Arie at een haring* (Arie ate a herring) and its pseudo-cleft version (69g) are action sentences according to logicians.

Before discussing a recent proposal by Davidson (1967) who gives a clear survey of the state of affairs in logic as far as the insights into the logical structure of action sentences are concerned, I shall first sketch some of Reichenbach's ideas about the description of entities (individuals) since they underlie Davidson's proposal and they can give an appropriate entry for the point at issue.[22]

In his analysis of the methods natural language has developed to characterize individuals, Reichenbach pointed out that the definition of the term 'individual' is a matter of convention rather than of physics. He rejects the idea that it could apply to "something occupying a continuous and limited part of space and time" (Reichenbach, 1966:266) in view of the simple fact that though we might agree upon the status of a chair as an individual as against the furniture which should be considered a class of individuals, from the physicist's point of view a chair is composed of atoms in the same way as furniture is composed of chairs and tables. Hence, we have to "drop the condition of physical connection of the parts and to consider the determination of the individual as a matter of convention" (*ibid.*:266–7). The insight that the determination of the individual is a matter of convention, also applies to temporal individuals, such as events. Our conception of what events are may vary "for the purposes of daily life".

Reichenbach made a distinction between individuals of the *thing type* ("aggregates of matter keeping together for a certain time") and individuals of the *event type* (entities which are space-time coincidences and do not endure). He observes that this distinction is also made in natural language: a sentence like *George VI was crowned in Westminster Abbey* (thing type) has its pendant in the sentence *the coronation of George VI took place in Westminster Abbey* (event type).

Reichenbach uses the term 'situation' to refer to the denotatum of a proposition. Now, "by describing a situation in a proposition composed of function and argument we split the situation into argument-object and predicate-object (or property)" (*ibid.*:268). The above distinction into individuals of the thing type and of the event type enables us to split a situation in two ways: "we distinguish these ways as *thing-splitting* and *event-splitting*". Thus a sentence like

(88a)   Amundsen flew to the North Pole.

can be analyzed in terms of thing-splitting as $'f(x_1, y_1)'$, where the two-place predicate *fly to*, represented as $'f'$, holds between x_1 (Amundsen)

[22] In this connection I would particularly refer to Kenny (1963). Davidson's paper discusses proposals by A. Kenny, R. M. Chisholm, G. H. von Wright, J. Austin, I. Scheffler and H. Reichenbach all concerning the logical structure of action sentences. His paper is followed by a discussion with E. J. Lemmon, H. N. Castaneda and R. M. Chisholm.

and y_1 (the North Pole). However, in terms of event-splitting we would obtain the following representation:

(88b) $(\exists v)\, [f(x_1, y_1)]^*\, (v)$

which should be read as 'a flight by Amundsen to the North Pole took place'. The variable 'v' ranges over temporal entities, events. In (88b) the predicate '$[f(x_1, y_1)]^*$', referred to by Reichenbach as an 'event-function' (or 'fact-function'), is assigned to the argument v. The asterisk is used to indicate that event-splitting is applied in the analysis of (88a). The expression (88b) can also be paraphrased as 'there is an event such that this event consists in the fact that Amundsen flew to the North Pole'.

Reichenbach's proposal introduces existential quantification over events into the analysis of action sentences. Events are taken as "entities about which an indefinite number of things can be said" (Davidson, 1967:91). Thus, for example, a sentence like:

(89a)   Amundsen flew to the North Pole in May 1926.

can be given the following logical form:

(89b) $(\exists v)\, [f(x_1, y_1)]^*\, (v, t_1)$

to be read as 'a flight by Amundsen to the North Pole took place in May 1926', where 't_1' stands for *May 1926*. In (89b) 'a flight by Amundsen to the North Pole' is taken as an event-unit. Not only can an indefinite number of things be said about it, it is also an unit of quantification.

However, we seem to be free to take 'a flight by Amundsen to the North Pole in May 1926' as an unit too, according to Reichenbach, as is expressed by his example:

(89c) $(\exists v)\, [f(x_1, y_1, t_1)]^*\, (v)$

to be read as 'a flight by Amundsen to the North Pole in May 1926 took place' or as 'there is an event which consists in the fact that Amundsen flew to the North Pole in May 1926'. Though we shall see that it is doubtful whether (89c) is a proper account of (89a), the point made by Reichenbach is that a temporal entity can be expanded: the event-unit in (89c) is expanded in comparison with the event-unit in (89b).

Analogously to (89b) a sentence like:

(90a)   Arie at gisteren een haring.
         Arie ate a herring yesterday.

can be analyzed as

(90b) $(\exists v)\, [(\exists z)\, \mathrm{Eat}\, (x_1, z)]^*\, (v, t_1)$

to be read as 'Arie's eating a herring took place yesterday, where the event-function is a two-place predicate holding between an event 'Arie's eating a herring' and the time-stretch 'yesterday' (*Cf.* Verkuyl, 1969b; 1970). We could also paraphrase (90b) as follows:

(90c)   ($\exists v$) (v consists in the fact that Arie ate a herring and v took place yesterday)

where conjunction makes it possible to "say a number of things" about some event. We can tack on new predications by means of conjunction, e.g. ... *and v took place in Amsterdam*, etc.

According to Davidson, Reichenbach's proposal has another merit: "it eliminates a peculiar confusion that seemed to attach to the idea that sentences like (89a) "describe an event". The difficulty was that one wavered between thinking of the sentence as describing or referring to that one flight Amundsen made in May 1926, or as describing a kind of event, or perhaps as describing (potentially?) several. As Von Wright pointed out, any number of events might be described by a sentence like "Brutus kissed Caesar". This fog is dispelled in a way I find entirely persuasive in Reichenbach's proposal that ordinary action sentences have, in effect, an existential quantifier binding the action variable. When we were tempted into thinking a sentence like (89a) describes a single event we were misled: it does not describe any event at all. But if (89a) is true, then there is an event that makes it true" (*id*:91).

Davidson showed, however, that Reichenbach's proposal concerning the logical form of the sentences under discussion cannot be maintained in view of some difficulties with the problem of extensionality, i.e. some problems arise with terms referring to the same object, which can be left out of consideration since they are not relevant to the point at issue here.

Now, rejecting forms like (90c) as a proper account of sentences like (90a), Davidson proposed that an action sentence like

(91a)   Shem kicked Shaun

normally analyzed as 'Kicked (Shem, Shaun)', i.e. in terms of a two-place predicate 'Kicked' and two arguments 'Shem' and 'Shaun', should be analyzed as follows:

(91b)   ($\exists v$) Kicked (Shem, Shaun, v)

where 'Kicked' is taken as a *three*-place predicate containing an event-place, where the two other places are occupied by 'Shem' and 'Shaun'. A proper paraphrase of (91b) is 'there is an event v such that v is a kicking of Shaun by Shem'. Davidson follows Reichenbach in describing the logical structure of action sentences in terms of events about which things can be predicated.

The new element in Davidson's analysis are (a) that it seeks to determine a "basic structural core of an action", and (b) that the predicate is analyzed as having a more complicated structure than its surface structure reveals.

As far as (a) is concerned, an action can be taken as "a relation between an agent, and an event, if the action is intransitive" or as "a relation among an agent, a patient or accusative of the action, and an event, if the action is transitive, i.e. has an object" (Davidson, 1967:105), as in example (91a), where Shem is the agent and Shaun the patient. I shall return to this point below.

As far as (b) is concerned, Davidson states that in describing the meaning of a predicate we should describe "how many places a predicate has", and "what sort of entities the variables that hold these places range over. Some predicates have an event-place, some do not" (id.:93).

Returning now to structure (XXXIX) underlying the action sentence (69h) *Arie at een haring* (Arie ate a herring), we can see that the deep structure of the predicate *eten* (eat) contains an event-place, since we have introduced v into TERM_2. Let us, for the sake of convenience, analyze (69h) in terms of a one-place predicate *een haring eten* (eat a herring), abbreviated as 'H'. Then (69h) can be represented as:

(69t) $(\exists v) [H (x_1, v)]$

where we express that there is a relation between x_1 ($=$Arie) and an event in which Arie occurs as the agent. This shows that our linguistic analysis can be translated into Davidson's logical analysis.

There are two points now which call for some discussion. First, our linguistic analysis seems more adequate than Davidson's in that it seems more complete. Davidson does not analyze the event-argument any further taking it as a primitive, whereas in structure (XXXIX) the event in question is analyzed. Moreover, the predicate 'kicked' in (91b) is not analyzed any further with respect to other predicates containing an event-place but occurring in non-action sentences. In structure (XXXIX) it is the presence of DO which accounts for the fact that Verbs like *eten* (eat) and *kick* can occur in action sentences, i.e. in sentences in which there is an agent-place, whereas such Verbs as *liggen* (lie) and *hangen* (hang) do not have this category in their underlying structure. In other words, though Davidson describes the logical form of action sentences, he does not explicitly account for the very element which makes Verbs like *kick* "Action Predicates".

In structure (XXXIX), however, the underlying category DO relates the agent to the event. We can describe the meaning of DO as 'be the (or an) agent in', or in terms of the analysis given in the preceding chapter as 'temporalize (an event) as agent'. In other words, DO accounts for the fact that an event is made extend in time. It gives expanse ("Ausgedehntheit") in time to an event.

Our second point is that structure (XXXIX) is the input to a rule which can determine the "basic structural core of an action". We observed under (a) above that Davidson aims to determine a minimal structure constituting events. Thus, in the case of (90b) it is Amundsen's flying to the North Pole which is taken as an event and not Amundsen's flying to the North Pole in May 1926. One of the participants in the discussion following Davidson's paper, Castaneda, suggested that sentences like (88a) should be analyzed as

(88c)   (∃v) [Flew (Amundsen, v) & To (The North Pole, v)]

where 'To' is taken as a two-place predicate. His argument was that (88a) entails *Amundsen flew*. If he is right, (88a) must be analyzed as 'there is an event 'Amundsen's flight' and this event has a "To-relation" to the North Pole'. He also argues that the logical form of a sentence like

(92a)   I flew my spaceship to the Morning Star.

should be:

(92b)   (∃v) [Flew (I, v) & Flew (v, my spaceship) & To (v, the Morning Star)]

thus suggesting that *my flying* can be taken as the smallest event about which things can be said.

Davidson very properly observed, however, that though *I flew my spaceship* may entail *I flew*, this is not a matter of logical form. There are cases like *I sank the Bismarck* which do not entail *I sank*.[23] His other counterexample *The King insulted the Queen* also clearly indicates that Davidson recognized the need for a lower bound of events, i.e. for the determination of the minimal structure some temporal entity should have to be termed 'event'. There are no temporal entities corresponding to 'The King's insulting' or to 'my sanking'. These expressions contain more-place predicates lacking, however, one of the arguments. Only if we enrich them by adding arguments, can we apply the term 'event' to the referents of the resulting

---

[23] Of course, *sank* should be analyzed in terms of an underlying Causative such as *I caused S*, where S stands for *The Bismarck sinks* (*Cf.* Lakoff, 1965; 1970). Note also that *I flew my spaceship to the Morning Star* can also be analyzed in terms of a complicated underlying structure, presumably containing a Causative.

expressions, in this case 'The King's insulting the Queen' and 'My sinking the Bismarck'. Davidson did not give an explicit criterion for determining the smallest entities the event-variables range over nor for their internal structure.

As far as I can see structures like (XXXiX) might serve as the basis upon which such a criterion could be formulated. This structure is the input to a transformational rule deriving our pseudo-cleft paradigm (72) which systematically determines the constituency necessary for reference to events. In fact, it is exactly what Lakoff and Ross (1966) implied when formulating their claim that *do so* replaces all and only constituents of the VP. Its amendment and extension (72) can determine a structural core: it is constituents that *must* occur in the Predicate Nominal of this paradigm which necessarily belong to the S referring to minimal events.

I shall now first discuss the "all and only"-claim in Lakoff and Ross (1966) and then continue by dealing with the pseudo-cleft paradigm (72) and its implications for the determination of the notion 'event-unit'.

3.4.2. *The "All and Only"-Claim by Lakoff and Ross*

In discussing the question as to which of the adverbials that occur in the Predicate Phrase are part of the constituent replaced by *do so*, Lakoff and Ross claim that *do so* "replaces all of the constituents of the verb phrase and only these" as we have already seen on page 119. However, the criterion for VP-constituency following from this claim has not been defined accurately. The relevant inferences must be drawn from their examples, which mainly contain coordinated sentences.[24]

Two kinds of coordination are at issue. Firstly, conjunction with *and*; secondly, adversative conjunction with *but*. Both can be found in examples separating *Time* and *Duration* from what was taken to be the VP:

(93)   John took a trip last Tuesday and I'm going to do so to-morrow.
(94)   John worked on the problem for eight hours but I did so for only two hours.

The underlying argument runs as follows: if *do so* in (74) were to refer back to *took a trip last Tuesday*, we would be forced to interpret the second part of this sentence as stating that I am going to take a trip last Tuesday to-morrow. Apparently, Lakoff and Ross hold, *do so* corresponds to *took a trip*. (See also (69d) and (71) on page 128). The same obtains for (94) as pointed out in Section 1.2.2.

However, it seems as if there were difficulties as far as the "only"-part

---

[24] Lakoff and Ross demonstrate the validity of their claim also with the help of sentences containing *do so* in embedded clauses.

of the Lakoff-Ross claim is concerned due to the referential "power" of the Pro-VP which seems to include the italicized constituents of the following sentences:

(93a)   John took a trip *on Tuesday* and I'm going to do so too.
(95)   John brought us home *in his Landrover* and Peter used to do so in his Buick.
(96)   John brought us home *in his Landrover* and he preferred to do so because he knew that we would feel as if we were on safari.

In (93a) it could be said that *on Tuesday* is included in the referential scope of *do so* since *I'm going to do so too* contains the information that I am going to take a trip on a coming Tuesday. On the other hand, sentence

(93b)   *John took a trip last Tuesday and I'm going to do so too

is ungrammatical, apparently due to the fact that *last Tuesday* refers to a stretch of time which cannot relate to my taking a trip in near future.

To my mind, the criterion formulated by Lakoff and Ross is unclear with respect to the opposition between the constituent containing *do so* and the constituent anaphorically referred to by *do so*, and to the possible extension of the scope of reference of *do so*.

The sort of conjunction in sentence (93) is not identical to the one occurring in such sentences as (93a) and (69a). The coordinated parts of (93) express an opposition between the Adverbials whose location is to be determined. Though this is nowhere stated explicitly in their paper, I take Lakoff and Ross to mean that this opposition is necessary for restricting the referential power of *do so*, or even for delimiting the scope of reference of *do so*. Their intention is most clearly visible in sentences containing the adversative Conjunction *but* as in (94).

The fact that *Time* and *Duration* cán occur after *do so* is indicative of their higher position in deep structure. Direct Objects, Directional Phrases, Indirect Objects and some other constituents can never occur after *do so*. Thus it appears as if the criterion by Lakoff and Ross should be formulated in terms of opposition.

As far as the second point is concerned, consider also sentence:

(93c)   John took a trip last Tuesday and I did so too.

In view of the consideration in the preceding paragraph this sentence cannot be taken as a real counterexample to the "only"-claim as was suggested by Michelson (1969), the point being that one can never show that *did so* corresponds to *took a trip last Tuesday*. Sentences like:

(93d)   John took a trip last Tuesday and I went to the cinema.

show that the Adverbial of Time can cover the stretches of time referred to by *John took a trip* and *I went to the cinema.* Sentence (93d) can assert that I went to the cinema last Tuesday. Moreover it might be *too* rather than *so* that can be held responsible for the interpretation that both John and I took a trip last Tuesday. (A sentence like *John took a trip last Tuesday and I did so too last Friday* has an air of redundancy about it on account of the presence of *too*). If we compare *last Tuesday* in (93c) with *on Tuesday* in (93a), which seems to fall inside the scope of *do so*, we observe that the reference of the former is far more definite than of the latter. In (93a) it is implied that there is a series of trips being taken on Tuesday such that John and I each relate to different specimina of this series. In (93c) no series of trips-on-Tuesday is implied whatsoever.

Much the same obtains for sentences like (96). The criterion by Lakoff and Ross predicts that *brought us home* in (95) is a VP since otherwise the terminal string of the second part would have the form **Peter used [to bring us home in his Landrover] in his Buick,* where *do so* corresponds to the part between the brackets, which is clearly impossible. However, in the case of (96) we cannot substitute *do so* for *brought us home* since we felt as if we were on safari not because of his bringing us home, but because of his bringing us home in his Landrover.

The above considerations lead to the conclusion that it is necessary to delimit the constituent corresponding to *do so* in terms of both oppositional conjunction with *and* and adversative coordination with *but*, and that under certain conditions this constituent may dominate constituents which strictly speaking are no part of it. However, it should be observed that even the restriction that the criterion intended by Lakoff and Ross should be stated in terms of opposition, notably in terms of adversative coordination with *but*, does not hold in cases resembling those mentioned in (96) and (93a), as can be seen from the following examples:

(97)   John worked for exactly three hours since he is an industrious person, but Peter did so since his boss was watching him.

(98)   John takes a bath once a week by reason of his dislike for water but Peter does so because he lives above the standard level of the municipal waterworks.

These sentences indicate that Durational Adverbials as well as Frequency Adverbials can fall inside the referential scope of *do so* even under the optimal conditions of adversative coordination. Peter worked for exactly three hours just like John, though for different reasons, and he shares John's habit of washing himself once a week.

In Verkuyl (1969b) facts like these were taken to be indicative of the need for a restriction on the referential power of *do so* displayed by the above examples.[25] It appeared to be possible to circumvent the above mentioned complications by using paradigm (72) to separate Adverbials from the (surface) VP. The paradigm lends itself better to introducing the notion 'minimal reference of *do so*' than the examples given by Lakoff and Ross, at least in Dutch, the advantage being that no superfluous elements like e.g. *too* in (93a) can blur our view on what is really at issue.

3.4.3. *Minimal Scope of Reference*

Let us once again consider paradigm (72):

$$
(72) \quad \left[\left[\begin{bmatrix} Wat \\ What \end{bmatrix} + \text{Subject} + \text{X} + \begin{matrix} doen \\ do \end{matrix} \right]_{S} \right]_{NP} \, _{VP}\left[\begin{matrix} zijn \\ be \end{matrix} + _{PN}[\text{Verb} + \text{Y}]_{PN} \right]_{VP}
$$

It can be observed that: (i) there are constituents that must occur in PN; (ii) there are constituents that cannot occur in PN; and (iii) there are constituents that can occur both in PN and in X. It appears necessary to account for the fact that Verb + Y, or more precisely its underlying source S_1 in structures like (XXXIX), constitutes a syntactic unit at some stage of the derivation.

The above tripartition can also be obtained by applying the following question-answer paradigm already given in (76):

(99)   *Wat + doen +* Subject + X?   Answer: Verb + Y
       What + do + Subject + X?   Answer: Verb + Y

I shall briefly discuss the tripartition so as to be able to determine the nature of the syntactic unit whose derived structural reflection occurs as nature of the syntactic unit whose derived structural relection occurs as $_{PN}[\text{Verb} + \text{Y}]_{PN}$. Our judgment on whether certain constituents can occur as part of PN depends on the possibility of having a rest after the Copula announcing as it were the Predicate Nominal. The ungrammaticality of pseudo-cleft sentences below can be explained by the fact that the italicized constituents in these sentences wrongly occur as their Predicate Nominal. The italicized constituents of corresponding grammatical sentences indicate which constituents rightly occur as their Predicate Nominal.

---

[25] The notion 'minimal replacement' by *do so* was developed in Verkuyl (1969b, Section 1.3) of which the subsequent section is an extended version. Recently it came to my attention that Michelson (1969) had independently worked out a similar restriction on *Do so-replacement* by distinguishing a 'Core-Predicate' including the Verb, Direct Object, Indirect Object and Directional Adverbials. However, Michelson does not indicate which criteria determine whether or not a given constituent belongs to this Core-Predicate. Besides, most of his examples countering the "all and only" claim turn out to be apparent counter-examples (See e.g. (93c)). Nevertheless Michelson is right in stating that the "only"-part of this claim is in need of some additional restrictions.

(i) Consider the following sentences:

(69f)   *Wat Arie een haring deed was *eten.*
         *What Arie did a herring was *to eat.*

(69g)   Wat Arie deed was *een haring eten.*
         What Arie did was *to eat a herring.*

Sentence (69f) clearly shows that the Direct-Object NP cannot be separated from its Verb in paradigm (72). Notice that *Wat deed Arie een haring? Eten.* (*What did Arie a herring? Eat.*) is also ungrammatical. Apparently it is his eating a herring rather than his eating which can be said to be Arie's action. Arie can only be the agent in an event which is described as his eating something (which is a herring) rather than as his eating. In this connection it is worth remembering our discussion about the King's insulting the Queen in Section 3.4.1. Consider also:

(100a)   Greetje reed naar huis.
          .   Greetje drove home.

(100b)   *Wat Greetje naar huis deed was *rijden.*
          *What Greetje did home was *drive.*

(100c)   Wat Greetje deed was *naar huis rijden.*
          What Greetje did was *to drive home.*

Sentence (100b) shows that the Directional Prep Phrase *naar huis* cannot be separated from the Verb. It must occur in PN. Consider further:

(101a)   Jan wachtte op zijn vader.
          Jan waited for his father.

(101b)   *Wat Jan op zijn vader deed was *wachten.*
          *What Jan did for his father was *to wait.*

(101c)   Wat Jan deed was *op zijn vader wachten.*
          What Jan did was *to wait for his father.*

The Prepositional Object *op zijn vader* (for his father) can not be separated from the Verb with which it occurs: *op zijn vader wachten* (to wait for his father) must be taken as a unit. Consider next:

(102a)   Jan verfde de deur groen.
          Jan painted the door green.

(102b)   *Wat Jan groen deed was *de deur verven.*
          *What Jan did green was *to paint the door.*

(102c)   Wat Jan deed was *de deur groen verven.*
          What Jan did was *to paint the door green.*

The Predicative Adjunct *groen* modifies the Direct Object: the result of Jan's painting the door is that this door has become green. *De deur groen verven* (paint the door green) must be taken as a unit. Note in passing, the absurdity as well as the ungrammaticality of **Wat deed Jan groen?* (What did Jan green?) Answer: *De deur verven* (Paint the door).

Though I do not pretend to give the complete list of constituents that must occur as a part of PN in (72), I think the following enumeration is not far from being exhaustive: Direct Object, Indirect Object, Prepositional Object, Prepositional Adjuncts of the Object, Manner Adverbials of Product ('Adverbiale bepalingen van Productshoedanigheid'; see for this term Kraak and Klooster (1968)), e.g. in *Katinka breide die Noorse trui grof* (lit.: Katinka knitted that Norwegian sweater coarsely), and Place Adverbials necessarily occurring as the complement of the Verb, e.g. *Ik bracht mijn vacantie door in Frankrijk* (I spent my holidays in France).

(ii) I shall now discuss some constituents which cannot occur in PN of our paradigm (72). It should be borne in mind that by saying that some constituents cannot occur in this PN as against other constituents which can, we pronounce upon the nature of the events corresponding to the structure underlying PN. Our distinctive predicates 'ungrammatical' and 'grammatical' assigned to sentences tested in paradigm (72) express certain assumptions about our universe of discourse. For example, by rejecting

(69u)   *Wat Arie deed was *graag een haring eten.*
*What Arie did was *to eat a herring readily.*

we claim, in fact, that there are no such events as 'Arie's eating a herring readily', just as there are no events 'The King's insulting'. If we want to say that Arie liked to eat herrings we would use:

(69v)   Wat Arie graag deed was *een haring eten.*
What Arie readily did was *to eat a herring.*
What Arie liked to do was *to eat a herring.*

rather than (69u). These facts correspond to the unacceptable combination of the following question and answer:

(69w)   *Wat deed Arie? *Graag een haring eten.*
*What did Arie do? *To eat a herring readily.*

whereas we find:

(69z)   Wat deed Arie graag? *Een haring eten.*
What did Arie do readily? *To eat a herring.*

Modal Adverbials cannot occur in PN of (72) as we can see from the following examples:

(103a)   Marcella heeft Phil waarschijnlijk weggestuurd.
          Marcella probably sent Phil packing.
(103b)   *Wat Marcella heeft gedaan is *waarschijnlijk Phil wegsturen.*
          *What Marcella did was *to send Phil packing probably.*
(103c)   Wat Marcella waarschijnlijk heeft gedaan is *Phil afpoeieren.*
          What Marcella probably did was *to send Phil packing.*

Consider also:

(103d)   Marcella stuurde Phil helaas weg.
          Unfortunately Marcella sent Phil packing.
(103e)   *Wat Marcella deed was *helaas Phil wegsturen.*
          *What Marcella did was *to send Phil packing unfortunately.*
(103f)   Wat Marcella helaas deed was *Phil wegsturen.*
          What Marcella unfortunately did was *to send Phil packing.*

It should be mentioned here that sentences like:

(103g)   Wat Marcella deed was helaas *Phil wegsturen.*
          What Marcella did was unfortunately *to send Phil packing.*

are acceptable when spoken with a rest after *helaas*, "announcing" the
italicized constituents. The Modal Adverbial is attached to the Verbum
finitum of the (surface) matrix constituent. This can be shown by the following sentence:

(103h)   Helaas was wat Marcella deed *Phil wegsturen.*
          lit: Unfortunately was what Marcella did *to send Phil packing.*

which is synonymous with (103g). Hence we can take the Modal Adverbial
in (103g) as a constituent occurring as X in paradigm (72) rather than as Y.
    Some other examples of constituents that cannot occur in PN contain Ad-
verbials of Reason and Concessive Adverbials:

(104a)   Jan verfde de deur derhalve groen.
          Jan painted the door green therefore.
(104b)   *Wat Jan deed was *derhalve de deur groen verven.*
          *What Jan did was *therefore paint the door green.*
(104c)   Wat Jan derhalve deed was *de deur groen verven.*
          What Jan did therefore was *to paint the door green.*

It is recalled to mind that (97) and (98) already suggested that Adverbials
of Reason are rather highly located in underlying structure. It should be
noticed in passing that the *doen dat*-test in the Lakoff-Ross version fails
to be accurate with respect to *derhalve*, since it does not account properly
for the ungrammaticality of:

(104d) *Jan verfde de deur groen en hij deed dat derhalve.
       *Jan painted the door green and he did so therefore.

It appears as if this sentence is ungrammatical for the same reason that e.g.

(102d) *Jan verfde de deur en hij deed dat groen.
       *Jan painted the door and he did so green.

is ungrammatical. If, however, we replace *derhalve* (therefore) in (104d) by *omdat hij van groen houdt* (because he likes green) or by *vanwege zijn voorkeur voor groen* (by reason of his preference for green), then we obtain a grammatical sentence.

Concessive Adverbials are also located in X of paradigm (72):

(105a) Jan heeft desondanks de deur groen geverfd.
       Nevertheless Jan painted the door green.
(105b) *Wat Jan deed was *desondanks de deur groen verven.*
       *What Jan did was *nevertheless to paint the door green.*
(105c) Wat Jan desondanks deed was *de deur groen verven.*
       What Jan nevertheless did was *paint the door green.*

The Lakoff-Ross version of the *doen dat*-test fails to be accurate with respect to *desondanks* (nevertheless) for exactly the same reason as in the case of *derhalve* (therefore). To my mind, this can be explained by the fact that both *derhalve* and *desondanks* can refer back to some sentential constituent preceding such sentences as (104a), (104c), (105a) and (105c). Neither in (104d) nor in:

(105d) *Jan verfde de deur groen en hij deed dat desondanks.
       *Jan painted the door green and he did so nevertheless.

is this antecedent present. If we replace *desondanks* (nevertheless) by e.g. *ondanks mijn advies om hem wit te laten* (in spite of my advice to leave it white), we can see that Concessive Adverbials fall outside the scope of *doen + dat* under the appropriate conditions. Paradigm (72) appears to be indifferent as to the anaphoric reference of *desondanks* and *derhalve* as we see from the c-sentences.

However, there appear to be some problems with respect to Concessive Adverbials which cannot be ignored here. Some of my informants consider sentences like:

(105e) ?Wat Jan deed was *ondanks mijn advies de deur groen verven.*
       lit: ?What Jan did was *to paint the door green in spite of my advice.*

grammatical. In their dialect the italicized constituent must refer to an event 'Jan's painting the door green in spite of my advice'. It is worth remembering here Reichenbach's contention that the determination of individuals is a matter of convention. To my feeling (105e) is far less normal than

(105f)   Wat Jan ondanks mijn advies deed was *de deur groen verven.*
          What Jan did in spite of my advice was *to paint the door green.*

At any rate, (105f) and not (105e) is synonymous with:

(105g)   Ondanks mijn advies verfde Jan de deur groen.
          In spite of my advice Jan painted the door green.

(105h)   Jan verfde de deur groen (,) ondanks mijn advies.
          Jan painted the door green (,) in spite of my advice.

Note that we can insert a comma in (105h) separating the Concessive Adverbial from the rest of the sentence.

We are discussing here judgments on rather subtle questions such as the acceptability and the grammaticality of sentences. However, as far as the main point of this section is concerned cases like (105e) do not form counter-examples. At best we can say that in the dialect of those who regard (105e) as a grammatical sentence, Concessive Adverbials belong to the class of constituents which can occur both in Y and in X, to be discussed below. Finally consider sentences containing Adverbials of Time:

(106a)   Arie at gisteren een haring.
          Arie ate a herring yesterday.

(106b)   *Wat Arie deed was *gisteren een haring eten.*
          *What Arie did was *to eat a herring yesterday.*

(106c)   Wat Arie gisteren deed was *een haring eten.*
          What Arie did yesterday was *to eat a herring.*

The ungrammaticality of (106b) can certainly be explained by the fact that *gisteren* (yesterday) occurs as a part of Y in paradigm (72), which appears to conflict with its structural position with respect to *een haring eten.* An Adverbial of Time like *gisteren* must occur in the position of X in (72). Note that (106a) is a normal answer to the question *Wat deed Arie gisteren?* (What did Arie do yesterday?) rather than to *Wat deed Arie?* (What did Arie do?)

It should be noted here that *gisteren* has a definite reference to a stretch of time, just as in the case of *last Tuesday* in sentence (93). It appears, however, that constituents which can occur as Adverbials of Time can also appear in PN of (72) under certain conditions having to do with reference. This brings us to the third category of constituents to be distinguished from (i) and (ii) because its members can occur as Y and X in (72).

(iii) Consider first the following examples:

(106d)   Wat Arie moet doen is *op Koninginnedag een haring eten op de Dam*.
          What Arie should do is *to eat a herring on the Dam on the Queen's Birthday*.

(106e)   ?Wat Arie niet had moeten doen was *tijdens een vergadering van de Boerenpartij een haring eten*.
          What Arie shouldn't have done was *to eat a herring during a meeting of the Farmers' Party*.

(106f)   ?Wat Arie heeft gedaan was *op Koninginnedag oranje strikjes verkopen*.
          What Arie did was *to sell orange bows on the Queen's Birthday*.

To some of my informants these sentences are hardly acceptable. They can only be used under the appropriate conditions which are met by a certain type of presumption. It appears as if selling orange bows on the Queen's Birthday is a specific sort of activity distinguishable from other *modes* of selling orange bows. The same obtains for eating a herring on the Dam on the Queen's Birthday or during a meeting of the Farmers' Party. As far as the temporal adverbials in (106d)–(106f) are concerned, we can say that they do not refer to a particular stretch of time during which some activity took place as in the case of real Adverbials of Time. Semantically they add features to the activities in question. For example, *op Koninginnedag* (on the Queen's Birthday) adds features to Arie's activity of just eating a herring which are in contrast with a class of other features assignable to this activity, e.g. his eating a herring with a knife. Arie's eating a herring on the Queen's Birthday is considered a special type of event. The same applies, *mutatis mutandis*, to the Place Adverbial *op de Dam* (on the Dam). The crucial point here is that the event 'Arie's eating a herring' is extended so as to contain the extra specifications. This is exactly what Reichenbach had in mind when he said that our definition of what individuals are may vary dependent on "the purpose for daily life". In the case of constituents which normally occur as Adverbials of Time the definiteness of reference to stretches of time is impaired as in (106d)–(106f).

In this connection I refer back to the difference between Reichenbach's examples (89b) and (89c) on page 158. By analyzing (89a) *Amundsen flew to the North Pole in May 1926* in terms of (89c), Reichenbach assumes there to be an underlying S including the Adverbial of Time and referring to a particular event. Consider the difference between:

(89b′)   Wat Amundsen in mei 1926 deed was *naar de Noordpool vliegen*.
          What Amundsen did in May 1926 was *to fly to the North Pole*.

(89c′) *?Wat Amundsen deed was *in mei 1926 naar de Noordpool vliegen.*
        ?What Amundsen did was *to fly to the North Pole in May 1926.*

In my dialect (89c′) is ill-formed. At any rate, it does not correspond to (89a) in the same way as (89b′) does: (89c′) is an unnatural answer to the question *Wat deed Amundsen?* (What did Amundsen do?). Put differently, this question is inappropriate to invoke (89c′) as an answer. Hence I would conclude that (89c) should be rejected as an account of the logical structure underlying (89a). Consider now the following sentences:

(107a) Jan verfde de deur groen met een kwast.
        Jan painted the door green with a brush.
(107b) Wat Jan met een kwast deed was *de deur groen verven.*
        What Jan did with a brush was *to paint the door green.*
(107c) Wat Jan deed was *de deur met een kwast groen verven.*
        What Jan did was *to paint the door green with a brush.*

Though (107b) and (107c) are not synonymous they can both be used to state that John used a brush rather than a spray-gun or a roller to paint the door green. In (107c) Jan's painting the door green with a brush is taken as a whole, just as in the case of Arie's eating a herring on the Dam.

Frequency Adverbials can also occur as a part of PN though their regular place is the position of X in paradigm (72). Consider:

(108a) Piet heeft hem toen drie keer een waarschuwing gegeven.
        Piet then warned him three times.
(108b) Wat Piet toen drie keer heeft gedaan is *hem een waarschuwing geven.*
        What Piet then did three times was *to warn him.*
(108c) Wat Piet toen heeft gedaan was *hem drie keer een waarschuwing geven.*
        What Piet then did was *to warn him three times.*

The difference between (108b) and (108c) can be brought out as follows:

(108b′) Wat Piet toen drie keer heeft gedaan was *hem een waarschuwing geven* en dat heeft hij daarna nog een keer gedaan.
         What Piet then did three times was *to warn him* and after that he did so once more.
(108c′) Wat Piet toen heeft gedaan was *hem drie keer een waarschuwing geven* en dat heeft hij daarna nog een keer gedaan.
         What Piet then did was *to warn him three times* and after that he did so once more.

In my dialect (108c′) can only be interpreted as asserting that Piet warned him six times, whereas (108b') says that he was warned four times by Piet. Piet's warning him three times is taken as a whole in (108c') and since Piet repeats what he has done he repeats his warning him three times. Note also that sentences like:

(108d) Wat je moet doen is *drie keer bellen*.
        What you should do is *to ring three times*.

express that your inging three times is conceived of as one single event, consisting of three subevents.

Finally consider such sentences as:

(109a) Piet hamerde een uurlang op dat punt.
        Piet hammered at that point for an hour.
(109b) Wat Piet een uurlang deed was *hameren op dat punt*.
        What Piet did for an hour was *to hammer at that point*.
(109c) Wat Piet deed was *een uurlang hameren op dat punt*.
        What Piet did was *hammer at that point for an hour*.

We meet the same situation here as in the above cases. *Een uurlang* modifies 'Piet's hammering at that point'. It can be observed that Durational Adverbials can occur much easier in PN of (72) than Adverbials of Time. This can be taken as an indication that the former are located lower than the latter.

Summarizing our considerations with respect to the constituents which can occur both as (part of) Y and of X in paradigm (72), we can safely state that the margin in our conception of what events are is determined by the nature of these constituents. They all concern certain properties of events which can be included in our definitions "for the purpose of daily life". We can expand events according to our wish. If we include the constituents in question into the Y of (72), we expand the events we are speaking about: if on the other hand we restrict ourselves to constituents only occurring in Y of (72) we restrict ourselves to the basic structural core of events. Thus we reach a position to define the terms 'event unit' and 'minimal event'. The term 'event unit' can be used to refer to a temporal entity corresponding to the S underlying the PN of paradigm (72), where the variable Y ranges over constituents which *can* occur in PN. The term 'minimal event' can be applied to a temporal entity corresponding to the S underlying $_{PN}[Verb + Y]_{PN}$ in (60) where Y ranges over constituents which *must* occur in PN. The events described under (i) and (iii) can all be considered event-units, i.e. the corresponding S's can be marked as entities which can be pluralized. However, the events described under (iii) are not minimal events as we have seen.

3.4.4. *Minimal Events and the Upper Bound of the Aspects*

We can now question the implication of the fact that Direct Objects, Indirect Objects, Prepositional Objects, Directional Objects, etc. can only occur in PN of (72).

In my opinion, we may assume the existence of a degree of cohesion between the Verb and constituents occurring obligatorily in PN, which is absent in the relation between the Verb and constituents which can occur in X. Thus we can relate the notion 'degree of cohesion' occurring in Chomsky (1965:101) to paradigm (72), in fact to the scope of reference of *wat* (what).

As far as I can see, we can explain the difference between the presence and absence of a certain degree of cohesion between the Verb and other constituents in terms of a difference between grammatical rules. The relation between the Verb and constituents under (i) already seems to hold in semantic representation (deep structure) itself, whereas the relationship of cohesion between e.g. Verb and Adverbials of Time – if this relationship indeed holds – is a matter of derived structure. Adverbials of Time relate to the (surface) Verb or to the VP (which is a derived constituent) after having been introduced transformationally into the Predicate Phrase. The same applies to all Adverbials having been discussed under (ii) and (iii).

The point at issue can be demonstrated with the help of a distinction between so-called *operators* and what is referred to as the *nucleus*. This distinction, well known in symbolic logic, was introduced into linguistic theory by Seuren (1969) after having been developed gradually in the work of Katz and Postal (1964) and Kraak (1966) and some others. Analogously to what is being done in logical analyses, the structure of sentences is divided into operator-like constituents such as existential and universal quantifiers, modal operators, tense operators and some others among which *Time*, on the one hand and the nucleus on the other. The nucleus "conforms to a relatively simple pattern of *subject-verb-object-indirect object-prepositional object*, or *subject-copula-predicate nominal*" (Seuren, *ibid.*: 112). Operators must be introduced transformationally into the nucleus. Hence the degree of cohesion between the Verb (originating in the nucleus) and Adverbials of Time (incorporated into the nucleus) cannot be as strong as the degree of cohesion between constituents dominated by the node *Nucleus* in deep structure.

The above bipartition can also be found in the work of scholars like Lakoff (1965; 1970), Ross (1967), McCawley (1969; 1970) and others, where operators are sometimes taken as predicates located higher in deep structure than the lowest S, which can be compared with Seuren's nucleus. Thus, a sentence like *Arie had die avond een haring gegeten* (Arie had been eating a herring that evening) can be analyzed as is shown in diagram (XLIII), where I follow the Ross/McCawley representation.

(XLIII)

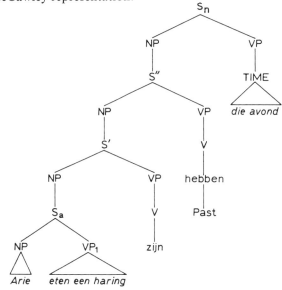

The Adverbial of Time *die avond* (that evening) as well as the Auxiliaries *have* and *be* are considered to be located outside the nucleur node S_a. They must be introduced into S_a by transformational rules whose ultimate output resembles structures which were generated by the base rules in *Aspects* (Chomsky 1965) as shown in (XLIV).

(XLIV)

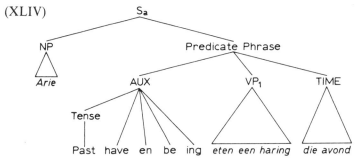

The relationship between (XLIII) and (XLIV) is similar to the relationship holding between (XXVId) and (XXVIe) in Section 3.2 on pages 113 and 114.

---

[26] The example is partly taken from McCawley (to appear). Diagram (XLIII) represents a proposal by Ross as far as *be* and *have* are concerned. Ross argued that (XLIII) underlies a surface structure of the form $_{NP}$[Arie]$_{NP}$ $_{VP}$[$_V$[have]$_V$ $_{VP}$[$_V$[been]$_V$ $_{VP}$[$_V$[eat]$_V$ $_{NP}$[herring]$_{NP}$]$_{VP}$]$_{VP}$]$_{VP}$. Whatever the resulting surface structure may be, the general principle is clear. A relatively rich underlying structure of the form sketched in (XLIII) is the input to rules incorporating operators into the Nuclear S-node.

The event node S' in (XXVId) is in exactly the same position as the node S_a in (XLIII). Both are nuclear nodes in the sense described above.

The node S' in (XXVId) was taken to be the upper bound of the Aspects as followed from our analysis. If it is correct to state that S_a in (XLIII) can be identified with this S', then it follows that our pseudo-cleft paradigm (72) can be used to determine the upper bound of the Aspects since this upper bound coincides with the minimal scope of reference of [PRO+[WH+ PRO]]. As we have seen it is reasonable to assume that the upper bound of the Aspects can be identified with this minimal scope, because if we compare the constituents contributing to the composition of the Aspects with the constituents discussed in the present section we see that none of the constituents mentioned under (ii) and (iii) contribute to the composition of the Aspects. It is only constituents necessarily occurring as (part of) Verb+Y in (72) that are involved.

3.5. CONCLUSION

In conclusion of the present chapter I would like to summarize the essentials by giving the outline of the argument.

In Section 3.1 evidence was given for the view that the term 'Aspects' applies to configurations of categories dominated by an S. On the basis of the material presented we were able to develop a Durative scheme and a Nondurative scheme. Sentences characterized by the presence of a Nondurative Aspect fit into the latter, sentences characterized by the presence of a Durative Aspect into the former. Since the opposition between the Durative and the Nondurative Aspects relates to the possibility for sentences to contain Durational Adverbials or not, it appeared to be a proper solution to the problem of selection to formulate a constraint on a transformational rule developed in Klooster and Verkuyl (1971), called *Adverbialization*. This constraint has the effect of blocking the single-event reading of sentences fitting into the Nondurative scheme while allowing for their frequency reading.

In view of the opposition between 'single-event reading' and 'frequency reading' it became necessary to determine the event-unit which can be pluralized to obtain frequency. The term 'frequency' applies to a series of similar events and consequently we ought to know the unit of quantification.

In Chapter II it had gradually become clear that the underlying V-node involved in the composition of the Nondurative Aspect has something to do with what I have called "the temporalization of abstract entities". Sentences like (69h) *Arie at een haring* (Arie ate a herring) can be described in terms of such a node, viz. DO. This fact relates the analysis of the Aspects to a proposal by Lakoff and Ross (1966) concerning VP-constituency. This proposal made a claim about the hierarchical status of Durational Adverbials in underlying structure. Their transformational rule *Do so-replacement* turned out to be descriptively inadequate. An attempt was made to relate sentences like (69a) *Arie at een haring en Piet deed dat ook* (Arie ate a herring and Piet did so too) to (69g) *Wat Arie deed was een haring eten* (What Arie did was to eat a herring). This was necessary to account for the scope of reference of *dat* (that) in (69a) and *wat* (what) in (69g).

The assumption that (69h) and (69g) should be derived from one common underlying source (setting aside different topicalization elements) is elaborated with the help of Gruber's framework extended by recent proposals concerning the underlying structure of Noun Phrases formulated in Bach (1968) and McCawley (1968a; 1968d). It was argued that the underlying category DO is not introduced transformationally into the categorial tree. Its lexical entry is deviced so as to prevent lexicalization unless DO occurs with a NP dominating PRO.

Our claim that the underlying structure of (69h) contains a category DO whose sister NP dominates a sentential complement, is supplemented by the introduction of temporal variables into our description. This step made it possible to relate our analysis to proposals made by Reichenbach (1966) and Davidson (1967) about the logical form of action sentences. It became clear that the term 'event' can be applied to the referent of the sentential complement of DO in the underlying structure of (69h) and (69g). This referent can be taken as an event-unit, i.e. as the unit of quantification over events.

However, as Reichenbach pointed out, the determination of individuals is a matter of convention: events can be expanded. This insight is supported by the flexibility of the scope of reference of *dat* (that) in (69a) and *wat* (what) in (69g). In other words, the sentential complement of DO in underlying structure can be expanded. The pseudo-cleft paradigm (72) complementized by the question-answer paradigm (99) seems to be able to account for the minimal structure of the sentential complement of DO (occurring as the Predicate Nominal of (72)) as well as for its possible expansions. In the former case we can use the term 'minimal event' for the referent of the sentential complement of DO; in both cases, however, we can speak of event-units.

As far as the frequency reading of sentences fitting into the Nondurative scheme (50a) is concerned, we have made the claim that the upper bound of the Aspects coincides with the sentential structure referring to minimal events. Those constituents which fall under the minimal scope of *dat* (that) in (69a) and *wat* (what) in (69g) are exactly those which contribute to the composition of the Aspects.

It will be clear that many problems concerning the Aspects remain to be solved. For example, the relationship between the structures of Noun

Phrases given in Chapter II and those under analysis in the present chapter should be specified. Obviously, the quantificational information contained by the structures fitting into the Durative and Nondurative schemata takes rise in the same underlying source as the information located in Numerical elements and Frequency Adverbials. It will be necessary to gain a deeper understanding of the operatorlike part of TERMS. Very little is known of this matter, however, and therefore I have restricted myself to giving some outlines.

As far as I can see the present study provides for an account of the problem raised by the examples (1)–(5) in Chapter I. The single-event reading in the b-sentences of (1)–(4) can be blocked by a constraint on a transformational rule, *Adverbialization*, which also accounts for their frequency reading. Whatever the formal apparatus necessary to describe the opposition between the Durative and Nondurative Aspects may ultimately look like, I hope to have shown that the generalizations made in this study should be accounted for in grammar.

BIBLIOGRAPHY

Akmajian, A.: 1970, 'On Deriving Cleft Sentences from Pseudo-Cleft Sentences', *Linguistic Inquiry* **1**, 149–68.

Bach, E.: 1968, 'Nouns and Noun Phrases', in: Bach and Harms (eds.) 1968, pp. 91–122.

Bach, E.: 1970, 'Problominalization', *Linguistic Inquiry* **1**, 120–1.

Bach, E. and Harms, R. T., (eds.): 1968, *Universals in Linguistic Theory*. New York, etc.

Behaghel, O.: 1924, *Deutsche Syntax. Eine geschichtliche Darstellung*. II. Die Wortklassen und Wortformen. B. Adverbium. C. Verbum, Heidelberg.

Botha, R. Ph.: 1968, *The Function of the Lexicon in Transformational Generative Grammar*, The Hague/Paris.

Bowers, F.: 1969, 'The Deep Structure of Abstract Nouns', *Foundations of Language* **5**, 520–33.

Bresnan, J. W.: 1970, 'On Complementizers: toward a Syntactic Theory of Complement Types', *Foundations of Language* **6**, 297–321.

Brugmann, K.: 1904, *Kurze vergleichende Grammatik der Indogermanischen Sprachen*, Strassburg.

Chomsky, N.: 1957, *Syntactic Structures*, The Hague.

Chomsky, N.: 1964, *Current Issues in Linguistic Theory*, The Hague.

Chomsky, N.: 1965, *Aspects of the Theory of Syntax*, Cambridge (Mass.).

Chomsky, N.: 1968a, 'Remarks on Nominalization', in Jacobs and Rosenbaum (eds.), pp. 184–221.

Chomsky, N.: 1968b, *Language and Mind*. New York, etc.

Davidson, D.: 1967, 'The Logical Form of Action Sentences', in N. Rescher (ed.), *The Logic of Decision and Action*, Pittsburgh, pp. 81–120.

Delbrück, B.: 1897, *Vergleichende Syntax der Indogermanischen Sprachen*. II, Strassburg.

Deutschbein, M.: 1917, *System der neuenglischen Syntax*, Köthen.

Dougherty, R. C.: 1969, 'An Interpretive Theory of Pronominal Reference', *Foundations of Language* **5**, 488–519.

Es, G. A. van: to appear, 'Het aspect als syntactische functie', Submitted to *Tijdschrift voor Nederlandse Taal- en Letterkunde*.

Grinder, J.: 1971, 'Chains of Coreference'. *Linguistic Inquiry* **2**, 183–202.

Grinder, J. and Postal, P. M.: 1971, 'A Global Constraint on Deletion', *Linguistic Inquiry* **2**, 110–2.

Gruber, J. S.: 1967a, 'Look and See', *Language* **43**, 937–47.

Gruber, J. S.: 1967b, 'Disjunctive Ordering among Lexical Insertion Rules', Unpublished paper M.I.T.

Gruber, J. S.: 1967c, *Functions of the Lexicon in Formal Descriptive Grammars*, Technical Memorandum 3776/000/00. SDC, Santa Monica (Cal.).

Herbig, G.: 1896, 'Aktionsart und Zeitstufe. Beiträge zur Funktionslehre des Indogermanischen Verbums', *Indogermanische Forschungen* **6**, 157–269.

Hermann, E.: 1927, 'Objektive und subjektive Aktionsart', *Indogermanische Forschungen* **45**, 207–28.

Hertog, C. H. den: 1903, Nederlandsche spraakkunst; handleiding ten dienste van aanstaande (taal)onderwijzers. 3 Vol., 2nd impr. Amsterdam, 1903–1904.

Jacobs, R. A. and Rosenbaum, P. S.: 1968, *English Transformational Grammar*, Waltham (Mass.), etc.

Jacobs, R. A. and Rosenbaum, P. S., (eds.): 1970, *Readings in English Transformational Grammar*, Waltham (Mass.), etc.

Jacobsohn, H.: 1926, 'Wackernagel, Vorlesungen über Syntax', *Gnomon* **2**. 379–95.

Jacobsohn, H.: 1933, 'Aspektfragen', *Indogermanische Forschungen* **51**, 292–318.

Katz, J. J. and Postal P. M.: 1964, *An Integrated Theory of Linguistic Descriptions*, Cambridge (Mass.).

Kenny, A.: 1963, *Action, Emotion and Will*, London/New York.

Kiefer, F. and Ruwet, N. (eds.): 1972, *Generative Grammar in Europe*, Dordrecht, to appear.

Klooster, W. G.: 1971a, 'Reductie in zinnen met "maatconstituenten"', *Studia Neerlandica* **2**, 62–98. An English translation 'Reduction in Dutch Measure Phrase Sentences' is to appear in Kiefer and Ruwet (eds.).

Klooster, W. G.: 1971b, *The Structure Underlying Measure Phrase Sentences* (Diss. University of Utrecht).

Klooster, W. G. and Verkuyl, H. J.: 1971, 'De transformationele relatie tussen *duren* + Specificerend Complement en bepalingen van duurmeting'. *Tijdschrift voor Nederlandse Taal- en Letterkunde* **87**, 29–63. An English translation 'Measuring Duration in Dutch' is to appear in *Foundations of Language*.

Klooster, W. G., Verkuyl, H. J., and Luif, J. H. J.: 1969, *Inleiding tot de Syntaxis. Praktische zinsleer van het Nederlands*, Culemborg/Keulen.

Kraak, A.: 1966, *Negatieve zinnen. Een methodologische en grammatische analyse*, Hilversum.

Kraak, A.: 1967a, 'Perfectief en duratief als syntactische en morfologische categorie', *Handelingen van het XXVIe Vlaams Filologencongres*. Gent, pp. 589–602.

Kraak, A.: 1967b, 'Presuppositions and the Analysis of Adverbs', Unpublished paper M.I.T.

Kraak, A.: 1968, 'A Search for Missing Agents'. *Le Langage et l'Homme* **8**, 146–56.

Kraak, A. and Klooster, W. G.: 1968, *Syntaxis*, Culemborg/Keulen.

Kuehner, R.: 1898, *Ausführliche Grammatik der Griechischen Sprache*, II, 1. Satzlehre, Hannover/Leipzig.[5]

Kuehner, R. and Stegmann, C.: 1962, *Ausführliche Grammatik der Lateinischen Sprache*. Satzlehre I, München[4] [1912].

Lakoff, G.: 1965, *On the Nature of Syntactic Irregularity*, Report NSF-16, The Computation Laboratory, Cambridge (Mass.).

Lakoff, G.: 1966, 'Stative Adjectives and Verbs in English', *Report NSF-17*, The Computation Laboratory, Cambridge (Mass.).

Lakoff, G.: 1967, 'Pronominalization and the Analysis of Adverbs', *Report NSF-20*, The Computation Laboratory, Cambridge (Mass.).

Lakoff, G.: 1968, 'Instrumental Adverbs and the Concept of Deep Structure', *Foundations of Language* **4**, 4–29.

Lakoff, G.: 1970, *Linguistics and Natural Logic*, Ann Arbor (Mich.).

Lakoff, G and Ross, J. R.: 1966, 'A Criterion for Verb Phrase Constituency', *Report NSF-17*, The Computation Laboratory, Cambridge (Mass.).

Langacker, R. W.: 1969, 'On Pronominalization and the Chain of Command', in Reibel and Schane (eds.), pp. 160–86.

Lees, R. B. and Klima, E. S.: 1963, 'Rules for English Pronominalization', *Language* **39**, 17–28.

Leskien, A.: 1919, *Grammatik der altbulgarischen (altkirchenslavischen) Sprache*, Heidelberg.[2]

Massey, G. J.: 1970, *Understanding Symbolic Logic*, New York, etc.

McCawley, J. D.: 1967, 'Meaning and the Description of Languages', *Kotoba no uchu* **2**, 10–8, 38–48, 51–7.

McCawley, J. D.: 1968a, 'The Role of Semantics in a Grammar', in Bach, E. and Harms, R. T. (eds.), pp. 124–69.

McCawley, J. D.: 1968b, 'Lexical Insertion in a Transformational Grammar without Deep Structure', *Papers from the Fourth Regional Meeting of the Chicago Linguistic Society*, Chicago.

McCawley, J. D.: 1968c, 'Concerning the Base Component of a Transformational Grammar', *Foundations of Language* **4**, 243–69.

McCawley, J. D.: 1968d, 'Where Do Noun Phrases Come From', In: Jacobs, R. A. and Rosenbaum, P. S. (eds.), pp. 166–83.

McCawley, J. D.: 1970, 'English as a *VSO* Language', *Language* **46**, 286–99.

McCawley, J. D.: to appear, 'Tense and Time Reference'.

Michelson, D.: 1969, 'An Examination of Lakoff and Ross' Criterion for Verb Phrase Constituency', *Glossa* **3**, 146–64.

Miller, J. E.: 1970, 'Stative Verbs in Russian', *Foundations of Language* **6**, 488–504.

Moravcsik, J. M. E.: 1970, 'Subcategorization and Abstract Terms', *Foundations of Language* **6**, 473–87.

Overdiep, G. S.: 1937, *Stilistische grammatica van het moderne Nederlandsch*, Zwolle.

Perlmutter, D.: 1968, 'The Two Verbs "begin"', in Jacobs, R. A. and Rosenbaum, P. S. (eds.), pp. 107–19.

Porzig, W.: 1927, 'Zur Aktionsart indogermanischer Präsensbildungen', *Indogermanische Forschungen* **45**, 152–67.

Postal, P. M.: 1964, *Constituent Structure; A Study of Contemporary Models of Syntactic Description*, The Hague.

Postal, P. M.: 1970, 'On Coreferential Complement Subject Deletion', *Linguistic Inquiry* **1**, 493–500.

Poutsma, H.: 1926, *A Grammar of Late Modern English*. II: The Parts of Speech, Section II: The Verb and the Particles, Groningen.

Quine, W. V. O.: 1965, *Mathematical Logic*, Revised edition, New York [2]. [1940, 1951].

Quine, W. V. O.: 1960, *Word and Object*, Cambridge (Mass.).

Reibel, D. A. and Schane, S. A. (eds.): 1969, *Modern Studies in English. Readings in Transformational Grammar*, Englewood Cliffs (N.J.).

Reichenbach, H.: 1966, *Elements of Symbolic Logic*, New York/London. [1947].

Rosenbaum, P. S.: 1967, *The Grammar of English Predicate Complement Constructions*, Cambridge (Mass.).

Ross, J. R.: 1966, 'A Proposed Rule of Tree-Pruning', *Report NSF-17*, The Computational Laboratory, Cambridge (Mass.). Also in: Reibel, D. A. and Schane, S. A. (eds.), pp. 288–99.

Ross, J. R.: 1967, 'Auxiliaries as Main Verbs', Unpublished paper-preliminary version, M.I.T.

Ross, J. R.: 1968, 'On Declarative Sentences', in Jacobs, R. A. and Rosenbaum, P. S. (eds.), pp. 222–72.

Ross, J. R.: 1969, 'On the Cyclic Nature of English Pronominalization', in Reibel, D. A. and Schane, S. A. (eds.): pp. 187–200.

Rijk, R. P. G. de: 1968, 'A Note on Prelexical Predicate Raising', Unpublished paper M.I.T.

Seuren, P. A. M.: 1969, *Operators and Nucleus. A Contribution to the Theory of Grammar*, Cambridge.

Seuren, P. A. M.: to appear, 'The Comparative', in: Kiefer, F. and Ruwet, N. (eds.).

Staal, J. F.: 1967, 'Some Semantic Relations between Sentoids', *Foundations of Language* **3**, 66–88.

Streitberg, W.: 1889, *Perfective und imperfective Actionsart im Germanischen*. I, Halle a.S.

Vendler, Z.: 1957, 'Verbs and Times', *The Philosophical Review* **66**, 143–60.

Verkuyl, H. J.: 1969a, 'Nederlandse taalkunde en methodologie', *De Nieuwe Taalgids* **62**, 251–63.

Verkuyl, H. J.: 1969b, *De constituentenstatus van tijdsbepalingen*, Internal Publication Instituut voor Neerlandistiek, Universiteit van Amsterdam.

Verkuyl, H. J.: 1970, 'De relevantie van logische operatoren voor de analyse van temporele bepalingen', *Studia Neerlandica* **1**, 7–33. A revised version 'Temporal Prepositions as Quantifiers' is to appear in Kiefer, F. and Ruwet, N. (eds.).

Verkuyl, H. J.: 1971, 'Aspekten als kompositionele kategorieën', in *Taalwetenschap in Nederland 1971* (to appear).

Verkuyl, H. J.: forthcoming, 'Syntactic evidence for a Tripartition into Durative, Terminative and Momentaneous Constituents'.

Wijk, N. van: 1928, '"Aspect" en "Aktionsart"', *De Nieuwe Taalgids* **22**, 225–39.

INDEX

Abstraction operator, *see* operator
Accusativus affectivus, 86–96
Accusativus effectivus, 53, 85–96
Action predicate, 160
Action sentence, 99, 100, 142–62
Action variable, 159
ADD TO, *see* Verb
Adjective, 12
Adjunct
  attributive –, 78–80
  prepositional – of the object, 167
  – to predicates, 116
  predicative –, 166
Adverbial
  – of circumstance, 109
  concessive –, 169, 170
  – of degree, 149
  directional –, 19, 33, 41, 42–46, 64, 80, 81,
    89, 93–96, 104, 105, 121, 165n, 166
  durational –, *see* durational adverbials
  frequency –, 3, 61, 116–8, 164, 172
  – of goal, 19
  instrumental –, 16n, 109, 172
  manner –, 16, 20, 109
  manner – of product, 167
  modal –, 167, 168
  place –, 167, 171
  – of reason, 109, 168, 169
  – of time, 8, 56, 107ff, 162, 163, 170–2, 174
  see also prepositional phrase
Akmajian, A., 142n
Article, *see* Determiner
Aspects, *passim*
  classification of the –, 4–8, 100, 107, 110,
    111
Austin, J. L., 157n
Auxiliary, 175

Bach, E., 137, 138, 139, 143–145, 177
Base component
  – with Chomsky, 9–29
  – with Gruber, 29–39
  homogeneity of the –, 31ff
Behaghel, O., 4n, 7n, 99
Botha, R. Ph., 10
Bowers, F., 61n
Bresnan, J., 128n

Brugmann, K., 4

Castaneda, H. N., 157n, 161
Categorial node, 30
Causative, 161n
Chisholm, R. M., 157n
Chomsky, N., 1, 7, 8, 9–39, 51, 59, 60, 68, 69,
  80n, 99, 110, 114, 118, 121, 123, 137, 139,
  147–50, 153, 155, 174, 175
Cleft sentence, 152–155
Cohesion
  degree of –, 82, 99, 119, 121, 155, 174
  Comment of, 124–6
Complementizer, 127, 128n
Complementizer Placement, *see* trans-
  formation
Complex symbol, 11–6, 19
Cooccurrence relationship, 30ff
Coordination
  adversative –, 162ff
  conjunction, 162ff
Copula, 112ff, 143–50, 165, 174
Core predicate, 165n
Countability, 59–62

Dalen, D. van, 140n
Davidson, D., 24n, 100, 156–62, 177
Declarative performative, 62–4
Deep structure vs. underlying structure, 7n, 8
Delbrück, B., 4
Designated element, 68ff
Determiner, 37, 58–61, 76, 98, 108, 111
Deutschbein, M., 4n
Directional Phrase, *see* adverbial
Direct Object, 14, 21, 46–97, 105, 106, 121,
  165n, 166, 174
DO, *see* Verb
Dougherty, R. C., 135, 137
Durational adverbial, *passim*
Duration-dating adverbial, 98, 99, 107, 108,
  111
Duration-measuring adverbial, 98, 99, 111–8
Durative scheme, 51, 64, 71, 73, 77, 82, 87, 94,
  96, 98–109, 176, 178

Elffers, E., 143
Es, G. A. van, 8n, 101n

Please send:
Veuillez m'envoyer:
Bitte zu senden:
Sírvanse remitirme:
Vogliate spedirmi:
Gelieve te zenden:

7, 18, 19, 24n, 27n, 30,
135, 136n, 137, 139,
168, 169, 175, 176
41

9–29, 30ff, 48
29–39, 46–49, 72,

31–39, 111–5, 130–4,

nent, 33–39, 75, 114,

nment, 33–39, 44, 75,

143n

IN BLOCK   12n, 22, 30, 32n, 62,
CAPITALS   5–9, 143ff, 154, 155,

12, 113
25, 40, 112–6

Name: ....

Address: ....

....

....

City: ....

Country: ....

erbial
rator
ects, 7ff

Na
Ad
City
Cou

gation, 100–9
Node
non-branching –, 34, 35n
Node admissibility conditions, 32
Nominalization, *see* transformation
Nondurative scheme, 64, 73, 82, 94, 96,
98–109, 115–8, 155, 156, 176, 178
Noun
abstract –, 53–73
animate –, 11, 13, 31, 32, 34
common –, 11, 31
concrete –, 11, 22, 32, 34, 73–85
count –, 11, 36, 59–61
female –, 31
human –, 11, 13, 32, 34, 143

iota operator, *see* operator

Jacobs, R. A., 142, 143
Jacobsohn, H., 4n, 7n, 8, 42, 53, 54, 86–90,
101n
Junggrammatiker, 4

Katz, J. J., 68, 69, 125, 174
Kenny, A., 157n
Klima, E. S., 135
Klooster, W. G., 24, 29, 60, 98, 111–8, 119,
154n, 167, 176
Kraak, A., 6, 8n, 9, 14, 18, 60, 69, 82n, 117,
119, 167, 174

mass –, 32, 59
non-count –, 11, 20, 59–61
non-human –, 11
proper –, 11, 32, 104, 144
quantity –, 21–4, 53–78
temporal –, 12–29, 55, 57
Noun Phrase
    descriptional part of the –, 139–56
    operator-like part of the –, 139–56
    plural –, 22, 50, 51, 109
    questioning of the –, 124–6
    singular –, 22, 50, 51, 109
Nucleus, 174, 175, 176
Numerical element, 60, 61, 116–8, 134, 151

Operator
    abstraction –, 140–1
    future tense –, 88
    incorporation of -s into the nucleus, 174, 175
    iota –, 139–41
    modal –, 174
    past tense –, 88
    PRO, 143–7, 150–155
    tense –, 174
Overdiep, G. S., 4n, 8, 101n, 131n

Partitive, 79–82, 89,90
Passive sentence, 100
Past tense operator, see operator
PERFORM, see Verb
Performative, see Verb
Peripheral environment, see lexical entry
Perlmutter, D., 139
Pluralization of S, 116–8
Polycategorial lexical attachment,
    see lexical attachment
Porzig, W., 4n, 7n
Postal, P. M., 32n, 68, 69, 125, 135, 136n, 137, 139, 155, 174
Poutsma, H., 4n, 5, 42, 99
Predicate
    logical –, 5n, 87, 88, 144ff, 156–62
Predicate nominal, 122, 123, 142–55, 165–73, 177
    dummy –, 147–50
Predicate Phrase, 99, 110, 114, 118, 119, 129, 155, 162, 175
Predication, 5n, 98
Preposition
    – as a predicate, 16, 24–7, 107, 108
    setting –, 107f
    temporal –, 55, 61, 107, 108, 114
Prepositional object, 166, 167, 174
Prepositional phrase

– as transform, 24–27, 79, 80n
    see also adverbial
Pro-form, see Pronoun, Pro-VP
Pronominalization, see transformation
    backward –, 135
Pronoun
    indefinite –, 51, 52, 68–70, 77–9, 133, 134
    plural –, 133, 134
    PRO, 118–155
    relative, 144–55
    unspecified dummy –, 53–98, 100–109, 148–50
Proposition, 87, 88, 129, 140f
Propositional function, 140f, 152
Pro-VP, 17, 118–23, 148, 155
Pseudo-cleft sentence, 99, 121–55, 165–73, 176, 177
    – paradigm, 122, 165

Quantification
    – over events, 116–8, 156–62
    unit of –, 116–8, 156
Quantifier
    existential –, 88, 107, 108, 111, 148, 156–62
    universal –, 107, 108, 111
Quantifying complement, 40, 94–7, 104, 105, 106
    dummy –, 94f
Question, 62, 124–6
Quine, W. V. O., 139, 140n

Recoverability, 69
Reference
    – and meaning, 129
    anaphoric –, 121, 134–41
    pronominal –, 120–55
    scope of –, 122, 156, 162–76
Referential identity, 17, 120–3, 134–41
Reichenbach, H., 100, 129, 139, 156–160, 170, 171, 177
Relative Clause, 112–4, 143–55
Relative Clause reduction, see transformation
Relativum, 112, 144
Rosenbaum, P. S., 128n, 136, 137, 139, 142, 143
Ross, J. R., 10, 16, 17, 18, 19, 27n, 30, 34n, 62, 99, 118–34, 135, 155, 156, 162–5, 168, 169, 175, 176
Rule
    branching –, 10, 31ff
    non-branching –, 32
    restructuring –, 35, 72
    selectional –, see subcategorization
    strict subcategorization –, see subcategorization

transformational –, *see* transformation
Rijk, R. de, 29, 154

Scheffler, I., 157*n*
Selection, 10–39
  – between non-lexical categories, 16, 21–4, 27–8
Semantics,
  generative vs. interpretive –, 7*n*, 30
Semicopula, 111*ff*
Sentoid, 124, 125
Seuren, P. A. M., 152*n*, 174
Simultaneous environment, *see* lexical entry
Specifying complement, 112
Staal, J. F., 124–33
Stegmann, C., 79*n*
Streitberg, W., 4, 5, 7, 99
Subcategorization
  – of verbs, 10, 12–6, 18–29, 35–39
  – rules, 10–29
  strict – rules, 10–29
Subject, 14, 40, 98, 100–9, 127, 174
Syntactic feature, *see* feature

TAKE, *see* Verb
Tense, 34, 114, 127, 128
Tense carrier, 127
Tense logic vs. tenseless logic, 87, 88
TERM, 143–55
Time axis, 55–8, 63, 64, 88, 89, 93–96
Topicalization, 99, 124, 142, 146, 151*n*
Transformation
  adverbialization, 98, 113, 114–8
  Chomsky-adjunction, 34, 35*n*, 113, 114, 153
  complementizer placement, 127, 128
  do so-replacement, 17, 99, 119–34, 155, 162–5, 177
  equi-NP-deletion, 137, 152
  extraposition, 136*n*, 150
  nominalization, 113
  predicate raising, 154
  pronominalization, 120, 134–42, 155
  PRO-replacement, 151*ff*
  pseudo-cleft –, 123, 142–55, 165–73
  relative clause reduction, 112, 144–55

relative raising, 152*n*
S-deletion, 136, 155
subject raising, 118*n*
TRANSITION, *see* Verb
Transitive, *see* Verb
Tree pruning, 34, 35, 72

Underlying structure vs. deep structure, 7*n*, 8
Unit of quantification, *see* quantification
Unspecified dummy, *see* Pronoun, Predicate Nominal

Vendler, Z., 5, 8*n*, 93
Verb
  ADD TO, 90–6, 119
  AGENTIVE, 51–3, 84, 87, 96
  CONSTRUCT, 89–96
  CONSUME, 75
  disambiguation of the term 'Verb', 46–9
  DO, 49, 84, 106, 118–56
  durative (imperfective) –, 3*ff*, 29, 35–9, 41–4, 54, 86
  empty –, 131*n*
  intransitive –, 46–9
  MOVEMENT, 36, 41–6, 88, 93–6, 102–6, 119
  nondurative (perfective) –, 3*ff*, 29, 35–9, 41–4, 54, 86
  nonstative –, 57*n*, 120, 130, 132
  PERFORM, 53, 54–73, 96, 106, 119
  performative –, 62–4
  pseudo-intransitive –, 49–97
  stative –, 57*n*, 93, 130
  strictly transitive –, 46–9
  TAKE, 49, 53, 73–84, 96, 106, 119
  TRANSITION, 103

Verb Phrase
  – as a deep structural category, 118, 155
  durative –, 17, 44–6, 93, 110–1
  nondurative (terminative and momentaneous) –, 17, 44–6, 91, 92, 110–1, 117

Wright, G. H. von, 157*n*, 159
Wijk, N. van, 4*n*, 7

FOUNDATIONS OF LANGUAGE

SUPPLEMENTARY SERIES

Edited by Morris Halle, Peter Hartmann,
K. Kunjunni Raja, Benson Mates, J. F. Staal,
Pieter A. Verburg, and John W. M. Verhaar

1. John W. M. Verhaar (ed.), *The Verb 'Be' and its Synonyms. Philosophical and Grammatical Studies*. Part I: *Classical Chinese. Athapaskan. Mundari*. 1967, VIII + 100 pp.
Dfl. 23,—

2. Nicholas Rescher, *Temporal Modalities in Arabic Logic*. 1967, IX + 50 pp.   Dfl. 16,—

3. Tullio de Mauro, *Ludwig Wittgenstein. His Place in the Development of Semantics*. 1967, VIII + 62 pp.   Dfl. 19,—

4. Karl-Otto Apel, *Analytic Philosophy of Language and the Geisteswissenschaften*. 1967, X + 63 pp.   Dfl. 16,—

5. J. F. Staal, *Word Order in Sanskrit and Universal Grammar*. 1967, XI + 98 pp.
Paper   Dfl. 32,—

6. John W. M. Verhaar (ed.), *The Verb 'Be' and its Synonyms. Philosophical and Grammatical Studies*. Part II: *Eskimo Hindi. Zuni. Modern Greek. Malayalam. Kurukh*. 1968, IX + 148 pp.   Dfl. 30,—

7. Hugo Brandt Corstius (ed.), *Grammars for Number Names*. 1968, VII + 123 pp.
Dfl. 32,—

8. John W. M. Verhaar (ed.), *The Verb 'Be' and its Synonyms. Philosophical and Grammatical Studies*. Part III: *Japanese. Kashmiri. Armenian. Hungarian. Sumerian. Shona*. 1968, VIII + 125 pp.   Dfl. 28,—

9. John W. M. Verhaar (ed.), *The Verb 'Be' and its Synonyms. Philosophical and Grammatical Studies*. Part IV: *Twi. Modern Chinese. Arabic*. 1969, VIII + 125 pp.   Dfl. 28,—

10. F. Kiefer (ed.), *Studies in Syntax and Semantics*, 1969, IX + 242 pp.   Dfl. 50,—

11. A. C. Senape McDermott, *An Eleventh-Century Buddhist Logic of 'Exists'*. 1969, X + 88 pp.
Dfl. 25,—

12. Karl Aschenbrenner, *The Concepts of Value. Foundations of Value Theory*. 1971, XVII + 462 pp.   Dfl. 100,—

In Preparation:

13. F. Kiefer and N. Ruwet (eds.), *Generative Grammar in Europe*.

14. John W. M. Verhaar (ed.), *The Verb 'Be' and its Synonyms. Philosophical and Grammatical Studies*. Part V: *Urdu / Turkish / Bengali / Amharic / Indonesian / Telugu / Estonian*.

16. Charles H. Kahn, *The Verb 'Be' in Ancient Greek*.

16. W. G. Klooster, *The Structure Underlying Measure Phrase Sentences*.

SOLE DISTRIBUTORS IN THE U.S.A. AND CANADA:
Volumes 1–12: Humanities Press / New York